# Safe & Sound Child

By Leslie Stone, Larry Stone, and Laurie Levy

Illustrated by Julie Breslin

GoodYearBooks

*An Imprint of ScottForesman*
*A Division of HarperCollinsPublishers*

**Dedication**

To Madeline and Jake
May you always be safe and sound, and may your warmth and gentle smiles continue to light up the lives of those around you.

The text of this book has been technically reviewed by the National Safety Council.

**GoodYearBooks**
are available for most basic curriculum subjects plus many enrichment areas. For more GoodYearBooks, contact your local bookseller or educational dealer. For a complete catalog with information about other GoodYearBooks, please write:

> GoodYearBooks
> ScottForesman
> 1900 East Lake Avenue
> Glenview, IL 60025

Cover photograph © Jeff Noble/Noble Stock, Inc.
Book design by Karen Kohn & Associates, Ltd.
Copyright © 1996 Leslie Stone, Larry Stone, and Laurie Levy.
All Rights Reserved.
Printed in the United States of America.

ISBN 0-673-36243-4

1 2 3 4 5 6 7 8 9 - DP - 02 01 00 99 98 97 96

Only portions of this book intended for classroom use may be reproduced without permission in writing from the publisher.

# Preface

Children inspire us, enlighten us, and add warmth to our lives, and as adults, we must return that inspiration with constant love, care, education, understanding, and, of course, communication. Combine the aspirations of children with the care of adults, and our future looks bright. Our aim should be to cherish the young and innocent and help them to grow strong and wise and confident.

While most of us, as parents and teachers, strive to make our homes and schools havens of love, learning, safety, and peace, we reluctantly realize that, in our present society, such is not always possible.

Depressing . . . but not defeating.

We prefer to be optimists, to hope that parents and teachers have the fire and the fortitude to accept the challenges of an often turbulent society. We believe not only in our best and brightest, but in all who work to improve their lives and the lives of those around them. This includes keeping them safe.

If you are responsible for a child, all aspects of safety deserve your attention, whether you are a parent, grandparent, teacher, caregiver, or sibling. We all agree that to keep our children safe and sound, we must all pitch in to educate them about the numerous hazards they'll encounter as they head down the paths of their lives.

After you review the array of safety issues compiled in our book, we urge you—parents, teachers, and others—to work with children to help inform and educate them. Because these topics are new and exciting to children of all ages, we hope we can safely say that in this instance, "learning can be fun."

While various natural disasters, such as floods and fires, do tend to make us all feel helpless, the truth is that many types of potentially tragic accidents and calamities can be avoided or averted if we take time to learn how. That is the point of *The Safe & Sound Child*.

We have always believed that the more you know, the better prepared you are to avoid trouble, from auto safety to poison prevention. As parents of two children, and also because we are in the safety business, safety is always on our minds. And just as we practice at home what we learned in business, we wish for you to gain the security of knowing what to do to keep your family safe and sound. We hope you will let us be your guides in the world of child safety.

## Acknowledgments

We wish to offer special thanks to the plethora of organizations and individuals we interviewed either in person or by phone. Without their specific knowledge and expertise, especially that of our writer, Laurie Levy, this all-encompassing child safety book could not have come to fruition.

Thanks to the following contributors:

First, our great appreciation goes to researchers Julia French and Cory Hance, as well as to assistants Tina Beltramo, Maura Madden, Barbara Milsner, and Margarite Reilly.

The following were consulted in the course of writing this book, and we thank them all:

Dr. Tim Adkins, Ernest E. Allen, J.D., Meri-K Appy, Detective J. J. Bittenbinder, Officer Jane Bolek, Dr. Daniel Broughton, Dr. Jeffrey L. Brown, David Buckshaw, Todd Cabanban, Diane Cardinale, Julia Cartwright, Dr. Richard Chase, Phipps Cohe, Joe Crawley, Sgt. Lawrence Deck, Barbara Dunn, David Eagle, Mark Ellinger, Dr. Joseph T. Esser, John Eyler, Firefighter Dan Fuhs, Dr. Theodore L. Gehrig, David Glowacz, Meg Grattan, Anne Green, Lyndsay Green, Dr. Vivian Hernandez, Pat Hines, Eric Hruda, Diane Imhulse, Dr. Marjorie Jeffcoat, Dr. Gary J. Kinley, Firefighter Sue Lencioni, Donna Leonhardt, Dr. Mark Mannenbach, Dr. Glenn Mayer, Frank McDonough, Dr. Terri Merens, Dr. Marla Minuskin, Dr. Howard Mofenson, Shin Nihon, Jean O'Neil, Joan Oppenheim, Fire Commissioner Raymond E. Orozco, Peter Reynolds, Don Richardson,

David Rodelius, Gail Shrawder, Linda Sharkey, Carrie Sibley, Jerry Slater, Rose Ann Soloway, Dr. Neil Starkman, Laurie Strong, Judy Teibloom-Mishkin, R. N., Office Bill Talone, Mitch Tracy, Dr. Dana R. Walters, Bernice Weissbourd, Dr. Burton L. White, Susan Whitehead, Gertrude Williams, and Marian Willinger.

Amerex Corporation, American Academy of Allergy, Asthma, and Immunology, American Academy of Pediatrics, American Airlines, American Association of Poison Control Centers, American College of Obstetricians and Gynecologists, American Medical Association (Chicago), American Red Cross, Asthma and Allergy Foundation of America, Bicycle Federation of America, Bicycle Helmet Safety Institute, Canadian Toy Testing Council, Chicago Fire Department, Chicagoland Safe Kids Coalition, Chicago Police Department, Chicago Veterinary Medical Association, Children's Safety Network National Injury and Violence Prevention Resource Center, Closure Manufacturers Association, Council on Family Health, Easter Seal Society National Headquarters, Edward Hospital, F.A.O. Schwarz, Federal Aviation Administration, Food Allergy Network, General Motors (Detroit), Harrods of London, Highland Park, Illinois, Police Department, Illinois Department of Transportation, Johnson & Johnson, Juvenile Products Manufacturers Association, Kidscare National Program/Product Safety Bureau, Kidslife Resources, Macfarlan Smith, Ltd., Midas International Corporation, National Association for the Education of Young Children, National Center for Health Statistics, National Center for Missing and Exploited Children, National Fire Protection Association, National Head Injury Foundation, National Highway Traffic Safety Administration, National Institute of Child Health and Human Development, National Safe Kids Campaign/National Safety Council, National Toy Manufacturers Association, Nonprescription Drug Manufacturers Association, Operation Lifesaver, Inc., Poison Control Center of Rush-Presbyterian-St. Luke's Hospital, Polly Klaas Foundation, Robotronics, United Hospital and Medical Center, United States Consumer Product Safety Commission, United States Department of Transportation, and United States Power Squadrons.

# Contents

**1   The Fury of Fire** — 1
   **The Awful Truth** — 2
   **The Anatomy of a Fire** — 3
   **Teaching Young Children About Fires and Fire Safety** — 5
     At Home — 5
     At School — 7
   **Smoke Detectors** — 10
   **Heat Detectors** — 12
   **Fire Extinguishers** — 12
   **The Family Escape Plan** — 14
   **Fire Safety Away from Home** — 20
   **Burns** — 20
     Preventing Burns — 22
     What to Do in Case of Burns — 26
   **VITs** — 28

**2   Medic Alert! Physical Injuries and Treatments** — 29
   **Safety for Babies and Toddlers** — 30
     Preventing Falls in the Home — 30
     Sudden Infant Death Syndrome — 32
   **Injury Treatments** — 35
     Minor Scrapes, Cuts, and Bruises — 35
     Puncture Wounds and Bleeding — 36
     Fractures and Sprains — 38
   **Injuries to Teeth** — 39
   **Choking and Suffocation** — 41
     The Heimlich Maneuver — 44
   **CPR** — 49
   **VITs** — 69

## 3  Medic Alert! Poisons, Medicine Overdoses, and Treatments — 71

- Household Poisons — 72
  - Plants — 72
  - Household Chemicals — 77
  - Pesticides — 80
- Medicines — 81
  - Do You Take Medicines Safely? — 81
  - Child-Resistant Packaging — 81
- Poison Education — 86
- Diagnosing and Treating Household Poisonings — 89
- Poison Control Centers — 91
- Systemic Poisoning — 95
  - Lead Poisoning — 95
  - Carbon Monoxide: The Silent Killer — 100
  - Other Gases and Toxic Substances — 103
- Drugs — 105
- Prevention Programs — 107
- VITs — 112

## 4  The Toyland Safety Zone — 115

- Regulating the Toy Industry — 116
- Choosing Safe Toys for Your Child — 118
  - Safety Guidelines — 118
  - Choosing Appropriate Toys — 123
  - Age-Appropriate Toys for Safe Play — 125
- Safe Toys for Outside Fun — 129
- Unsafe Toys — 131
  - Loud Toys — 131
  - Projectiles — 131
  - Electric Toys — 131
- The Importance of Toy Maintenance — 132
- VITs — 133

## 5   The Childproofed Home    135
**Some Basic Childproofing Equipment**    137
    Safety Latches    137
    Room Monitors    138
    Fire Ladders    138
    Doorstops    138
**The Kitchen**    138
    General Hazards    138
    Poisons    140
    Furniture and Appliances    140
    Electrical Concerns    141
**The Dining Room**    142
**Stairways**    143
    Gates    143
    Banisters and Posts    144
    Stair Steps    145
**The Family Room**    145
    Furniture    145
    Gun Cabinets    146
    Appliances    146
    Electrical Outlets    147
    Fireplaces    148
    Sliding Glass Doors    148
**Bathrooms**    148
    Tubs, Showers, and Toilets    148
    Electrical Appliances    150
    Floors    150
    Medicine Cabinets    150
**Bedrooms**    151
    Children's Rooms    151
    All Bedrooms    154
**Basements and Exercise Rooms**    156
**The Garage**    157
**Outdoors**    157
**VITs**    158

## 6 Oh, What Fun It Is to Ride!: Planes, Trains, Automobiles, and Other Conveyances   161

**Automobile Safety**   162
- Buckling Up Kids: The Statistics   162
- Child Safety Seats   164
- Seat Belt Use   170
- Other Auto Safety Tips   172
- Pedestrian Safety   175

**Train Safety**   178
**Bus Safety**   180
**Boat Safety**   181
**Plane Safety**   186
**VITs**   189

## 7 Oh, What Fun It Is to Ride!: Strollers, Bicycles, and Skates   193

**Stroller Safety**   194
**Bicycle Safety**   195
- Injury Statistics   195
- Younger Riders   195
- Older Riders   199
- Using Helmets   200
- Rules for Safe Cycling   204
- Selecting and Inspecting a Bike   205

**Skating Safety**   208
**VITs**   212

## 8 Outdoor Safety: Playgrounds and Pools   215

**Playground Safety**   216
- Safety in Your Own Backyard   217
- Playground Safety Away from Home   223
- Supervision Away from Home   225
- Treating Head Injuries   226

| | | |
|---|---|---|
| **Pool Safety** | | 227 |
| Safety in the Home Pool | | 228 |
| Swimming in Public Pools and Other Bodies of Water | | 233 |
| What to Do in Case of Submersion or Drowning | | 235 |
| **VITs** | | 237 |

## 9 "Stranger Danger": The Child Stands Alone — 239

| | |
|---|---|
| **What Is a Stranger?** | 242 |
| **Low-Risk vs. High-Risk Adults** | 243 |
| **Programs That Make Children "Stranger Aware"** | 246 |
| McGruff, the Crime Dog | 246 |
| Play It Safe | 247 |
| The Polly Klaas Foundation | 249 |
| **Keeping Your Kids Safe Away from Home** | 250 |
| Bolstering Self-Esteem | 251 |
| Knowing the Basics | 251 |
| Giving the Password | 251 |
| Establishing a Landmark | 252 |
| Combating Older and Bigger Aggressors | 252 |
| Providing Children with Identification Cards | 253 |
| Encouraging Two-Way Communication | 254 |
| **Home Alone** | 255 |
| Knowing Your Child's Schedule | 255 |
| Giving Your Child a Key | 255 |
| Answering the Door and Phone | 256 |
| Using the Phone in Emergencies | 256 |
| **Tips from Police and Educators** | 257 |
| **VITs** | 260 |

## 10 Seasonal Safety — 261

| | |
|---|---|
| **Winter Wonderland** | 262 |
| How to Dress for Outdoor Activities | 262 |
| Smart Sledders | 264 |

|   |   |
|---|---|
| Snowboarding | 265 |
| Skating | 266 |
| Skiing | 269 |
| Winter Injuries and Dangers | 273 |
| Other Potential Hazards | 275 |
| Winter Holidays | 278 |
| **Summer Sense** | **281** |
| Sunburn and Sunscreen | 281 |
| Summer Injuries and Dangers | 283 |
| **Safe Holidays** | **289** |
| Fourth of July Fireworks | 289 |
| Happy Halloween | 290 |
| **VITs** | **294** |

## 11 For Pet's Sake — 297

|   |   |
|---|---|
| **Selecting a Pet** | **299** |
| **Dogs** | **300** |
| Selecting a Dog | 300 |
| Bringing the Dog Home | 302 |
| Training | 304 |
| Dogs and Babies | 305 |
| Walking Dogs Safely | 306 |
| Diseases | 308 |
| Strays | 311 |
| **Cats** | **312** |
| Selecting a Cat | 312 |
| Cats and Babies | 313 |
| Claws | 314 |
| Diseases | 315 |
| Strays | 316 |
| **Birds** | **316** |
| Domestic Birds | 317 |
| Wild Birds | 319 |
| **Fish** | **320** |

| | |
|---|---|
| Hermit Crabs | 323 |
| Reptiles | 323 |
| Rabbits | 327 |
| Hamsters | 327 |
| VITs | 329 |

# Resources 331

# References 334

# Index 335

# Chapter 1

# The Fury of Fire

FIRE! THE VERY WORD sends shivers up and down your spine, no matter how old you are. Parents and teachers need to inform the children in their care about all the up-to-the-minute facts when it comes to fighting fire. No, not the way trained firefighters do. The way people trained in fire safety do, in battling even the most horrible catastrophes. It's important for every family member to learn about everything he or she can do to prevent fires and burns, and how to get out of the house in case a fire should start. This chapter offers details you should know, appropriate for children of various ages, as well as for their parents and teachers.

## The Fury of Fire

# The Awful Truth

While it never pays to generalize about the tragedy of fire, certain facts are known. Fire strikes a home somewhere in the United States once every one to two seconds, and fires serious enough for the fire department to respond strike nearly once a minute. Every year, roughly 4,500 lives are lost in fires; of those, around 80 percent are home fires. Of the fatalities, one-third are children under age twenty. Approximately 1,100 are children ages nine and younger, including about 900 children under age five, notes the National Fire Protection Association (NFPA).

That's why Mom and Dad have to know what to do in case of fire. It is also important for older brothers and sisters in every family to learn enough to battle these statistics.

Deaths are not the only horror. Data from NFPA and the U.S. Fire Administration's National Fire Incident Reporting System show that, on average, 4,900 children ages nineteen and younger are injured each year in reported fires at home. Of these, 1,800 are children five and younger. Even more shocking is that among these preschoolers, blazes started by children playing with fire—typically matches or lighters—are the leading cause of both fire deaths and injuries. One of every three fire deaths and two of every five fire injuries result from such careless play. These fires can cause serious injury in seconds, and their prominence makes prevention the number-one goal. For home fires in general, smoking (one-fourth of home fire deaths) and arson (one-sixth of home fire deaths) are the leading causes. Arson in the home most often involves juvenile firesetters. Again, children are involved and prevention is crucial.

The National Fire Protection Association divulges further figures. Did you know that more than 450,000 home fires occur annually, causing more than 20,000 injuries a year? And while most measures of fire safety have improved dramatically, the fire injury figures haven't decreased in at least a decade and a half.

Each year, one to two million people suffer home fire injuries, including 300,000 to 400,000 children under age eighteen. Hundreds of thousands of victims suffer disabling injuries that confine them to bed, including tens of thousands of children.

And it is not the licking flames that kill. Smoke and deadly gases, principally carbon monoxide, are the culprits. In fact, deaths from smoke inhalation outnumber those from burns by more than two-to-one.

Loss of life and the pain of injury are the most crucial concerns in fire safety. But damage to the home should not be underestimated, either. Home fires cause more than $4 to $5 billion in annual property losses.

The most important factor in fire safety at home (and at school) is the use of smoke detectors (since they make a noise, many refer to them simply as *smoke alarms*) and other proper equipment. Two-thirds of home fire deaths occur in homes that do *not* have smoke detectors. It has been proven that families cut their risk of dying nearly in half when they install smoke detectors. When you remember the many victims who perish from the inhalation of smoke and toxic gases, as well as in the flames, the necessity of smoke detectors seems even more evident.

If you are thinking that it's easy for adults to pick up safety tips and learn how fire prevention works, but that this knowledge is over the heads of most children, you're wrong. Kids who learn about fire safety in school often bring home the information to their parents; they want to discuss it. And it's up to you to find out whether they've picked up on all the facts (or not) after a visit from their local Firefighter Friendly. If your child's school doesn't include visits from local firefighters as part of its curriculum, work with your local school board or parent-teacher association to instigate these all-important visits.

If your school does schedule firefighter visits, go over the booklets your child brings home and be sure to reinforce what she's learned. (Later in this section, you'll learn how to spell out a workable family escape plan, in case of fire.)

## The Anatomy of a Fire

Right from the start you should understand the elements of fire. When kids ask how fires start, you should be able to tell them in very simple terms about the *Fire Triangle*.

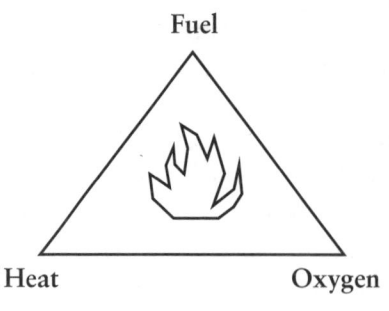

The Fire Triangle

The three parts of the triangle are fuel, heat, and oxygen. Something *fuels* the fire. That fuel may be wood, or anything that burns. The second corner of the triangle is *heat*. This can come from matches, lighters, or any source that ignites, including sparks from faulty wiring in any part of the home.

Without *oxygen* (air, the third element) to stir the flames, fuel would be ineffective. All fuels must be converted to vapor and combined with oxygen to begin the burning process. Most fires will continue to burn only when all parts of the Fire Triangle are in place.

Are all fires bad? There are two schools of thought when it comes to that question. Some people believe children rightly should be afraid of fires—all fires. Other people disagree. They know about the pleasure of lighting birthday candles, or any candles, for that matter. They enjoy sniffing the fragrance in the autumn air when folks sit around an outdoor campfire; no camper can deny the warmth and comfort provided by that campfire on a cold night. Others revel in fires kindled in an indoor hearth, come winter. And can anything be more delectable, not only for kids but also for adults, than hamburgers and hot dogs on the barbeque on a summer night? Indeed, cooking is one of the good uses of fire. Another good use? Blowing glass. It may interest older children to read about glass blowing and learn how fire is instrumental in creating a thing of beauty.

No, fire is not all bad. We just have to know how to light and control the fires we use in our homes. Total fear is not the point. What is? A lot of healthy respect and caution on everyone's part.

# Teaching Young Children About Fires and Fire Safety

## At Home

Grills and barbeques in the yard require the use of matches and lighters. The same goes for those cozy fireplace blazes inside. But every child should learn that matches and lighters are not toys. Fire safety experts have informed the public that children *as young as three years old* (and even younger, if they have the manual dexterity) play with matches.

If your child can count, tell her that temperatures of real fires can be more than 600°F. Tell your child the temperature outside right now and ask her to imagine how much hotter 600°F would be. Explain that fires are so dark from smoke, you can't see or breathe. You want her to be aware of the danger involved. The rule should not be hard for her to grasp: *Never* play with lighters or matches.

The best way to prevent problems, of course, is to place the matches and lighters in your home in a cabinet with a lock. But be sure to tell your child to report to you if she finds matches or lighters lying around. Making her responsible enables her to feel she has a part to play in family safety.

Adults must be in charge, whether it's a fire in the fireplace or an outdoor campfire. Nothing's more fun than roasting marshmallows (can anything top the temptation of s'mores?), but the motto remains: "Adults in Charge." (That goes for lighting birthday or holiday candles, too.)

When your child is of preschool age, it is likely that she has not yet experienced the typical school visit from a firefighter. (And, frankly, most firefighters can be scary. They are big and tall, and they wear an outfit the children may never have seen before. If a firefighter, in fact, did attempt to save a child caught in a home fire, the child might even be too frightened to leave the house with this strange creature.) That is why it is a good idea, as soon as your child can identify people, places, and things shown in pictures, for you to show the child a picture of a firefighter dressed

## The Fury of Fire

for work. Then, explain what the firefighter does, what is worn from hat to boots, and why he or she is a friendly figure.

As the child grows a little older, you're likely to find that she learns fire safety in school; nursery school children may be taught what the firefighter does and what the firefighter looks like in full regalia. Learning can sometimes include listening to the firefighter's voice through a mask (which, again, can be alarming to a child). Discuss the firefighter's outfit with your child at home. Tell her the safety reasons the firefighter needs a helmet, an airpack, a long jacket, pants, gloves, and boots. Tell the child how heavy all of the firefighter's equipment is. Familiarity breeds security.

## The Fury of Fire

## At School

The helpful and dedicated National Fire Protection Association (NFPA) devotes a vast amount of work to teaching children about fire safety. According to Ms. Meri-K Appy, NFPA Vice-President for Public Education, 1996 marks the hundredth anniversary of the NFPA. In addition to developing and publishing the highly technical National Fire Codes, the NFPA is committed to addressing the problem of fire in our country by educating people to make wiser choices about fire and burn prevention.

One of the best ways to do that is to teach children when they're young, before they learn risky behaviors that get them into trouble. That is why the NFPA developed the *Learn Not to Burn* curriculum for schools. The NFPA decided to implement the program in the schools because it found that adults often don't know correct fire and burn prevention behaviors, and children are learning dangerous things from parents and other caregivers. The U.S. has one of the worst records of fire death and injury in the industrialized world.

People make mistakes while cooking, using electricity, and heating their homes. They make all kinds of unwise judgments, such as using cigarettes and matches, and children tend to mimic parents and other caregivers. So, it is important to intervene at a very young age to teach fire and burn prevention, then rely on the children to go home and help the adults around them understand how to correct *their* risky behaviors. The NFPA hopes to educate future generations of fire-safe adults while teaching children to make wise choices right now.

The NFPA has been able to document the hundreds of lives saved through its curriculum. Even very young children survive often devastating fires in their homes because they've been taught, for example, how to crawl low under smoke, or if they encounter smoke and flames, to use an alternate exit. They go home, practice with their families, and in the event of a fire, they're not guessing—they know what to do.

The NFPA believes that fire is a community problem, and a good approach to solving it involves not only fire departments but schools and families. According to Ms. Appy: "In terms of future

## The Fury of Fire

goals, one of the changes we find taking place at the community level is that fire departments are beginning to see their role broadening. Because fire departments are first on the scene of most emergencies, it's becoming a part of their commitment to prevent some of these other kinds of injuries beyond fires and burns. So, NFPA is beginning a new comprehensive injury prevention program that will include fire and burn prevention education, but will also address the unintentional injury areas that most affect kids from preschool to grade eight—traffic accidents, drowning, poisonings, mechanical suffocation, firearm injuries, and falls."

The NFPA hopes to make the program available in 1997. With the fire department's role in the community really growing, the NFPA wants to assure availability of the same kinds of tools that *Learn Not to Burn* provides, developing additional tools to look at fire and burns in the context of injury prevention as a whole.

Currently, *Learn Not to Burn Resource Books* are used in more than 50,000 classrooms across the country, from kindergarten to high school. In the *Learn Not to Burn Preschool Program,* kids learn to recognize the firefighter as a helper. They also learn seven other top tips, and parents should review them:

1. Stay away from hot things that can hurt (irons, coffeemakers, all appliances that transmit heat).
2. Tell grownups when you find matches or lighters.
3. Learn appropriate behavior if fire strikes:
   (1) STOP (don't run, which fans the flames),
   (2) DROP (fall to the floor to prevent rising smoke and flames from reaching your lungs), and
   (3) ROLL (cover your face with your hands, hold arms close to the body, and roll back and forth to smother flames). Note: The reasons behind this procedure may be beyond most preschoolers, but the basic idea of Stop-Drop-Roll shouldn't be too hard to learn.
4. Crawl low under smoke.

## The Fury of Fire

5. Immerse any burn in cool water for ten to fifteen minutes.
6. Know the sound of a smoke alarm.
7. Practice an escape plan.

As children progress through school, fire safety instruction becomes more sophisticated. For instance, by first grade, children are taught what fire is, as well as what to do. They learn more about Stop-Drop-Roll and the Get Out! Stay Out! formula (which basically means escape first, then call the fire department from the neighbor's home). They learn to test the doors for heat, and why it's important to crawl low below the smoke. They learn how hot the room is at ceiling level, and that it's so hot because heat rises.

By fourth grade, children are taught more advanced information about dealing with fire. If a child smells smoke, she should not run for her parents. Instead, she should do as she's been taught: roll out of bed to the floor and crawl on hands and knees to the bedroom door. She should touch the door with the back side of her hand. (The back is more sensitive, and the palm has more nerves that you don't want to damage; you don't want to lose your sense of touch.) Then she should follow these procedures:

1. If the door is hot, put a towel or a sheet from the bed under the door to keep smoke out. (You may be safe up to one hour with the door closed.) Then go to the window. Always make sure the door is closed before opening the window, otherwise the air will suck the fire and smoke upstairs immediately. Escape through the window if possible. If trapped, stay inside the room with the door closed and with a towel or clothing underneath the door. If there is one, use the phone to dial 911 for help. (Never dial this number unless there's an emergency. The people who answer are busy helping other people and can't waste time on mistakes or jokes.) If you don't have 911 service in your area, ask your mom or dad what numbers to use in emergencies. Speak clearly and calmly into the phone and tell the person who answers

exactly what is wrong. Next, give your name and the address of the house with the fire. Don't hang up until the person at the other end hangs up in case he or she has more questions.

If you don't have a phone, yell for help and wave a blanket, sheet, pillowcase, towel, or an item of clothing until the firefighter comes to get you, but be ready to close the window if smoke is coming in from outside.

2. If the door is cool, open it a bit, bracing it with your foot and keeping your face away from the opening, to see if there is smoke in the hall. If so, close the door and use the window. If the hall is clear, go downstairs and outside quickly and immediately. Cover your mouth and nose with your hand if nothing else is available. Having decided upon a place outside the home to meet, such as a lamppost, fire hydrant, or other designated meeting place, go to that prearranged area so that everyone can be accounted for. Never arrange to meet at a car (it can move).

    Never try to save pets; you should concentrate on saving yourself. Animals sense the fire and are likely to escape before you.

3. Tell your child never to go into a burning building.

## Smoke Detectors

The importance of smoke detectors cannot be overstated. It is therefore important to know how they work and how they're maintained. One smoke detector is better than none, but one on every level (basement, first floor, and upstairs) is best. Follow installation instructions provided by the manufacturer. Keep alarms away from air vents.

Smoke alarms alert people because they make a noise. An excellent pamphlet issued on fire safety by the National Safe Kids Campaign notes that the very first "smoke alarm" was a canary.

**The Fury of Fire**

In the 1880s, factories used canaries to smell smoke; their chirping alerted workers to get out fast. In the 1920s, a merchant mariner invented a smoke detector that pumped air from below the ship's deck into a glass box. He knew there was a fire if the smoke turned dark. In the late 1930s, a doctor from Switzerland discovered electricity couldn't pass through smoky air. He invented a system that set off an alarm when the air in the detector's special chamber became smoky. The first smoke detectors cost more than $100 each; today, some top models can be purchased from as low as $5 up to $85, or more. Look for those approved by an independent testing facility, such as Underwriters Laboratory.

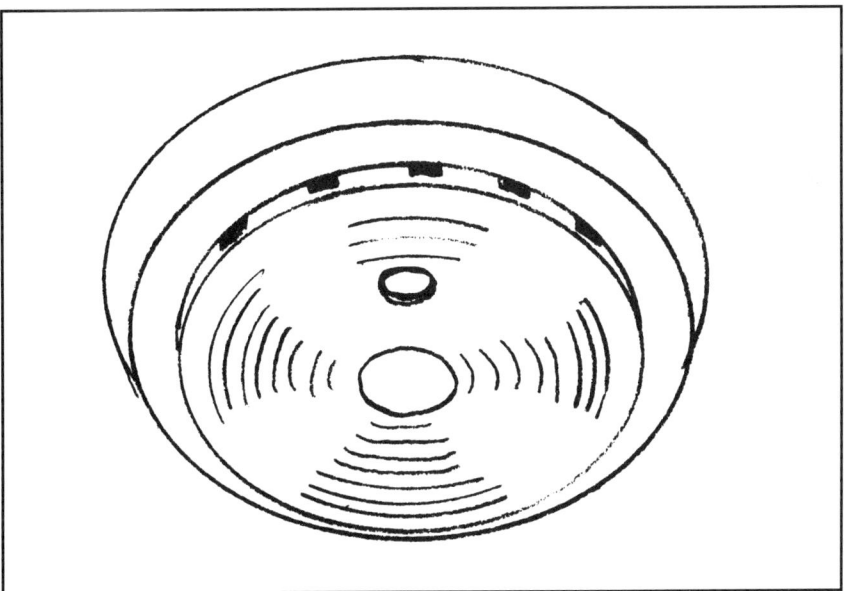

Of course, it doesn't matter how many smoke detectors you have in the house if they're not in working condition with the batteries functioning properly. So, the number-one "must-do" is to be sure your smoke detector is operating. Even if your smoke alarm hasn't been used, replace the batteries twice a year when you change your clocks in fall and in spring. Some battery-operated smoke detectors will make a chirping sound when batteries need replacing, but yours may not.

Ask the salesperson to show you how to test your smoke detectors. If you have to press a test button, do it monthly. Vacuum the grillwork of the detector periodically to keep it dust free. Be sure your child recognizes the sound of the smoke detector so she knows how to respond; it should make a startling noise.

One more thing to tell your child: Your smoke detector provides you with a maximum of three minutes in which to escape. That's *not* time enough to go to the phone to report the fire. *Get out first.* Then, phone to report the fire from a neighbor's house.

## Heat Detectors

Heat detectors are newer than smoke detectors, but they are increasing in use. When these devices detect heat, not smoke, they sound an alarm. There are two types of heat detectors, rate-of-rise and fixed temperature. They are available in many models and in two ratings: 135°F and 200°F. A rate-of-rise detector detects heat by responding to a rapid temperature increase, approximately 15°F per minute. Fixed temperature detectors respond to a specific temperature setting. Either type protrudes a little more than an inch from the ceiling, with a junction box that is easily installed.

It is important to remember that heat detectors should be used for property protection, not personal safety. They should be used in conjuction *with* a smoke detector, not in place of one.

## Fire Extinguishers

Legislation requires fire extinguishers in all commercial, institutional, and government buildings, but it's a good idea to buy several for the home as well. You should familiarize yourself with the various types of fire extinguishers and how they operate. When you buy one, ask the salesperson to demonstrate it. What good is an important piece of equipment in your home if you don't know how to use it? Like your smoke alarms, fire extinguishers should carry the Underwriters Laboratory label. Ask your salesperson how to have one serviced and inspected.

## The Fury of Fire

Some fires are small enough to be doused with a good fire extinguisher, so make sure yours is the right size and is of good quality. Models rated ABC can be used for fires involving wood and cloth, flammable liquids, or electrical equipment.

A supplier of fire equipment, among them fire extinguishers, explained this ABC rating: the class A fire involves combustible materials; class B fires originate from flammable liquids; and class C fires are electrical fires. It is important to have ABC-rated multipurpose extinguishers, therefore, for all classes of fires, such as kitchen grease fires or wastebasket fires.

Keep fire extinguishers out of children's reach, and follow the manufacturer's instructions. If dislodged, they can be dangerous. Spraying someone in the face could do considerable damage. The chemical agent comes out with considerable pressure, and carbon dioxide can seriously burn because it is really cold.

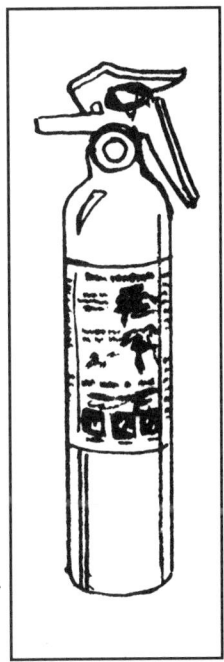

Learn how to use a fire extinguisher correctly in advance. In a panic situation when the adrenalin flows, who bothers to read the instructions? Each extinguisher comes with a label that has pictogram instructions on it, so language is not a barrier and everyone should be able to understand them. Underwriters Laboratory requires an owner's manual to be packed with every extinguisher.

If you practice with the extinguisher and discharge even just a bit, it could leak. (Most commonly, a dry chemical will exit.) As you depress the lever and open the valve, the chemical will shoot through it. When you close it, particles of the chemical could become lodged and cause it to leak. If the valve leaks, the extinguisher becomes useless, losing pressure and fire-handling capability. You will need to have it properly refilled and checked by your local fire department, who may give demonstrations on how to use an extinguisher. If you live in an involved neighborhood, maybe your neighbors could get together to purchase a spare extinguisher and try it out.

# The Fury of Fire

Always locate the fire extinguisher next to the exit of a room so you can fight the fire from the exit side. Otherwise flames may cut off your escape route. (Remember to keep the extinguisher out of the reach of children.) If you operate a home tool shop or any home workroom where you engage in an art or science (sculpting, chemistry, etc.) that requires heated tools or appliances, mount a fire extinguisher there, too. In using most fire extinguisher models, the key word is P-A-S-S:

1. Pull the pin.
2. Then Aim the nozzle at the base of the flames.
3. Then Squeeze (or press) the handle.
4. Then Sweep from side to side.

## The Family Escape Plan

If fire strikes, every single second counts. An escape route is essential. While the child may hear about this first at school, discussing it—and acting on it—can only be done at home.

Chances are, you and your family will never have to escape from a fire; nevertheless, waiting until disaster strikes is no time to decide how to get out. Deciding now could save your life and the lives of those you hold dear. The entire family should sit down and plan what to do in case of a home fire, making sure your child has a voice in the plan, too.

Devise at least two escape routes. Some parents sit down with their children and plan escape routes from every room. Be sure you choose rooms with windows that could serve as exits. Perhaps your first consideration should be how to flee from upstairs

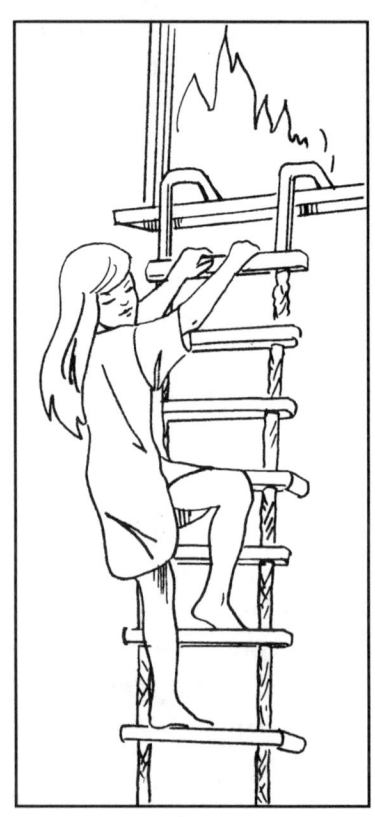

## The Fury of Fire

bedrooms, if there are any. The primary routes are of course through the doors; but if fire blocks them, alternate escape plans are vital. In most cases, the secondary route is out the bedroom window(s). Are those windows low enough to hang from and drop to the ground?

If you live in an apartment building, are the fire escapes safely maintained? If you live in a large home, with two- and three-story windows too far from the ground, buy fire escape ladders (be sure they are approved by Underwriters Laboratories), and store them near the windows you expect to use. Try out your escape ladders as you make your plan so that you'll know how to get them working at once in a real fire. The rule is Hook, Heave, and Hurry: *hook* the ladder to the windowsill—many are equipped with a strap to pull them open—then *heave* or throw it to the ground, and start your climb down carefully but as fast as you can.

Once you have devised the escape plans and discussed them, practice them: schedule a fire drill. The National Fire Protection Association calls this EDITH (Exit Drills in the Home). Both kids and their parents can learn from EDITH. Try to hold drills in at least two different seasons (summer and winter or spring and fall) so that parents as well as children know how to respond in different circumstances. Check to see if furniture and other heavy objects block any doors and windows, and clear them now. Outside, make sure your house numbers aren't hidden, so that the fire department can find you.

Your child may want to know what to do about saving pets. The answer is, sadly: There's no time to rescue pets, unless the pet is with the child and follows as she crawls low to safety. *Under no circumstances* should the child go to look for the pet to try to save it. The good news, however, is that animals are better able to sense fire than humans, and they will wait at an exit, or may be outside before you.

Tell babysitters in your home everything about fire safety. Just as you always leave appropriate emergency phone numbers, don't neglect to share your family's escape plan in case of fire. Babysitters should benefit from the same rules of safety that you and your children follow.

# How Safe Is Your Home?
# A Checklist

### Indoors
Take a tour of your home and check for the hazards and safeguards on this list.

### Throughout the House
- ❑ Are important numbers posted near the phone in every room? In addition to 911, post the numbers of your local fire department, hospital, police department, and poison control center right up there with the names and numbers of important family members, friends, and neighbors.

### Garage, Basement, and Workshops
- ❑ Make sure there aren't too many appliances plugged into the same electrical socket.

Properly dispose of:
- ❑ Incendiary materials (piles of newspapers and magazines, old clothes, paper goods, and old furnishings), especially if they're left too close to fireplaces, heaters, radiators, or any flammable source
- ❑ Gasoline or other flammable liquids stored near gas and hot water heaters or in other indoor spaces
- ❑ Propane cylinders and flammable gases and liquids stored in basements and workshops
- ❑ Rags soaked in oils or paint thinners
- ❑ Gasoline substituted for charcoal lighter or used as a cleaning solution

### Kitchen
- ❑ Consider proper use of cooking and heating equipment. In the kitchen, look for flat bottoms that steady cookware; look for insulated handles so that no pot is literally too hot to handle. Preventing burns from hot liquids is crucial. (Most scald victims are under five years old.) Keep all hot items near the center of the kitchen table and turn pot handles to the rear

**The Fury of Fire**

of the stove. Keep children away from hot stoves (with extra caution when using deep-fat cookers and fryers).
- Never leave cooking foods unattended; they can burn when moisture cooks away, and grease fires can start when fats or oils are allowed to overheat. (It's important to keep the top of the stove clean; grease piles up, and food scraps act like kindling.) Don't use water on a grease fire; smother it instead. You must deprive the fire of air. On the stove, turn off the heat and cover the pot or pan; in the oven, turn off the broiler at once and close the oven door. Suffocate fires!

- The National Safety Council advises never to carry a flaming pan; that just gives the fire more air. Also, if you spill the contents, the fire can quickly spread to floors, walls, and furniture.
- Check placement of chemicals in the kitchen (detergents, cleaning agents, bleaches); keep them in locked cabinets.
- How about microwave cord placement and preventing burns when using the microwave? Consult your microwave user's guide for the proper placement of the microwave.
- Keep the microwave off-limits to kids under twelve. According to the National Safety Council and many pediatricians, six- or seven-year-olds are too young to be allowed to use the microwave, even under adult supervision. (Be sure to tell your babysitter.) Microwave operation is more complicated than it seems. You must remember which dishes are microwave-safe, how long certain foods should be cooked, and to use oven mitts, along with the basics, such as how the controls work. (Actually, both safety experts and microwave oven manufacturers seem to agree that regardless of the child's chronological age, it is her maturity that determines if she is able to handle the responsibilities associated with the microwave.)

## The Fury of Fire

Kids can burn themselves when removing food from the microwave, just as they might when using a conventional oven. Some microwaves are built high into the wall—fine for Mom or Dad to reach, but difficult for small children. Children also may be burned by steam that escapes when they remove the lid from a hot dish, or if they open a bag of microwave popcorn.

❑ Should you microwave infant formula? If you do, the American Academy of Pediatrics (AAP) recommends heating at least four ounces of formula at a time. Use plastic bottles, standing them up straight and uncovered. *Don't* use plastic liners; they can explode. How long you heat the bottle depends upon the wattage of the microwave. Turn the bottle upside down at least ten times before serving to eliminate hot spots. Always test the temperature of any formula or food before feeding it to a child.

### Living Room and Family Room

❑ Check for appliances with old or shabby cords, electrical cords under rugs, unsecured portable heaters, and faulty space heaters. Most fire departments will tell you to keep space heaters at least three feet from curtains, furniture, and walls (painted or wallpapered).

❑ Correct dangerous placement of appliance cords: if baby can crawl to the cord and pull it, its placement is wrong. Also, appliance cords that are not rated for the electrical load create a fire hazard.

## The Fury of Fire

### Bedrooms
- Are your windows painted shut? Do they open properly? Once you have unstuck windows sealed by paint, rub the tracks with a bar of soap. This helps windows to open and shut.

### Outdoors
Survey your yard for safe and unsafe conditions:
- Dispose of piles of leaves and prune dead dry tree or bush branches.
- If your house has a chimney, clean it regularly. In winter when a cozy fire is just the ticket, keep your roof safe from sparks by placing a screen on the chimney. (This also keeps out pesky raccoons in some suburban areas.) Contractors recommend installing both a cap and a screen on the top of the chimney, because it's extremely important to keep the chimney clear. A resident animal, leaves, or a bird's nest will prevent a good draft in the fireplace, causing the fire to smolder and release poisonous gases.
- Chimneys connected to heating units must also be kept clear of debris and animal infestation because carbon monoxide can back up into the home.
- Be sure to have your chimney cap and screen installed by a licensed contractor. You can buy these devices to install yourself; however, most people are novices when it comes to this, so it may be best—unless you know what you're doing—to call in an expert. Remember, chimneys vary in size, so it's important to get yours fitted properly.
- Watch for special dangers associated with holidays, such as dry trees and candles at Christmas and Hanukkah, firecrackers on the Fourth of July, and candles in pumpkins and non-flame-retardant costumes at Halloween.

## Fire Safety Away from Home

What about fire safety away from home? Observe safety habits when you're away just as you observe them at home. When you are camping, campfires must be tamped out, grills must be dead, and ashes buried before you leave the campsite. Many state and federal parks no longer want you to bury ashes but instead to place them in appropriate fire-safe collection containers, so check to be sure. Proper care and usage of all fire equipment applies no matter where you are.

If your child spends the night at Grandma's, she should know how to deal with emergencies (just as she knows how to dial 911 at home). Of course, children always should be taught how to help the elderly and/or people with disabilities. If Grandma refuses to consider herself elderly, assure her she's young-at-heart enough to share her family's safety values, so she should post emergency numbers near her phones, too!

## Burns

Burns are the second leading cause of unintentional injury-related deaths among children in the United States. Each year, burns kill more than 1,300 children and disable 3,900. In 1991 unintentional injuries from fires caused the deaths of 114 children under the age of one, 608 children between ages one and four, and 582 children between the ages of five and fourteen. According to the National Electronic Injury Surveillance System (U.S. Consumer Product Safety Commission), each year, 37,000 children ages fourteen and younger are treated in emergency rooms for hot liquid, food, and tap-water scald burns (in addition to those who do not report to emergency rooms). Of these, 16,400 (45 percent) are under the age of five. The commission also notes that every year, 32,000 children are scalded by hot substances, most often in the kitchen. Hot tap-water scalds 5,000 children annually, usually in the bathtub. In fact, the hospital admission rate for children with

### The Fury of Fire

tap-water scalds is 17 percent annually, compared to 5.5 percent for hot liquid scalds. The average stay in the hospital for a tap-water scald burn is seventeen days, note M. S. Baptiste and G. Feck in *Preventing Tap Water Burns* (1990).

Another source of burns in children is chemicals from a number of sources. In 1993, for example, ovens caused 28.6 percent of the burns experienced by children under four years old, while gas furnaces caused 33.3 percent of the burns in children between the ages of five and fourteen. Turpentine is especially harmful, causing 55.6 percent of the burns experienced by children under age four. A dangerous source of chemical burns in children under four is flashlights or battery-powered lanterns, and fireworks caused 59.9 percent of the burns experienced by children between the ages of five and fourteen.

In all, approximately one million children every year endure burns serious enough to require medical attention. Finally, E. McLoughlin and A. McGuire note in *The Causes, Cost and Prevention of Childhood Burn Injuries* (1990) that for all burns sustained by children fourteen and under in just one year, societal losses (such as loss of wages and medical expenses) are valued at approximately $2.02 billion. Children under four account for $916 million of these losses.

There are three categories of burns:
1. First degree: the mildest, causing redness and perhaps a slight swelling of the skin.
2. Second degree: blistering and considerable swelling of the skin results.
3. Third degree: the most severe. The skin may appear white or charred, and serious injury is not only evident on the surface but also can affect deeper skin layers.

The causes vary in intensity—everything from sunburn and hot-water scaldings, to burns caused by fire, electrical contact, or

## The Fury of Fire

chemicals. Any of these can cause permanent injury and scarring of the skin. Actually, a burn is the most devastating injury a human being can suffer, and because children have thinner skin, they sustain more severe burns at lower temperatures than adults. Children under five are at the greatest risk of scalds as they begin to walk, climb, and reach. Hot liquid and food burns often occur when children grab dangling appliance cords, pull pots off the stove, or pull hanging tablecloths or placemats.

Deaths are more common and injuries more severe from bathtub scalds than from hot liquid and food scalds. It takes just three seconds for a child to sustain a third-degree burn from water at 140°F, which would require hospitalization and skin grafts.

For children ages three to eight, curiosity about matches and lighters is normal. But the sobering fact is that more than one-third of the burns to children in the three- to eight-year-old age group are the result of playing with matches.

### Preventing Burns

Less time could be spent talking about treatment if more time were spent talking about prevention. An ounce won't do it; think pounds. Naturally, accidents happen. But by practicing preventative measures around the house, you're ahead of the game.

Here are some of practices to adopt. They are divided into four categories to simplify them, though sometimes they overlap.

SCALDS
- Lower the thermostat of your hot-water heater to below 120°F or 48.8°C. Test the water with a bath or cooking thermometer. Some hot-water heaters have low, medium, or hot settings. Keep yours at medium or lower.
- Keep hot foods and drinks away from the edges of tables and counters. Don't put them on a tablecloth that little hands may yank. If you wish to use a tablecloth at all, be sure it's firmly anchored with a stable centerpiece and keep tabletop items centered (serving dishes, etc.).

**The Fury of Fire**

- Don't hold a cup of coffee (or something equally hot) and your child at the same time.
- Never hold your child when you cook. Keep your child away from the stove while you are cooking; if possible, use rear burners and always turn pot handles to the back of the stove.
- Watch out for dangling appliance cords.
- Don't allow your baby to crawl around hot stoves, floor heaters, or furnace vents.
- If you have a gas stove, turn dials firmly to the *off* position, and if they're easy to remove, do so when you are not cooking, so your child can't accidentally turn the stove on. If they can't be removed, block as much access to the stove as possible. Stove shields or knob covers are available for purchase.
- Do not store snacks in cabinets above the stove.
- When your child is old enough to turn on water faucets in the kitchen sink, bathroom sink and tub, teach her to turn on the cold before the hot.
- Install antiscald devices in faucets, bath spouts, and shower heads. Use a bath-spout cover.
- Always turn on the cold water first in baby's bath and then add the hot water. Always turn hot water off first.
- Before plunking baby in the bath, always test the water temperature with the inside of your wrist or forearm.

FLAME BURNS
- Avoid fireworks.
- Never allow anyone to smoke around your baby or child.
- Keep oven mitts, table napkins, and other flammable kitchen and dining linens at least three feet away from the stove.
- Lock away flammable liquids in the garage or workshed (and not in the basement). Get rid of those greasy oil rags in Dad's workroom. Don't keep piles of old newspapers lying around.
- Keep matches and lighters out of children's reach by locking them up.
- Install smoke detectors on every floor; check batteries.

## The Fury of Fire

- Keep a fire extinguisher in the kitchen.
- Equip fireplace with a screen and spark arrester.

- Set up your computer equipment with proper air space around each electronic device to ensure proper ventilation. Keep their vents clear of animal hair and dust so that heat doesn't build up in the equipment. To deal with power surges, it's wise to buy a line conditioner. A power surge can create a lot of heat within the outlets, which might cause a fire. The line conditioner can be bought as part of a package that includes a battery backup, along with your surge protector. In the event of a power surge, the line conditioner does its best to even out the surge, and the battery backup switches your computer off the outlet onto a battery source, thus offering protection from a fire and preserving your equipment. Of course, none of these devices guarantees safety if your power cord wires are exposed (as is true of any electric appliance).

## The Fury of Fire

- Never pour lighter fuel on lit flames, no matter how slowly those steaks are grilling.
- Place space heaters away from drapes and furniture.

### CONTACT BURNS
- Use potholders or oven mitts when handling hot objects.
- Cover home radiators.
- Never leave irons unattended. Even when cool, lock them away.
- Children should never use heating pads, curling irons, or sunlamps. And lock away Dad's electric razor.
- Keep oven door closed when cooking.
- Wisely dispose of hot charcoal from barbeque grills.
- Check metal playground equipment exposed to direct sun before allowing children to use it.
- Provide adequate ventilation when you use portable gas or kerosene space heaters. (It is a good idea to keep children away from them.) If you use an electric heater, select one that shuts off automatically if it tips over.

### ELECTRICAL INJURIES
- Don't use inadequate extension cords or old, unsafe electrical equipment.
- Place plug covers over all outlets.
- Read and follow directions when using electrical appliances. It seems so simple, but if you use an appliance incorrectly, chances for a fire do increase. Someone recently used a toaster oven to heat a toy that had been left out on an icy sidewalk. The toy was not fireproof.
- In the bedroom, never tuck in the sides or end of an electric blanket, and be careful not to place anything on top of it (even a sleeping pet), for this can cause heat to build up and start a fire.

### The Fury of Fire

- Never overload wall outlets or extension cords; that is, don't plug more appliances into a socket than it can hold.
- Don't run extension cords under rugs or through door jambs.
- Do replace a burned-out fuse with one that's rated for that circuit. If the fuse is too large, it could overload the circuit and cause a fire.
- If any outlet or wall switch feels hot to the touch, have it checked by an electrician.
- Avoid sources of high-voltage power and never touch anything near fallen electric power lines.

## What to Do in Case of Burns

1. Soak the burn immediately in cool water for ten to fifteen minutes. Don't use ice. Run cool water over the area long enough to cool it and relieve the pain.
2. Remove any clothing from the burned area unless it's stuck firmly to the skin. In that case, cut away as much clothing as possible.
3. If the injured area is not oozing, cover the burn with a sterile gauze pad. If the burn *is* oozing, cover it lightly with a sterile gauze pad, or leave it open, in which case you should seek medical attention immediately.
4. Don't rely on so-called home remedies: Putting butter, grease, or powder on a burn can actually cause more injury.
5. Your physician should determine the seriousness of the burn. If it isn't too serious, he or she will show you how to clean and care for it at home, using medicated ointments and dressings. The physician may determine, however, that the child needs to be hospitalized. This usually occurs under the following circumstances:
   - if the burns are third degree;
   - if 10 percent or more of the body is burned;
   - if face, hands, feet, or genitals are burned;
   - if the child is too young (or fussy) to be at home.

### The Fury of Fire

When you're treating a burn or scald at home, keep an eye on the burned area for change in color, swelling, or a bad odor or discharge. These developments may signal an infection.

For *minor burns without blisters,* cover the burn immediately with cold water (for at least fifteen minutes). Then, cover loosely with a bandage or clean cloth and call your doctor.

Treat *burns with blisters* the same way. Do not break the blisters. Call your doctor and ask how to cover the burn. Any burn on face, hands, feet, or genitals and any large burn should be seen by a doctor.

For *large or deep burns,* call 911 or an emergency number for help. Remove clothing. Do not apply any medication. Keep the child warm with a clean sheet and then a blanket until help arrives.

For *chemical or electrical burns,* disconnect electrical power. Do not touch the victim with bare hands. Move the victim away from the power source with wood or a thick, dry cloth. All electrical burns need to be seen by a doctor.

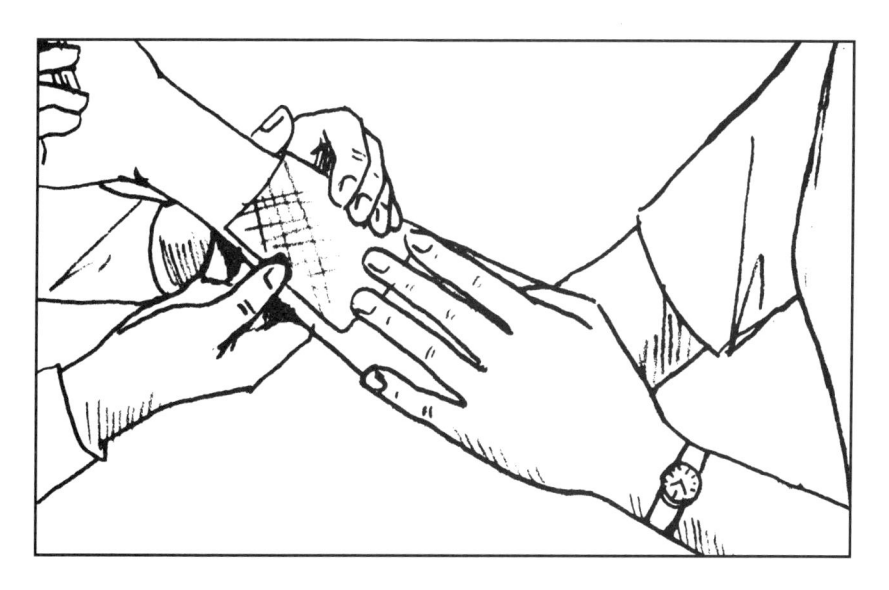

# Very Important Tips

*One of the best summations of fire safety tips was published by the American Academy of Pediatrics' Injury Prevention Program:*

**BIRTH TO SIX MONTHS:**
*Don't* carry a baby while you're simultaneously toting hot liquids or foods; baby waves her fists and grabs at things from three to six months. For bath time, turn down your hot-water heater temperature to 120°F. Be sure you have working smoke detectors.

**SIX TO TWELVE MONTHS:**
Everything above goes double (except that baby's bath can stay at 120°F). Babies now grab at everything, so don't leave cups of hot coffee on tables or counter edges. Keep crawling babies at this age away from stoves, wall or floor heaters, and hot appliances; use a playpen, high chair, or crib.

**TWO TO FOUR YEARS:**
Keep kids from underfoot while you're cooking in the kitchen. (Grease, hot foods, and hot liquids can spill.) Toddlers and hot appliances (irons, toasters, waffle irons, and the like) don't mix.

**FIVE YEARS:**
You won't have to remind her not to play with matches and lighters if you keep them out of your child's reach. Don't smoke at home; cigarettes, improperly extinguished, can cause fires. Check your smoke detector batteries.

**SIX YEARS:**
This is a good time to map out your family fire escape plan. Go over what to do if the smoke alarm rings. Go over what you and your child would do in case of fire.

*Some additional tips:*
1. Store matches and lighters in a metal container out of your child's reach.
2. Children under twelve and microwave ovens don't mix.
3. Buy and install smoke detectors and keep them working.
4. Devise two escape routes from your house and practice.
5. Ask your doctor about appropriate remedies and medications to have on hand for household burns—sterile gauze pads and so on. (Let's hope you don't need to use them.)

**Chapter 2**

# Medic Alert! Physical Injuries and Treatments

IF THERE'S ANYTHING A GRANDPARENT WILL TELL YOU, it's that every mom and dad in history has had to face the unpleasant fact that no child can grow up without suffering any number of bumps and bruises. Babies are curious; toddlers are (like Alice in Wonderland) "curiouser." Add curiosity to the fact that homes contain stairs, furniture, and countertops, and that the outdoors is full of natural obstacles—trees to climb, ponds to fall into—and you have a potentially lethal combination. An older child's daily routine of riding his bike, running, climbing, and participating in sports activities virtually guarantees an accident happening sometime during the childhood years.

Medic Alert! Injuries

This chapter tells you how to avoid as many of those obstacles and potentially dangerous situations as possible, as well as how to treat the injuries caused by these situations. Unfortunately, that knowledge won't prevent accidents and even tragedies from happening, but the more you know, the more secure you'll feel in an emergency.

# Safety for Babies and Toddlers

## Preventing Falls in the Home

When it comes to falls inside the home, a number of safety measures prevent problems. The National Safe Kids Campaign in Washington, D.C., has stated that more than 120 children under the age of fourteen die annually as the result of falls in the home. More than ninety of these children are under age five. They also have noted that falls resulted in more than three million trips to the emergency room for kids age fifteen and under in 1993.

Babies lie still the first month or two, but later, as early as four or five months, they can be in constant motion. They tend to roll off changing tables if they are not watched constantly. They will fall off beds, couches, or chairs, as well. Obviously, never leave baby alone on a raised surface. Don't sit baby on the kitchen counter in an infant seat. He may be placed too near the edge, hot food might splatter, or any number of unpleasant things can happen. Place baby in some protected spot away from kitchen hazards, but not out of sight and hearing. Wherever you place him, be sure the surface is stable, not an oh-so-soft couch pillow, and that baby is not in danger of falling.

Babies can't fall down steps if a gate prevents them from entering the staircase. Most important, forget baby walkers. They are more injurious than helpful. *Parents* magazine reported that in 1991, walkers sent 27,000 children fifteen months or younger to emergency rooms; many of these accidents involved falls down stairs.

Use safety straps wherever they are provided to stabilize your child in infant seats, in high chairs, and in strollers or cars. And, remember, don't leave baby unattended.

Once baby can pull himself to his feet, he learns to climb. He will climb on a couch; he will pull himself up in his crib, climb up on the bumpers, then stand on a large teddy bear to look around. Bumpers may serve a purpose by filling the space between the mattress and crib railings, but the toys in the crib pose a different kind of hazard and should be kept to a minimum. And lower the crib mattress as far as it will go, while you keep the drop side locked in its highest position.

Baby doesn't pay too much attention to his feet before he can pull himself up. Bare feet are fine, because baby can use his toes to grip surfaces across which he's crawling. When winter comes, on go the socks. But walking calls for shoes, and these shouldn't be neglected, for safety's sake as well as for the child's health. The foot has twenty-six bones in it, and in children, these bones are partly cartilage. If you buy shoes that are too tight, too loose, or ill fitting in any other way, your child's foot growth pattern may be damaged and the child can suffer unnecessary pain. Ill-fitting shoes that are not properly laced can cause a child to lose his balance and fall. Be sure the shoes aren't tight or rigid. They should be flexible and allow air to circulate around the foot; choose a material that breathes well. (Rubber and patent leather don't.)

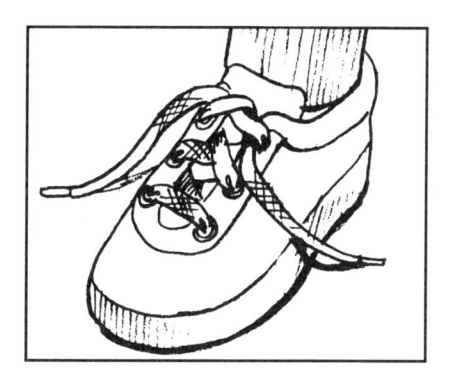

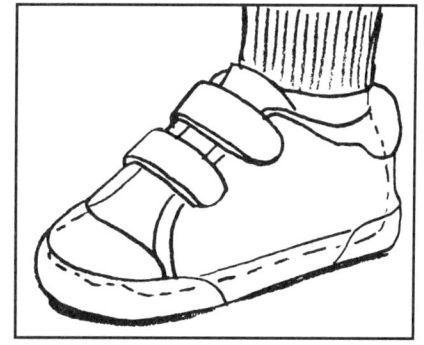

When you fit the shoes, there should be about a half-inch of room for the longest toe of the larger of the two feet. Soles shouldn't be slick (you can put pieces of tape across them or rough them up with sandpaper) or too narrow. Check carefully that the heel is snug inside the shoe and is supported so it doesn't slip; toes shouldn't be cramped. Pay attention to your baby's feet. They grow fast and need to be constantly checked when the baby is between the age of one and two. By the time the baby is three years old, he's likely to tell you himself if his shoes are too tight!

## Sudden Infant Death Syndrome

THE RESEARCH. No one knows what causes Sudden Infant Death Syndrome, or SIDS, but doctors and safety counselors are beginning to talk resoundingly about what to do to reduce its risk. Most infants who die before they have reached their first birthdays—almost 95 percent of them before they've reached the six-month mark—do so suddenly and unexpectedly in their sleep. About 6,000 babies die from this unexplained and horrifying affliction every year—the equivalent of about one to two out of every thousand babies born. That makes SIDS the biggest threat to infants and one that has researchers all over the world on a medic alert.

The syndrome was identified as a medical disorder in 1969, and some progress has been made since to solve its mystery. According to the director of SIDS research at the National Institute of Child Health and Human Development (NICHD), the federal government spent more than $11 million in 1994 studying SIDS. NICHD and other researchers are exploring the development and function of the nervous system, the brain, the heart, breathing and sleep patterns, body chemical balances, autopsy findings, and environmental factors. These studies have found that it is likely that SIDS may be caused by a subtle developmental delay, functional failure, or anatomical defect in particular babies.

What is *known* about SIDS?
- Boys seem to be more prone to SIDS than girls.
- SIDS is more common among twins, triplets, and other multiple births.
- The younger the mother, the greater the risk.

- It is also statistically significant that winter, when the incidence of respiratory and bronchial infections increases, and houses are closed and overheated, is a more dangerous time for SIDS than any other season.

This respiratory connection seems to be receiving a good deal of study. Colds, flu, and allergies reduce a baby's oxygen supply. Normally, when a decrease in oxygen creates a build-up of carbon dioxide in the system, a baby will awaken. Are there certain cells in SIDS babies that fail to warn them of the rise in carbon dioxide and prevent that awakening? Some scientists believe that certain enzymes could be at the bottom of the mystery, such as *tryptase,* which is released during allergic reactions.

Finally, a current study published in the *Journal of the American Medical Association* (March 8, 1995) states that research has confirmed that infants who breathe secondhand smoke face an increased risk of SIDS. The *Journal* reports that the more cigarette smoke an infant is exposed to, the higher the risk of SIDS. A study of 200 cases of SIDS indicates that a baby exposed to the smoke from more than twenty-one cigarettes a day was twenty-three times more likely to die than an infant not exposed to cigarette smoke.

Research by the National Center for Health Statistics indicates that SIDS is not only related to smoking during pregnancy, but to a mother's postpartum smoking. In other words, even if you smoke only *after* the baby is born, you're putting that baby at risk through passive smoke. The center studied data on 10,000 normal birth-weight infants and 6,000 infant deaths in three categories: those whose mothers smoked during and after pregnancy; those whose mothers didn't smoke at all; and those whose mothers smoked only after their babies were born. Babies exposed only after birth were twice as likely to die from SIDS as those whose mothers didn't smoke. Those mothers who smoked both during and after pregnancy *tripled* the chance for SIDS. Because the study relied on self-reported smoking data and didn't take into account the baby's actual smoke exposure from all sources (a nurse, nanny, or caregiver who exposed the baby to more smoke), the study results aren't completely conclusive (except for this one point: passive smoke is harmful).

**PREVENTION.** Despite the extensive research, there is as yet no single solution to SIDS, but a number of findings have led to significant results. The number-one recommendation is that healthy infants be positioned for sleep on their sides and backs, not on their stomachs. The American Academy of Pediatrics (AAP) changed its policy in 1992, recommending the "tummy-up" position. The AAP based its findings on studies from Australia, New Zealand, Norway, the Netherlands, and Great Britain that associate particular sleep patterns with SIDS. The Academy studied the issue in great depth before making its recommendation. But it was clear that public education on the "on-their-backs" issue had created a statistic in Britain, where by December 1994 SIDS cases had decreased by 70 percent since 1991, the year parents were first urged to put infants to sleep on their backs. Reports from New Zealand, Australia, and Norway show that their SIDS rates have fallen dramatically: a 50 percent cut in the death rate is attributed to the sleeping position change.

The U.S. Public Health Service launched its nationwide "Back to Sleep" campaign in 1994 in partnership with the AAP, the SIDS Alliance, and the Association of SIDS Program Professionals. According to the U. S. Surgeon General, despite fears that back sleeping would cause babies to choke on regurgitated fluids, no adverse effects have been reported.

If your baby doesn't like sleeping on his back, carefully position him on his side by placing his lower arm at a right angle to his body; when he rolls from his side, he'll end up on his back. Or, if necessary, wait until baby falls asleep in his preferred position, then reposition him on his back. Also, you can keep baby in the less stable side position by bracing his back against the side of the crib (not with a pillow) and positioning the lower shoulder and arm farther forward than the upper. You can also purchase a product called Baby Sleep-Ez®, a terry-covered foam wedge used to prop sleeping newborns on their sides so they won't tumble over onto their tummies, from a Denver company named Basic Comfort, or you can use a rolled-up towel for the same effect. Both should be removed from the crib after baby has grown a bit and begun to move around. (If you have a premature baby with respiratory problems or a baby who vomits excessively, ask your pediatrician for guidance on the issue of sleeping position.)

Do not place babies on pillows or fluffy bedding. The Consumer Product Safety Commission (CPSC) found that up to 30 percent of the 158 babies it studied who died of SIDS had been sleeping on top of soft comforters and pillows. The supposition is that such bedding poses an added and sometimes insurmountable challenge to a baby already vulnerable to SIDS, molding around the child's mouth and nose and causing him to re-breathe trapped air he has exhaled. Always rest a sleeping infant on a firm, flat surface and avoid using soft, fluffy materials under him. CPSC officials say that while their two-year study does not conclusively prove a causal link between SIDS and fluffy bedclothes, it does underscore the advice on sleep positioning that the medical community has offered for the past several years.

## Injury Treatments
### Minor Scrapes, Cuts, and Bruises

To parents' great dismay, lacerations and scrapes (particularly facial ones) plague kids regularly, especially those under five. A bump or a scrape can be painful to the child. Ice wrapped in a towel should make the wound feel better, but you can do other things to help your child heal fast.

Thoroughly cleanse a surface cut or scrape with mild soap and water. Blot it dry with sterile gauze or cloth. Then use antibacterial spray, lotion, or cream and apply a bandage or use gauze plus bandage tape. If the scrape is very slight, remove the bandage after a day or so. If the cut is fairly large or oozing, use bandages and change them daily. A larger cut should be kept dry and clean and covered with gauze and bandage tape. See your doctor at any sign of infection: pus, swelling, tenderness, or reddening around the wound site.

Bruises can be painful for children, and though parents may tend to treat them more lightly than other wounds, they shouldn't. The American Academy of Pediatrics advises applying cold compresses for a half-hour. If the bruises are extensive, call your doctor. If pain or swelling continues, call your doctor.

## Puncture Wounds and Bleeding

What if your child suffers a puncture wound? The AAP warns: "Do not remove large objects, such as knives or sticks. Call your doctor. For minor puncture wounds, wash with soap and water and call your doctor. The child may need a tetanus booster." What about a tetanus shot? In years gone by, it was a parent's first question when a child stepped on a piece of jagged metal, or when a wound resulted from any contact with rusty or filthy material. These days, if your child has had DPT (diphtheria, pertussis, tetanus) immunizations as a baby or a booster shot (every ten years), a tetanus shot may not be needed. If there is any question (if the wound is particularly deep and filled with dirt), your pediatrician will tell you what to do.

Bleeding is almost as frightening to parents as it is to the young victims, and if certain parts of the body are involved—face, lips, and scalp with their many blood vessels, for example—then bleeding is sure to be considerable. Because this is so scary for a child, adults must learn to keep cool. The smaller the child, the more serious the bleeding can be, so it's important to go to the nearest hospital emergency room. In general, if blood is spurting or flowing from a wound, or if a cut or laceration is a gaping wound with jagged edges, you need to seek medical attention.

Johnson & Johnson and Walgreen's Drug Stores have created a poster outlining three tips for the treatment of bleeding:

1. Act quickly. Apply pressure directly and firmly on the wound with sterile gauze, sterile compress or a clean cloth to control the bleeding. Once the bleeding is controlled by this direct pressure, bandage firmly to protect the wound. Check for discoloration around the wound to make sure bandage is not too tight.
2. Have the victim lie down. Elevate the injured area higher than the heart if possible unless you suspect a broken bone.
3. Call for professional medical help IMMEDIATELY.

If you are bleeding and have no one to help you, apply direct pressure if possible as directed above. Call for help, lie down and elevate the affected area.

<small>Reprinted by permission of Johnson & Johnson Consumer Products.</small>

If a cut penetrates beneath the skin into muscle or tissue, your child may need stitches. Doctors advise that the skin and muscle should be joined to help the wound heal and to prevent scarring. Additionally, if the deep wound is on the face, you may wish to consult a plastic surgeon. Your pediatrician will help you with that decision.

Dr. Tim Adkins, medical director for Emergency Services at the Coral Springs Medical Center in Coral Springs, Florida, thinks a doctor should be consulted for treatment of deep wounds: "Usually, when you have a through-and-through penetrating wound that crosses the entire surface of the skin—where you have multiple layers of the skin and it goes all the way through the skin, so that you have protruding fat or an area where it stretches open—then, that usually needs closure. Superficial abrasions, little cuts that don't go all the way through the skin and don't stretch open when you spread them apart, frequently won't require sutures. And, obviously, if you are in doubt, the trained professional should take a look at those kind of wounds."

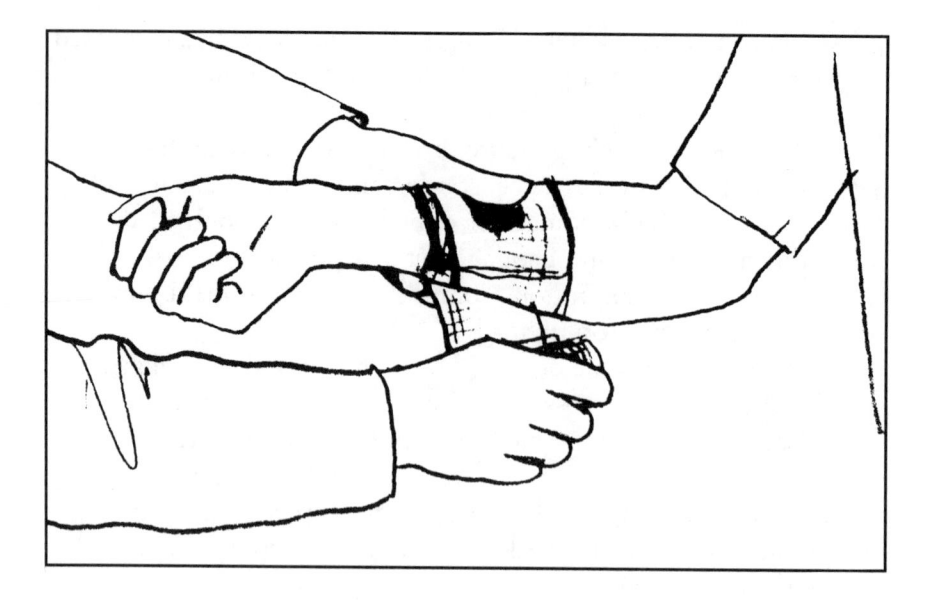

The nature of the wound determines whether Dr. Adkins will work with plastic surgeons. "Some of what would be considered plastic surgical procedures we do, such as subcuticular stitches or layered closures or whatever; other procedures that we consider beyond our expertise are referred to plastic surgeons." Dr. Adkins added that the use of sedatives while stitching children's wounds varies from doctor to doctor. He uses them only "in particular cases where a completely nonmoving child is important. That's frequently when you're doing very delicate plastic work or trying to work on fingers, where it's very difficult to immobilize them on a very young child. For the most part, we'll just use topical or injectable anesthetics that are local anesthetics—on the area, that is, where we're working."

## Fractures and Sprains

What about fractures and sprains? You should not move a child who may have a neck or back injury, because this may cause a worse problem. If an injured limb, such as an arm, leg, wrist, hand, ankle, or foot, is swollen and deformed, or if slight movement causes pain, you should suspect that it's broken. Remember, as a parent you must remain calm. Your child may be crying, but do not rush to pick him up. Get his attention by asking him where he hurts. Once the child responds to you, check to determine if he has feeling in his hands and feet. You may have to apply a temporary splint to stabilize the injured limb.

To make a splint, use any stiff material (wood, or even a rolled-up newspaper). Attach the splint to the injured limb with tape or cloth. Ideally, the splint should extend to include the joints above and below the injury. You can also splint a broken arm by wrapping it to the child's chest. The main point is not to let the arm dangle loosely as your precious cargo is being transported to the emergency room. Remember, if possible, someone other than the driver should attend to the child during the transport.

## Injuries to Teeth

Do teeth and the care of them have much to do with safety? Yes, indeed, and parents can do a number of things to protect their child's smile. First, children as young as twenty-four to thirty-six months should begin seeing a dentist and brushing their teeth. All children should practice good dental care, including regular visits to the dentist, daily brushing and flossing, and the use of fluoride or sealants. Dr. Theodore L. Gehrig of Chicago described a sealant as "a little protective resin filling that goes in the grooves of developmental teeth; it actually seals off the groove of the tooth in order to protect it to make it cavity proof. Until the adult tooth is in, it gets the kids through the formative years, when those grooves are most susceptible to decay."

In addition, older children who are active in sports should be fitted for and should wear a mouthpiece while playing those sports. Dr. Dana R. Walters in Columbus, Ohio, sees sports injuries from soccer, football, hockey, basketball, in-line skating, and skateboarding. He recommends that all children involved with these sports wear a mouth guard. Custom-made mouthpieces are more expensive, but the child can speak and breathe more easily. The mouthpiece, made of soft rubber shaped like a horseshoe, fits over the upper teeth. "It keeps the biting surface separated, and keeps teeth from banging against one another. Wearing a mouth guard actually reduces concussions. I do believe the mouth guard is the number-one piece of protective equipment to have. And, you can still wear braces and wear a mouth guard."

Dr. Marjorie Jeffcoat, professor of dentistry at the University of Alabama in Birmingham, stresses the importance of protecting children's teeth against injury, particularly the front teeth: "If the baby teeth come out too soon, the teeth tend to drift and then the permanent teeth don't necessarily come in in the right places. Of course, the tooth doesn't always fall out. The tooth can be broken, and there can be infection and pain for the child, which you'd rather avoid." After trauma, a tooth can die, even in an older child: "They can take a pretty good whack to the front of the face. The tooth can be loose and it may tighten up, but then, even five years later, the tooth may go dark, indicating it needs a root canal, and we'd rather save the child from that."

Dr. Walters notes that the most common incidents he sees result from falls in the home that cause the teeth to become either loose or wobbly. "The tooth will commonly firm back up within a few weeks. Usually these are still baby teeth. Other common injuries I see are cut lips and gums. These are not too serious, and will heal." After an injury, teeth may turn gray or red, the latter being more rare: "The gray tooth goes from gray to brown and in either case, the tooth is dead or dying. If the tooth is very bad, we can do a baby root canal. For children younger than four years old with a mouth injury, it's best to go to a children's hospital. If it is a tooth injury, look for a pimple on the gums. This also indicates the tooth is dead."

If your child's tooth is knocked out, don't wash it or brush off dirt: "Place it in a glass of milk and go to the dentist within one hour of the time the tooth was lost and you have a chance to replace it. If it's a baby tooth, it's not so vital. If an adult tooth breaks or chips, call your dentist and he or she can repair the tooth." If you have any doubt about the seriousness of the child's injury, see your family dentist. If it's a serious injury, see a pediatric dentist.

## **Choking and Suffocation**

Choking children and the specter of suffocation understandably frighten all adults. In fact, choking and suffocation are the most common causes of preventable death in children under one year of age, and the fourth most common cause of death in children under fourteen years of age. In 1993, the National Safe Kids Campaign in Washington, D.C., stated that approximately 325 children under four years old choked to death on food (170 children) and objects (155 children). Approximately 350 children under fourteen suffocate, and about 250 of those children are under the age of five.

Choking is such an emergency that adults *do* panic. Rather than panic, though, it is best to learn what to do in case it should ever happen to you. Ideally, after reading this book, all parents, teachers, and caregivers will be able to perform cardiopulmonary resuscitation (CPR) and the Heimlich maneuver, and, if need be, they will go for formal training from the American Heart Association or the American Red Cross.

Choking is caused by the inhalation of objects or food. Strangulation/suffocation is caused by constriction of the neck or blocking the nose and mouth. Both result in blockage of the airway passages, which interferes with breathing. If a child is choking, *don't* interfere if he can speak, cough, or breathe; he'll work to clear his own airway. *Do not* try to force open a choking child's mouth to pull out any object. Stay calm and reassuring. Check for the following:
- Is the child able to speak?
- Is the child able to cough?

## Medic Alert! Injuries

- Is the child grasping his throat?
- Is the child having difficulty breathing?
- Is the face turning blue, pale, or ashen?
- Is the child unconscious?

If the child *is* unconscious, open his mouth immediately. If you see the foreign object, carefully remove it. *Never poke your finger straight into the throat;* if you're too forceful, you may push down an object even further. When an infant under one year is choking, follow these steps:

1. If the infant can breathe, cough, or cry, let him try to expel the object, and do none of the following.
2. If baby is unable to make sounds, or if complete obstruction is the case, *don't* do the Heimlich maneuver (the abdominal thrust technique). This technique may damage the stomach, liver, or spleen of children under twelve months. Instead, immediately lay the infant face down across your lap or forearm with your hand firmly supporting the jaw. Turn the head to the side. Rest your forearm on your thigh to support the infant. Baby's head should be lower than his chest.
3. With the heel of your other hand, give five forceful and quick blows to the baby's back between his shoulder blades.
4. If the object is still not dislodged, turn the child faceup (with head still lower than the body). Support the baby's head and neck with one of your hands and position him faceup on your forearm. Turn the infant's head to one side. With two fingertips (middle and ring fingers) on the baby's chest near the center of the breastbone, between the nipples, give five quick downward presses or thrusts. (Note: If the baby is large, you may want to lay him over your lap. Firmly support the head, holding it lower than the trunk and begin with the back blows.)

5. If choking continues, repeat the entire procedure.
6. If the infant becomes unconscious, begin mouth-to-mouth resuscitation (see step 5 below for complete instructions).
7. *Don't give up.*
8. Call for emergency services.

When a child older than a year is choking, follow these steps:
1. If the child can cry, cough, speak, or breathe, don't interfere with her own efforts.
2. If the child is choking, can't cough or make sounds, and has increasing difficulty breathing, do the Heimlich maneuver (abdominal thrusts) immediately (see page 44 for instructions).
3. If you think the child has swallowed a sharp object, or if the pain persists more than five minutes, don't stop to worry about it. Go instantly to your nearest emergency room.
4. If you have successfully performed first aid, remember that *even if the child is more than one year old*, abdominal thrusts during the Heimlich maneuver can cause internal injury, and there could also be respiratory tract damage. Seek medical attention right away.
5. If the victim is unconscious, lower him to the floor and perform mouth-to-mouth resuscitation. Kneel close to the victim's side or straddle his hips. Open the victim's airway using a chin lift or a jaw lift. The jaw lift draws the tongue from the back of the throat and may help clear the airway. If you see a foreign object, sweep it out with your finger. Don't poke the finger straight into the throat. Tilt the child's head back. Seal your lips tightly around the child's mouth and pinch the nose shut. Give two slow breaths until the chest gently rises.

## Medic Alert! Injuries

6. If the chest doesn't rise and your breath won't go in, place the heel of one hand on the child's abdomen in the midline slightly above the navel and well below the rib cage. Press one hand into the abdomen with quick upward thrusts. If necessary, do a series of five thrusts. Each thrust should be a separate, distinct movement. Direct each thrust inward and upward in the midline and *not to either side of the abdomen.* Thrusts should be rapid; press firmly but gently.
7. After delivering five abdominal thrusts, attempt rescue breathing again. If the airway remains obstructed, repeat all of the above.

The American Academy of Pediatrics advises: Don't do blind finger sweeps down the child's throat. When chest thrusts or abdominal thrusts (under the diaphragm) are done for the unconscious, nonbreathing victim, open the victim's mouth by grasping both the tongue and the lower jaw between your thumb and finger and lifting. This is the *tongue-jaw lift.* It draws the tongue from the back of the throat and may itself partially relieve the obstruction. If you see the foreign matter, remove it. And remember, if the child has suffered severe choking, consult your pediatrician to be sure no pieces of the choked item have lodged in the lungs.

### The Heimlich Maneuver

The Heimlich maneuver is based on the concepts that four-fifths of normal respiration occurs using the diaphragm and that abdominal pressure compresses the diaphragm upward. This raises intrathoracic pressure, and it is this rapid intrathoracic pressure that can force the object out. The patient's muscle tone diminishes with every passing minute, so the repeated abdominal thrusts become effective. Remember, do not use this maneuver on infants under one year. Try instead the chest thrust technique, which uses sternal compression in an effort to expel the foreign object.

Follow these steps to perform the Heimlich maneuver:

# Performance Guidelines

## Relief of Obstructed Airway: Conscious Infant (younger than 1 year)

| | Objectives |
|---|---|
| | **Assessment:** Determine *complete* airway obstruction either by observing sudden onset of signs of complete airway obstruction or by the circumstances in which the infant is found. |
| | If the infant is *unable* to cry or cough effectively:<br><br>**Action:** Deliver up to 5 back blows. |

Reproduced with permission.
© *Pediatric Basic Life Support Textbook*, 1994.
Copyright American Heart Association.

| **Critical Performance** | **Reason** |
|---|---|
| Rescuer must identify *complete* airway obstruction by the presence of breathing difficulty, an absent or ineffective cough, dusky color, and an inability to make sounds.<br><br>*If the infant is able to cough or cry, do not interfere* with the infant's attempts to expel the object. | In the conscious infant it is essential to recognize the signs of *complete* airway obstruction and take prompt action.<br><br>If the infant is able to cough or cry, air is getting through the trachea (windpipe) and the obstruction is *not* complete. In such a situation, you may make things worse by interfering. |
| Support the infant's head and neck with one hand firmly holding the jaw. Place the infant face down on your forearm, keeping the head lower than the trunk.<br><br>With the heel of your free hand, deliver up to **5** back blows forcefully between the infant's shoulder blades. | You must hold the infant's head firmly to avoid injury. The back blows increase pressure in the airway and may help dislodge the object. |

Reproduced with permission.
© *Pediatric Basic Life Support Textbook*, 1994.
Copyright American Heart Association.

# Performance Guidelines

**Relief of Obstructed Airway: Conscious Infant (younger than 1 year) (continued)**

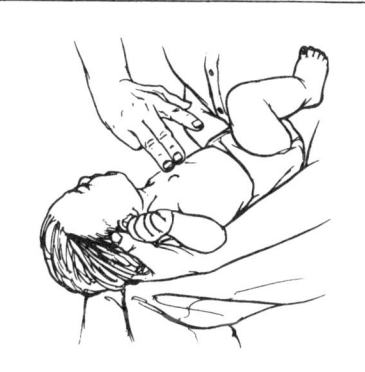

| | Objectives |
|---|---|
| | **Action:** Deliver up to 5 chest thrusts over the lower half of the sternum (avoid the xiphoid). |
| | **Action:** Repeat the sequence of 5 back blows and 5 chest thrusts until the object is expelled or until the infant becomes unconscious. Be persistent!<br><br>Reproduced with permission.<br>© *Pediatric Basic Life Support Textbook*, 1994.<br>Copyright American Heart Association. |

## Medic Alert! Injuries

| Critical Performance | Reason |
|---|---|
| Supporting the head, sandwich the infant between your hands and arms and turn the infant on his or her back, keeping the head lower than the trunk.<br><br>Deliver up to **5** thrusts over the lower half of the breastbone, using the same landmarks as those for chest compression. Make sure your fingers are not placed over the very bottom of the sternum (xiphoid).<br><br>Deliver the chest thrusts more slowly than when doing chest compressions. | Such thrusts can force air upward into the airway from the lungs with enough pressure to expel the foreign object. |
| Alternate these maneuvers in rapid sequence:<br>• Back blows<br>• Chest thrusts | Persistent attempts should be made to relieve the obstruction. As the infant becomes more deprived of oxygen, the airway muscles will relax, and maneuvers that were previously ineffective may become effective. |

Reproduced with permission.
© *Pediatric Basic Life Support Textbook*, 1994.
Copyright American Heart Association.

**Medic Alert! Injuries**

## CPR

You've heard the heart referred to as "the master pump," and this makes sense, when you come to understand the pumping system that goes on between the heart and the body. It all starts with the fact that air is about 21 percent oxygen at sea level. As the air sacs of the lungs fill with this air, the blood around the air sacs picks up oxygen from the air and carries it back to the heart, which pumps it everywhere we need it in the body.

As oxygen is taken from the blood by the body's cells, carbon dioxide is given off as a waste product, returned by the blood to the air sacs, then exhaled out of the body. When air is inhaled, only one-quarter of the oxygen gets taken up by the blood; the rest is exhaled. That's why mouth-to-mouth breathing can give the victim enough oxygen (about 16 percent of the rescuer's breath) to help prevent biological death.

Early prompt rescue can prevent the heart from stopping (otherwise known as cardiac arrest). What is this rescue? It's known as *cardiopulmonary resuscitation* (CPR)—an emergency procedure that combines mouth-to-mouth rescue breathing and chest compressions that can be performed until advanced life support care can be made available.

See the following pages for instructions for performing CPR.

# Performance Guidelines

## CPR: Infant (younger than 1 year)

| | Objectives |
|---|---|
| | **Assessment:** Determine unresponsiveness. Shout for help. |
| | **Action:** Position the infant on his or her back. |
| | **Action:** Open the airway (head tilt–chin lift). |
| | **Assessment:** Determine breathlessness. |

Reproduced with permission.
© *Pediatric Basic Life Support Textbook*, 1994.
Copyright American Heart Association.

**Medic Alert! Injuries**

| Critical Performance | Reason |
|---|---|
| Tap or gently shake victim's shoulder. Call out "Help!" If help arrives, send someone to activate the EMS system. | You do not want to begin CPR unnecessarily if the infant is sleeping. A call for help will summon persons nearby but allow you to begin CPR if necessary. |
| Turn the infant as a unit, supporting head and neck. Place the infant on a firm surface. If the infant's head or neck has possibly been injured, turn the infant carefully, holding the head and neck as a unit to avoid bending or turning the neck. | For CPR to be effective, the infant must be flat on his or her back on a firm surface. CPR cannot be performed if the infant is face down. |
| Lift the chin up and out gently with one hand while pushing down on the forehead with the other to tilt the head back into a neutral position. Don't close the mouth. If trauma is suspected, use the jaw thrust to open the airway. | The airway must be opened to determine whether the infant is breathing. Infants may be unable to breathe because the tongue is obstructing the airway. |
| Maintain an open airway. Turn your head toward the infant's chest with your ear directly over and close to the infant's mouth.<br>  *Look* at the chest for movement.<br>  *Listen* for the sounds of breathing.<br>  *Feel* for breath on your cheek. | Hearing and feeling are the only true ways of determining the presence of effective breathing. If there is chest movement but you cannot feel or hear air, the airway may still be obstructed.<br>Rescue breathing should not be performed on someone who is breathing effectively. |

Reproduced with permission.
© *Pediatric Basic Life Support Textbook*, 1994.
Copyright American Heart Association.

## Performance Guidelines
### CPR: Infant (younger than 1 year) (continued)

| | Objectives |
|---|---|
| | **Action:** If the victim is not breathing, provide rescue breathing. Give 2 slow rescue breaths (1 to 1½ seconds per breath). Observe the rise of the chest with each breath. |
| | **Assessment:** Determine pulselessness. |

Reproduced with permission.
© *Pediatric Basic Life Support Textbook*, 1994.
Copyright American Heart Association.

### Medic Alert! Injuries

| Critical Performance | Reason |
|---|---|
| Maintain pressure on the infant's forehead to keep the head tilted. With the other hand lift the chin, open your mouth wide and take a deep breath. Cover the infant's mouth and nose with your mouth, making a tight seal. Breathe into the infant's mouth and nose twice, completely refilling your lungs between breaths. Watch for the infant's chest to rise.<br><br>Each rescue breath is given over 1 to 1½ seconds, allowing the infant's lungs to deflate between breaths. If the rescue breaths do not cause the infant's chest to rise, the airway is obstructed. Reposition the head, lift the chin, and try again. If the chest still does not rise with the rescue breath, start the relief of obstructed airway sequence (page 50). | It is important to get as much oxygen as possible into the infant. If your rescue breathing is effective, you will<br>• Feel air going in as you blow<br>• Feel the air leaving your own lungs<br>• See the infant's chest rise and fall<br><br>The most common cause of an obstructed airway is that the airway has not been properly opened. |
| Place 2 or 3 fingers on the inside of the infant's upper arm, between the elbow and shoulder. Press gently on the inside of the arm with your index and middle fingers. Maintain head tilt with the other hand. Feel for the brachial pulse.<br>• If pulse is present and breathing has not resumed, breathe for the infant at the rate of 20 times per minute.<br>• If there is no pulse, start chest compressions. | This step should not take more than a few seconds. If the heart is beating effectively, you should be able to feel a strong, rapid pulse within a few seconds. If you do not feel a pulse, begin chest compressions.<br><br>Reproduced with permission.<br>© *Pediatric Basic Life Support Textbook*, 1994. Copyright American Heart Association. |

## Performance Guidelines

### CPR: Infant (younger than 1 year) (continued)

| | Objectives |
|---|---|
| | **Action:** Begin the first cycle of chest compressions. |
| | Reproduced with permission.<br>© *Pediatric Basic Life Support Textbook*, 1994.<br>Copyright American Heart Association. |

**Medic Alert! Injuries**

| Critical Performance | Reason |
|---|---|
| To begin the first cycle, imagine a line drawn between the infant's nipples. Place 2 or 3 fingers on the breastbone (sternum) about 1 finger's width below that line. Because of wide variations in the relative sizes of rescuers' hands and infants' chests, these instructions are only guidelines. After finding the position for compressions, make sure your fingers are not over the bottom of the sternum (xiphoid). Compress the infant's chest downward approximately one third to one half the depth of the chest (about ½ to 1 inch, but these measurements are not precise) at least 100 times per minute. | Proper finger placement is important to maximize the effectiveness of compressions and minimize the risk of injury to the infant. |
| Compress smoothly and evenly, and release pressure between compressions to allow the chest to return to its normal position. Do not lift your fingers off the chest. | With each compression, you want to squeeze the heart and increase pressure within the chest so that blood moves to the vital organs. |
| To achieve a proper rate and ratio, count aloud: "one-two-three-four-five-breathe . . . ." | |

Reproduced with permission.
© *Pediatric Basic Life Support Textbook*, 1994.
Copyright American Heart Association.

# Performance Guidelines

## CPR: Infant (younger than 1 year) (continued)

| | Objectives |
|---|---|
| | **Action:** Give **5** compressions and **1** breath. |
| | **Action:** Activate the EMS system at the end of 20 cycles or 20 rescue breaths (approximately 1 minute).<br><br>After EMS notification, resume CPR, beginning with chest compressions. Check every few minutes for return of pulse. |

Reproduced with permission.
© *Pediatric Basic Life Support Textbook*, 1994.
Copyright American Heart Association.

## Medic Alert! Injuries

| Critical Performance | Reason |
|---|---|
| Ventilate properly. After every **5** compressions, deliver **1** rescue breath. Pause briefly after each 5th compression to deliver the 1 breath. | Adequate oxygenation must be maintained. |
| Know your local EMS telephone number. If a second person is available, he or she should telephone the local EMS immediately while you continue CPR. If you are alone, perform CPR for approximately 1 minute *before* activating the EMS system.<br><br>• If the pulse returns, check for spontaneous breathing.<br>  — If there is no breathing, give 1 rescue breath every 3 seconds (20 breaths per minute) and monitor the pulse.<br>  — If breathing resumes, maintain an open airway and monitor breathing and pulse.<br>• If pulse *and* breathing resume and are regular and there is no evidence of trauma, turn the infant on his or her side, continue to monitor breathing and pulse, and await rescue personnel. | Notification of the EMS system at this time allows the caller to give complete information about the infant's condition.<br><br><br><br><br><br><br><br><br><br><br><br><br><br>Reproduced with permission.<br>© *Pediatric Basic Life Support Textbook*, 1994. Copyright American Heart Association. |

## Performance Guidelines
### CPR: Child (1 to 8 years)

| | Objectives |
|---|---|
| | **Assessment:** Determine unresponsiveness. Shout for help. |
| | **Action:** Position the child on his or her back. |
| | **Action:** Open the airway (head tilt–chin lift). |
| | **Assessment:** Determine breathlessness. |

Reproduced with permission.
© *Pediatric Basic Life Support Textbook*, 1994.
Copyright American Heart Association.

## Medic Alert! Injuries

| Critical Performance | Reason |
|---|---|
| Tap or gently shake the shoulder. Shout "Are you OK?" Call out "Help!" If help arrives, send someone to activate the EMS system. | One concern is the risk of possible damage from unnecessary CPR for children who are sleeping. A call for help will summon people nearby but allow you to begin CPR if necessary. |
| Turn the child as a unit, supporting head and neck. If head or neck injury is suspected, do not bend or turn the neck. | For CPR to be effective, the child must be flat on his or her back on a firm, hard surface. CPR cannot be performed if the child is face down. |
| Kneel beside the child's shoulder. Lift the chin up gently with one hand while pushing down on the forehead with the other to tilt the head back into a neutral position. Do not close the mouth. If there is evidence of trauma, open the airway using a jaw thrust. | The airway must be opened to determine whether the child is breathing. Children may be unable to breathe because the tongue is obstructing the airway. |
| Maintain an open airway. Turn your head toward the child's chest with your ear directly over and close to the child's mouth.<br>*Look* at the chest for movement.<br>*Listen* for the sounds of breathing.<br>*Feel* for breath on your cheek. | Hearing and feeling are the only true ways of determining the presence of effective breathing. If there is chest movement but you cannot feel or hear air, the airway may still be obstructed. Rescue breathing should not be performed on someone who is breathing effectively. |

Reproduced with permission.
© *Pediatric Basic Life Support Textbook*, 1994.
Copyright American Heart Association.

Medic Alert! Injuries

# Performance Guidelines
CPR: Child (1 to 8 years) (continued)

| | Objectives |
|---|---|
| | **Action:** If the child is not breathing, provide rescue breathing. Give 2 rescue breaths (1 to 1½ seconds per breath). Observe the rise of the chest with each breath. |

Reproduced with permission.
© *Pediatric Basic Life Support Textbook*, 1994.
Copyright American Heart Association.

| Critical Performance | Reason |
|---|---|
| Pinch the child's nostrils closed with the thumb and forefinger of the hand maintaining pressure on the child's forehead while lifting the chin with the other hand. Open your mouth wide, take a deep breath, and make a tight seal over the child's mouth. Breathe into the child's mouth twice, completely refilling your lungs between breaths. Watch for the child's chest to rise. Each rescue breath is given over 1 to 1½ seconds, allowing the child's lungs to deflate between breaths. | It is important to get as much oxygen as possible into the child. If your rescue breathing is effective, you will<br>• Feel air going in as you blow<br>• Feel the air leaving your own lungs<br>• See the child's chest rise and fall |
| If the rescue breaths do not cause the child's chest to rise, the airway is obstructed. Reposition the head, lift the chin, and try again. If the chest still does not rise with the rescue breath, start the relief of obstructed airway sequence (page 70). | Improper head tilt–chin lift is the most common reason that airway obstruction is not relieved. |

Reproduced with permission.
© *Pediatric Basic Life Support Textbook*, 1994.
Copyright American Heart Association.

**Medic Alert! Injuries**

# Performance Guidelines
## CPR: Child (1 to 8 years) (continued)

| | Objectives |
|---|---|
| | **Assessment:** Determine pulselessness. |

| Critical Performance | Reason |
|---|---|
| Using the hand that is farther from the child's forehead, place 2 or 3 fingers on the child's Adam's apple (voice box) just below the chin. Slide the fingers into the groove between the Adam's apple and the neck muscle on the side of the neck near you. Maintain head tilt with the other hand. Feel for the carotid pulse.<br>• If a pulse is present and breathing has not resumed, breathe for the child at a rate of 20 times per minute.<br>• If there is no pulse, start chest compressions. | This step should not take more than a few seconds. If the heart is beating effectively, you should feel a strong, rapid pulse within a few seconds. If you do not feel a pulse, begin chest compressions.<br><br><br><br>Reproduced with permission.<br>© *Pediatric Basic Life Support Textbook*, 1994. Copyright American Heart Association. |

## Medic Alert! Injuries

# Performance Guidelines
CPR: Child (1 to 8 years) (continued)

| | **Objectives** |
|---|---|
| | **Action:** Begin the first cycle of chest compressions. |
| | Reproduced with permission.<br>© *Pediatric Basic Life Support Textbook*, 1994.<br>Copyright American Heart Association. |

**Medic Alert! Injuries**

| Critical Performance | Reason |
|---|---|
| To begin the first cycle:<br>Move the hand that is not maintaining head tilt to the child's chest. Place the heel of the hand on the lower half of the breastbone (sternum). Do not place your hand over the very bottom of the sternum (the xiphoid). Compress the child's chest downward approximately one third to one half the depth of the chest (this is about 1 to 1½ inches, but these measurements are not precise) at a rate of 100 times per minute. | Proper hand placement is important to maximize effective compressions and minimize the risk of injury to the child. |
| Compress smoothly and evenly, keeping your fingers off the child's ribs.<br>Between compressions, release pressure and allow the chest to return to its normal position, but do not lift the hand off the chest. Say a mnemonic to maintain the proper rate and ratio. Count aloud to establish a rhythm: "one-two-three-four-five-breathe . . . ." | With each compression, you want to squeeze the heart and increase pressure within the chest so that blood moves to the vital organs. |

Reproduced with permission.
© *Pediatric Basic Life Support Textbook*, 1994.
Copyright American Heart Association.

## Performance Guidelines

CPR: Child (1 to 8 years) (continued)

| | Objectives |
|---|---|
| | **Action:** Give **5** compressions and **1** breath. |
| | **Action:** Activate the EMS system at the end of 20 cycles or 20 rescue breaths (approximately 1 minute of CPR). |
| | After EMS activation, resume CPR, beginning with chest compressions. Check every few minutes for return of pulse. |

Reproduced with permission.
© *Pediatric Basic Life Support Textbook*, 1994.
Copyright American Heart Association.

| Critical Performance | Reason |
|---|---|
| Ventilate properly. After every **5** compressions, deliver **1** rescue breath. | Adequate oxygenation must be maintained. |
| Know your local EMS telephone number. If a second person is available, he or she should telephone the local EMS immediately. | Notification of the EMS system at this time allows the caller to give complete information about the child's condition. |
| • If the pulse returns, check for spontaneous breathing.<br>  — If there is no breathing, give 1 rescue breath every 3 seconds (20 breaths per minute) and monitor the pulse.<br>  — If breathing resumes, maintain an open airway and monitor breathing and pulse.<br>• If pulse *and* breathing resume and are regular and there is no evidence of trauma, turn the child to the side, continue to monitor breathing and pulse, and await emergency personnel. | |

Reproduced with permission.
© *Pediatric Basic Life Support Textbook*, 1994. Copyright American Heart Association.

Medic Alert! Injuries

# The Family First-Aid Kit

Accidents do happen, unfortunately, so it is best to be prepared. One good way to be prepared is to gather the following items in your family's first-aid kit:

- Adhesive bandages (different sizes for minor wounds, cuts, and scratches)
- Butterfly bandage closures (to hold wound edges firmly together)
- Flexible rolled gauze in several sizes (one-, two-, and three-inch) to secure sterile pads or dressings and for wrapping joints and hard-to-bandage areas
- Adhesive pads for larger wounds
- Sterile gauze pads and/or nonstick sterile pads for bleeding and draining wounds; for burns and infections
- Tape for securing dressings
- Elastic tape
- Small scissors
- Safety pins
- Sterile cotton balls
- Soap or other cleansing agent
- Petroleum jelly or other lubricant (not for burns)
- Analgesic (to help relieve pain)
- Ice packs (small and large) for reducing pain and swelling
- Ipecac syrup to induce vomiting, but *not* to be used if victim has been poisoned by an unknown substance, a petroleum product, or a corrosive. As one nurse put it, "If it burns going down, it will burn coming up." A corrosive, such as cleaning fluid, lye, or drain cleaner, is an acid. Petroleum products include gasoline (kids could stumble over a can of this in the garage, which Dad keeps around for emergencies), turpentine, paint thinner, lighter fluid, and the like. (See Chapter 3 for more information on poisons.)
- Mineral oil (one somewhat offbeat use: to help dislodge ticks from a child's ears)

**Medic Alert! Injuries**

- ❑ Sterile eye wash
- ❑ Triangular bandage for arm slings, binders for splints, head dressings, and so on
- ❑ Tweezers to be sterilized for splinter removal
- ❑ Anti-itch cream or calamine lotion (or both) for insect bites
- ❑ Sunblock, sunscreen, sunburn prescription (physician-recommended)
- ❑ Antibacterial cream
- ❑ Chamomile ointment for a skin reaction to nickel or other metals
- ❑ Epsom salts (or chamomile or calendula tea)—for an allergic reaction that causes a skin rash
- ❑ Aveeno® for itching
- ❑ Instant cold pack to prevent swelling
- ❑ Hot water bottle for pain
- ❑ Hydrogen peroxide (wound disinfectant) or rubbing alcohol
- ❑ Baking soda (use in paste form to treat bee stings, insect bites, poison ivy, canker sores, sunburn, rashes, and skin irritations)
- ❑ Calendula ointment to inhibit infection
- ❑ A small flashlight or penlight. This is necessary if or when, for any reason, you need light to read the writing on any medicine bottle.

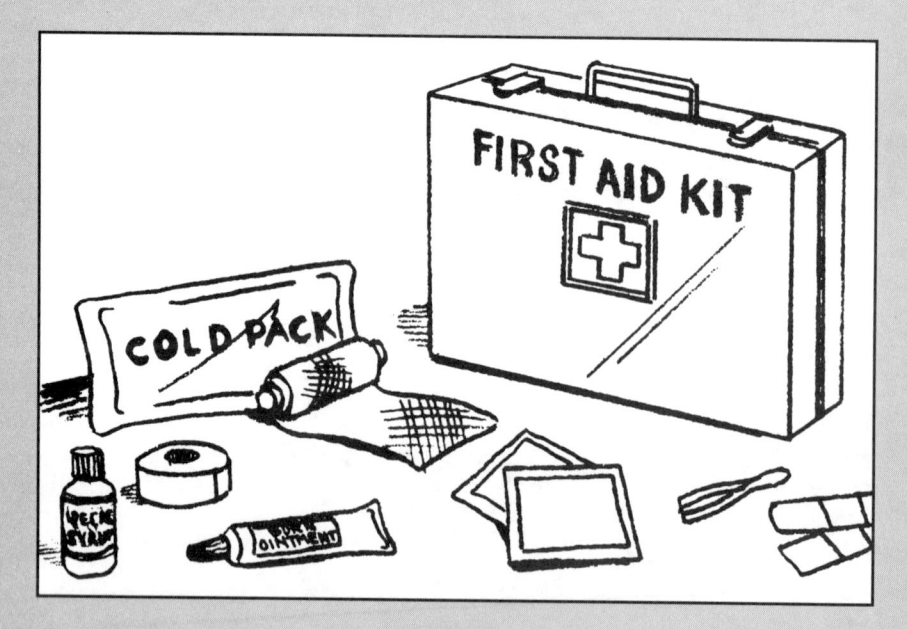

**Medic Alert! Injuries**

# Very Important Tips

**PREVENTING INJURIES FROM FALLS**

*In addition to referring to Chapter 5 on childproofing your home, check the following:*

1. Tack down rugs, including area rugs.
2. Use bath rugs that stick and aren't flimsy.
3. Keep floors clean but not slippery.
4. Install window guards and stops if you need them.
5. Keep stairs well lit and clutter free. Children should not be allowed to play on stairs. Infants and toddlers should be protected by safety gates at the top and, in some instances, bottom of the stairs.
6. Children don't belong on fire escapes, high terraces in apartment buildings, or balconies.
7. Fix loose boards and railings on staircases.
8. Move chairs and other items ideal for climbing away from windows in children's rooms.
9. Do not leave windows open more than five inches. These pose a safety risk for children.
10. In the kitchen, wipe up spilled liquids right away, especially if they are oily or greasy.
11. Outdoors, patch broken walks and driveways and fill in any holes in the lawn or garden. Be sure to secure objects in the yard or on the terrace, such as a swingset or playhouse. Store garden implements and hoses out of the way and get rid of loose boards or plywood sheets.
12. Clear wet leaves and snow from walkways, steps, and porches, and sprinkle icy patches with a de-icing solution. Make sure little ones can't slip or trip on ice on doormats.

**PREVENTING CHOKING AND SUFFOCATION**

1. Sit down at the table when you eat. Simple as that. Do not allow your child to eat while walking, running, or playing.
2. When you are feeding a toddler, cut up his food in appropriately small pieces and teach your child how to chew. (This is part of the fun of having new teeth!)

**Medic Alert! Injuries**

# Very Important Tips

3. Certain foods are more dangerous to eat than others. If your two-year-old loves seedless grapes, cut each grape in half, so he can manage them.

4. Don't prop baby's bottle to allow him to drink by himself.

5. Foods you should not give to children (under four years of age, say the American Academy of Pediatrics and the American Heart Association) include popcorn, hard candy, peanut butter chunks, raw carrots, nuts, and hot dogs.

6. Keep watch at the family dinner table. Sometimes older siblings offer something, such as a chunk of meat, to a smaller brother or sister, which could lead to choking. Thank your helpful one most kindly, but say, "Your sister doesn't have enough teeth to chew that, like you can do, so we can't give it to her. But it was very generous of you to share."

7. Toys with small parts are dangerous. Take a good look: If a toy has any part that could be swallowed, remove it. Keep coins, marbles, small button-type batteries, the tops of pens, and earrings and rings away from your child.

8. Watch out for balloons, especially when deflated. If your child receives an inflated balloon at a birthday party or store, don't allow him to leave it lying around while it loses air or until it breaks or bursts. Baby could discover one of these, months later, and put it in his mouth. According to the Consumer Product Safety Commission, more children choke to death on deflated balloons than any other toy. Get rid of any of the burst fragments and lock away collapsed balloons. All packages of latex balloons sold in the U.S. now carry a warning: "Choking hazard."

## Chapter 3

# Medic Alert! Poisons, Medicine Overdoses, and Treatments

IN THIS CHAPTER, you'll learn about poisons—the most obvious, and possibly the most accessible to children around the house, from aspirin to insecticides, as well as the least obvious, including the "silent" killers known as carbon monoxide and lead. The chapter will conclude with a discussion of what can be done to combat the deadly poisons known as drugs. It also should be noted that in contrast to unintentional poisonings, according to the National Safety Council, many poisonings result from intentional product misuse in an effort to get "high." The victims (or culprits) are more often youngsters in the eight-to-twelve age bracket, but sometimes adults abuse products as well.

Medic Alert! Poisons

# Household Poisons

In the booklet *Protecting Young Children from Poisoning*, Macfarlan Smith Ltd. and the National Safety Council characterized accidental poisonings: "Over 90% of poisonings occur in the home, usually between 9 A.M. and 11 P.M. Most poisonings occur in children who are younger than six years old, almost half are under the age of four. Most poisonings result from drinking or eating (rather than inhalation) and involve only one substance." Poisons around your house include household chemicals and cleaning agents, and other inedible substances found in the average home and/or garage, such as shoe polish, weed killer, rodent and insect poisons, and nail polish remover. One of the most important subjects in this chapter is the danger of certain poisonous plants. Who on earth would have dreamed that the pretty lily of the valley would NOT be so pretty if ingested by a tiny mouth, attracted by the lovely fragrance? (The flower is, in fact, toxic.)

## Plants

There are more than five hundred poisonous species of plants growing in the United States. Although only a few are dangerously poisonous in small amounts, even the least toxic plants can be harmful if ingested in large quantities. Don't assume that plants and flowers on your property are safe. Some are, some aren't. Even Christmas holly is toxic, not to mention philodendron, dieffenbachia, English ivy, Japanese yew, wisteria, morning glory, deadly nightshade, jimsonweed, oleander, and dozens more. Bulbs, seeds, fertilizers, herbicides, and insecticides should be kept out of the reach of children. Teach your child at a very early age to identify poisonous plants in the garden and in the home. Teach very young children not to put plant parts or dirt in their mouths. Dirt can cause choking, even if it may not be poisonous. Some dirt, however, may contain lead from peeled exterior paints, so it too can be dangerous.

When people use the word *toxic*, they usually mean "poisonous." But there can be different interpretations of plant toxicity, and sometimes an entire plant may not be toxic. One part of a plant can be potentially toxic, while the remainder can be neutral or even beneficial. For example, though the thick sap of the aloe plant is considered toxic, people cut open aloe leaves and apply it directly to burns. And some people drink the liquid from crushed/pressed aloe leaves. Check the vegetation in your yard against the following list of toxic plants.

## A Sampling of Toxic and Injurious Plants

*Adenium*—(alias Desert Rose, Mock Azalea)—All toxic.
*Aloe*—The thick sap is toxic.
*Amaryllis*—Bulb is toxic.
*Anthurium*—Leaves, stem burn mouth area.
*Avocado*—Leaves are toxic.
*Arum Lily*—Toxic.
*Autumn Crocus*—(Not a true crocus)—All extremely toxic.
*Azalea*—(Rhododendron)—Leaves and honey from nectar are toxic.
*Baby's Breath*—Causes contact dermatitis only.
*Baptisia*—(Wild Indigo)—All toxic.
*Begonia*—Toxic.
*Bird of Paradise*—Toxic.
*Black Calla*—All parts hurt mouth, throat area.
*Black Dogwood*—Bark and fruit are toxic.
*Black Eyed Susan*—Causes contact dermatitis only.
*Bluebell*—(Schila)—All toxic.
*Blue Taro*—Leaves burn mouth area.
*Box Wood*—(Buxus)—Irritates skin. If eaten, causes nausea.
*Buckeye*—(Horse chestnut)—Nuts and twigs are toxic.
*Burning Bush*—(Euonymus Europaeus)—Fruit is toxic.
*Buttercup*—Toxic.
*Caladium*—All parts burn mouth area.
*Calla Lily*—Burns mouth and lips.
*Castor Bean*—Plump seeds, usually white with black or brown mottling, are extremely toxic.

**Medic Alert! Poisons**

*Cowslip*—(Caltha)—All parts toxic and irritating.
*Daffodil*—(Narcissus, Jonquil)—Bulbs toxic.
*Daphne mezereum*—(February Daphne)—All toxic.
*Deadly Nightshade*—(Solanum)—Some species: all parts fatal.
*Dieffenbachia*—(Dumb Cane)—Leaves burn mouth area (have even caused temporary speech impairment); also irritates the skin.
*Duranta*—(Golden dewdrop)—Berries are toxic.
*Elephant's Ear*—Leaves burn mouth area.
*English Ivy*—Berries and leaves are toxic.
*False Acacia*—Bark, leaves, and seeds toxic.
*False Heather*—Toxic.
*Ficus Benjamina*—Sap is injurious.
*Fishtail Palm*—Fruit burns mouth area, irritates skin.
*Flowering Maple*—Causes contact dermatitis only.
*Four-O'Clock*—Toxic.
*Foxglove*—Leaves extremely toxic.
*Gloriosa Lily*—All toxic, especially tuberous root.
*Golden Chain Tree*—(Bean Tree)—All toxic, especially seed.
*Hanging Geranium*—Causes contact dermatitis only.
*Helleborous*—(Christmas Rose)—All toxic.
*Hills of Snow*—(Hydrangea)—Flower buds are toxic.
*Holly*—Berries are toxic.
*Horse Chestnut*—Nuts and twigs are toxic.
*Iris*—(Fleur de lis)—Roots are toxic.
*Jicama*—Root edible, but seeds and pods are toxic.
*Jimsonweed*—All toxic.
*Lily of the Valley*—All parts are extremely toxic, including any water the plant was in.
*Monkshood*—All toxic.
*Mock Azalea*—(Desert Rose)—All toxic.
*Mountain Laurel*—Texas Mountain Laurel seeds are toxic. New Zealand

74

Laurel fruit is extremely toxic.
*Oleander*—All parts extremely toxic, including smoke from branches, water plant was in, and branches used as barbecue skewers.
*Peony*—Toxic.
*Philodendron*—Leaves burn mouth and throat area, also irritate the skin.
*Potato*—Green tuber skin and uncooked shoots are toxic.
*Pothos*—All parts irritate skin, and, if eaten, can cause diarrhea.
*Privet*—(Lovage)—All toxic.
*Prunus*—(Apricot, Cherry, Nectarine, Peach, Plum, Prune)—Pit kernels of all are toxic.
*Pyracantha*—Berries and thorns are injurious.
*Rhubarb*—Stalks are good, leaves are toxic.
*Schefflera*—Causes contact dermatitis only.
*Snowberry*—Berries toxic in quantity.
*Spider Lily*—Bulbs toxic.
*Split-leaf Philodendron*—Leaves burn mouth area.
*Sweetpea*—Toxic.
*Tulip*—Toxic.
*Wisteria*—All toxic.
*Wonder Flower*—All toxic, especially the bulb.
*Yellow Oleander*—All toxic, especially seed.
*Yellow Sage*—Toxic.
*Yew*—(Ground Hemlock)—Most of plant, including seeds: toxic.
*Zephyr Lily*—Bulb is toxic.

## A Sampling of Nontoxic Plants

| | | |
|---|---|---|
| *African Daisy* | *Althaea Bush* | *Baby's Tears* |
| *African Violet* | *Aluminum Plant* | *Beauty Bush* |
| *Ageratum* | *Anthurium* | *Billbergia* |
| *Aglaonena* | *Ardisia* | *Bird's Nest Fern* |
| *Air Fern* | *Artillery Plant* | *Blood Leaf Plant* |
| *Air Plane Plant* | *Asparagus Fern* | *Boston Fern* |
| *Air Plant* | *Asperula* | *Bride's Bonnet* |
| *Alpine Currant* | *Aster* | *Bromeliad* |

## Medic Alert! Poisons

Burros Tail
Canna
Cape Jasmine
Cape Marigold
Carolina Hemlock
Cast Iron Plant
Cat Tail
Cauliflower Ears
Chestnut
China Doll Plant
Chocolate Soldier Plant
Chocolate Tree
Christmas Begonia
Christmas Cactus
Christmas Dagger Fern
Christmas Kalanchoe
Christmas Pride
Coleus
Coral Bells
Corn Plant
Cosmos
Crassula
Crataegus
Creeping Charlie
Creeping Mahonia
Creeping Mint
Creeping Jenny
Creeping Sailor
Crossandra
Dahlia
Dallas Fern
Dandelion
Day Lily
Dracaena
Dragon Tree

Dwarf Rubber Plant
Dwarf Silene
Dwarf Whitman Fern
Easter Cactus
Easter Cattleya
Easter Daisy
Easter Lily
Echeveria
Elephant Ear Begonia
Exacum-Affine
False Aralia
Fatsia Japonica
Felt Bush
Ficus Adenosperma
Ficus Rubinginosa
Fittonia
Flaming Sword
Forget-Me-Not
Forsythia
Freesia
Fuchsia
Gardenia
Gloxinia
Goldfish Plant
Gynura
Hawthorn
Hemlock Tree
Hens and Chickens
Hibiscus
High Bush Cranberry
Hindu Rope Plant
Hollyhock
Honey Locust
Honey Plant
Honeysuckle
Hosta
Hoya

Humble Plant
Impatiens
Jade Plant
Japanese Snowball/Snowbell
Japanese Spurge
Juneberry
Ladder Fern
Lilac
Lipstick Plant
Madagascar Jasmine
Maternity Plant
Mock Strawberry
Money Plant
Monkey Plant
Mountain Ash
Neanthebella
Orchid
Palm
Panda Bear Plant
Passion Flower
Peacock Plant
Peperomia
Pepper Face
Persian Violet
Petunia
Phlox
Piggy-Back Plant
Pilea
Pink Polka Dot Plant
Plectranthus
Pleomele Reflexa
Pocketbook Plant
Potentilla
Ponytail Plant
Prayer Plant
Purple Cone Flower

**Medic Alert! Poisons**

| | | |
|---|---|---|
| *Purple Passion Vine* | *Snap Dragon* | *Tiger Lily* |
| *Quince* | *Song of India* | *Touch-Me-Not* |
| *Red Bud* | *Sorbus* | *Valor Plant* |
| *Ressurrection Lily* | *Spider Aralia* | *Velvet Elephant Ear* |
| *Ressurrection Plant* | *Spider Plant* | *Velvet Leaf* |
| *Ribbon Plant* | *Spirea* | *Velvet Plant* |
| *Rosary Plant* | *Star Jasmine* | *Venus Fly Trap* |
| *Salvia* | *Straw Flower* | *Viburnum* |
| *Scabiosa* | *Streptocarpus* | *Violets* |
| *Sensitive Plant* | *Sunflower* | *Wandering Sailor* |
| *Service Berry* | *Swedish Ivy* | *Warneckei* |
| *Shame Plant* | *Sweet Camellia* | *Watermelon Plant* |
| *Silver Dollar* | *Sweet Woodruff* | *Weigela* |
| *Silver Queen* | *Sowrd Fern* | *Yucca Plant* |
| *Silver Weed* | *Sycamore* | *Zebra Plant* |
| *Skunk Bush* | *Tahitian Bridal Veil* | *Zinnia* |
| *Snake Plant* | *Ti* | |

Reprinted by permission of RUSH-PRESBYTERIAN-ST. LUKE'S POISON CONTROL CENTER, 1653 West Congress Parkway, Chicago, IL 60612.

## Household Chemicals

Nearly 5,000 people die each year from accidental poisoning caused by household products; of the 1.3 million poisonings annually, 800,000 happen to children. A good percentage of these accidents are avoidable. As a matter of fact, the number of fatal poisonings is declining. In 1959, 450 children under five died because of accidental poisoning. By 1988, that number was down to only 60 deaths. In 1990, the National Center for Health Statistics reported 49 deaths from all medicines and household chemicals, including a single fatality from aspirin products. The 1993 edition of the National Safety Council's Accident Facts listed approximately 40 children between the ages of one and five dying each year from accidental poisonings.

While these statistics do not cover deaths from poisonous plants and other substances, the decline is nevertheless impressive. Three reasons primarily account for this victory:
1. Education (such as the National Poison Prevention Week program)
2. Treatment (Poison Control Centers)
3. Prevention (such as manufacturer-required child-resistant packaging)

It's just common sense that all chemicals and cleaning agents should be out of the reach of children. Many products are so helpful in cleaning up the house, yet so potentially dangerous to children. They should be stored in upper cabinets, inaccessible to babies and toddlers, or kept stored behind locked doors (see Chapter 5 on Childproofing). Some cleaners are so potent that they may even be considered dangerous for adults (some may cause acidic burns on the skin, necessitating rubber gloves; some should be used only in well-ventilated areas, so that fumes cause no damage to throat and lungs). It's most important to *read the labels*. Common household products off-limits for children should include:

acids
aerosols
ammonia
antiseptics
antifreeze
automotive products, including waxes and engine fluids
bleach
bubble bath
button batteries
charcoal starter and benzene
colognes
copper and brass cleaners
cosmetics

## Medic Alert! Poisons

- dish detergents
- drain cleaners
- epoxy glue
- furniture polish
- garden sprays
- gun cleaners
- hair dyes
- iodine
- insulations
- kerosene
- lamp oil
- laundry detergents
- lye
- mace (chemical)
- model cement
- moth balls
- nail polish
- nail polish remover
- oven cleaner
- paint
- paint thinner
- paint varnish
- permanent wave solution
- peroxides
- pesticides and herbicides
- shampoos
- perfumes
- pet foods
- petroleum products
- pine oil
- plant food and fertilizers
- rodent and insect poison
- shaving lotion
- silver polish
- toilet-bowl cleaner
- turpentine
- typewriter cleaner
- weed killers
- window cleaner
- wood preservatives

Dr. Susan M. Sandbeck, assistant director of the Fort Lauderdale, Florida, Poison Control Center, says that household bleach causes most of their incoming calls: "We get at least seven or eight calls a day. Actually, it's nontoxic, as long as the child isn't choking. It requires giving the child a cupful of water; you don't want the child to vomit, to aspirate, where the contents of the stomach go into the lungs. Some stuff, when aspirated, impedes flow of oxygen into the lung tissue."

The greatest danger to little children, says Sandbeck, is "exposure to household cleaning products. Some dangers that might be in the garage are: antifreeze, gasoline, butane; then there are furniture polish, medications (especially older people's medications to treat heart and depression), and pain relievers." Sandbeck cautions everyone to "keep hazardous substances and medications out of the child's reach—stored up high, in locked cabinets. I also encourage parents to buy hazardous substances with safety-resistant tops and to use those caps properly. By that, I mean restoring the cap; some people don't take the time to tighten it up."

## Pesticides

Did you know that the United States Environmental Protection Agency lists chlorine bleach and your dog's flea shampoo right along with rat poison and insect sprays? "According to the American Association of Poison Control Centers," notes the EPA publication *Pesticides and Child Safety,* "in 1992 alone, an estimated 148,000 children were involved in common household pesticide-related poisonings or exposures in the United States.

"Almost half—47%—of all households with children under the age of five had at least one pesticide stored in an unlocked cabinet, less than 4 feet off the ground (i.e., within the reach of children). Approximately, 75% of households without children under the age of five also stored pesticides in an unlocked cabinet, less than 4 feet off the ground. This number is especially significant because 13% of all pesticide poisoning incidents occur in homes other than the child's home."

Law requires most residential-use pesticides (roach sprays, kitchen and bath disinfectants, rat poison, repellents and baits, swimming pool chemicals, weed killers, and the like) that bear the signal word "danger," "caution," or "warning" to be in child-resistant packaging. This helps, but precautions should still be taken, such as putting all containers labeled with those words in a locked cabinet, high out of a child's reach.

Before applying pesticides, indoors or outdoors, remove children and their toys as well as pets from the area, and keep them away until the pesticide has dried or as long as is recommended by the pesticide label. *Don't* place rodent or insect baits where small children can get to them, and *do* teach children that pesticides are poisons.

Medic Alert! Poisons

# Medicines
## Do You Take Medicines Safely?

Are there different ways to take medicines *correctly?* Yes, of course. Sometimes we don't even need a medicine at all. Most of us take medicine because a doctor tells us to; we should learn not to improvise. Lately, there has been a rash of news about people who overmedicate, who take medicines routinely, having started for one reason or another, and who go on taking them needlessly. For example, the trouble with taking antibiotics over and over again for illnesses such as colds or sore throats is that they can lose their effectiveness unless their strength is increased.

When one medicine doesn't do the job, another is prescribed, and the medicating cycle begins. If your child has something as common as a cold, all she may need is good old-fashioned rest, a lot of fluids, and a healthful diet. Talk it over with your pediatrician: Do you overmedicate?

Is it safe to give a child a dose of medicine with the same eyedropper used when a sibling recently was sick? No. If you're sharing a bottle of an over-the-counter medicine, such as a liquid acetaminophen, the medicine can become easily contaminated. After giving the medication, place the dropper in boiling water (two to three minutes) before you return it to the medicine bottle. Washing it off thoroughly in hot water is enough if you are treating just one child.

Some prescribed liquid medications and vitamins should be kept in your refrigerator to slow bacterial growth. It's always a good idea to throw out remnants of the medicine.

## Child-Resistant Packaging

The Closure Manufacturers Association in Washington, D.C., wants to be sure parents know all about child-resistant packaging. Under the Poison Prevention Packaging Act, the Consumer Product Safety Commission (CPSC) requires safety caps on all aspirin, oral prescription drugs, and many hazardous household products. So a joint industry/government effort aimed at preventing accidental poisonings among children came up with the child-resistant cap. According to the CPSC, "Child resistant packaging is . . . designed and constructed to be significantly difficult for children under five years of age to open, or to obtain a toxic or harmful amount of the substance contained in the package, within a reasonable time; and is not difficult for adults to use properly."

Child-resistant packaging appears to be strikingly effective. In 1972, when drugs first were required to have child-resistant packaging, 96 children died from drug ingestion (5.6 deaths per million children under age five). By 1974, the first year in which child-resistant packaging was required for most prescription drugs, according to the Closure Manufacturers Association, fatalities decreased to 57 (3.4 deaths per million children under age five). By 1984, there were only 31 drug-ingestion fatalities (1.7 deaths per million children under five). Additionally, the National Center for Health Statistics now has data showing that all aspirin-related deaths of children under five were eliminated in 1985. However, when only deaths of children are compared, the statistics fail to bring out the massive numbers of children who end up in emergency rooms and survive. Yet, the figures are impressive.

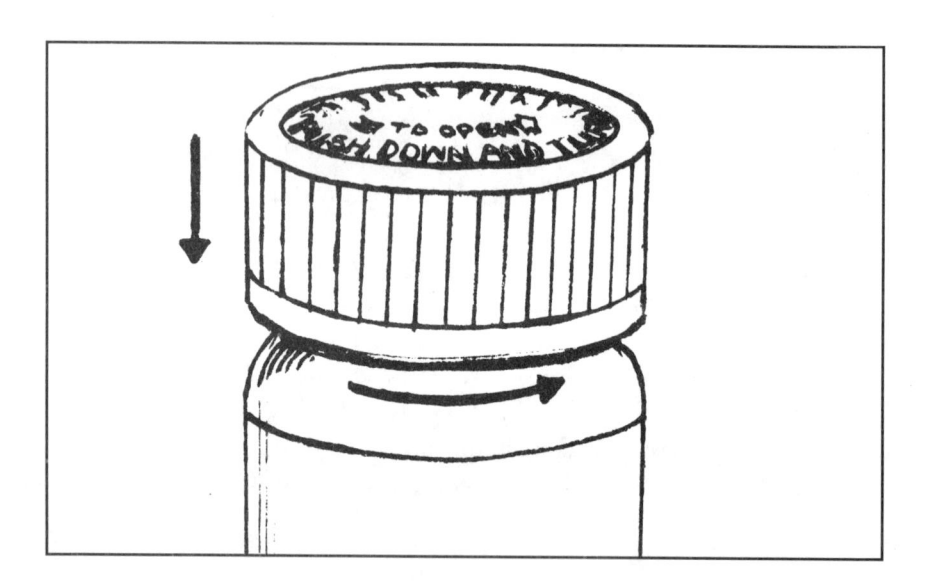

### Medic Alert! Poisons

In its brochure titled *Tips for Child Safety* (1988), the Closure Manufacturers Association advises: "Make sure that medicines and household chemicals are kept out of the reach of children, and be sure to resecure your child-resistant cap after each use. Isn't it worthwhile taking a little extra time and saving a life?" What if Grandpa has arthritic hands, and when he comes to visit, he brings bottles without child-resistant caps. Does it matter? Yes, it does. It's true that Grandpa, and other arthritics, may request aspirin and drugs without child-resistant caps from their druggists, but when Grandpa visits you, he'll have to be careful. If Grandpa keeps his medication virtually locked away in a childproofed bathroom cabinet, or takes the time to lock it into his luggage, your child won't find it.

It may be hard to remember to replace those safety caps; it's tempting to leave them off or loose because they're so hard to open. There are ways, says the Closure Manufacturers Association, to make using these caps easier. First, read the directions for opening that are printed or embossed on the cap. "*Think* carefully about it for a moment and you understand the motions required." Next, calmly remove the cap. If you hurry or pull hard the wrong way, you won't succeed ("that's why they're safe for youngsters"). If the cap doesn't open at the first try, try again. Are you following the directions? If it says "match the arrow on the cap with the arrow on the bottle," that's the key. Then, of course, replace the cap securely when you are finished.

The association offers a number of ideas in *Tips on Child Safety*:

- Replace child-resistant caps on all medicines and household products after every use.
- Keep potentially harmful drugs, poisons, and household products out of the reach of youngsters, especially while in use.
- Because toddlers can climb and conquer most obstacles, keep poisons in locked cabinets.
- Never refer to medicine as "candy" to get a child to take the recommended dosage. Since children tend to believe

everything adults say, this appealing and sweet-sounding term may encourage the child to take more medicine than is healthy when you are not around.
- Watch for any visitor not used to having young children around who may leave toxic drugs within reach.
- Youngsters love to imitate Mom and Dad, so if you take a medicine of any kind, do it when the kids aren't around.
- Set an example as a safety-oriented parent. Children will observe and learn to be cautious when handling potentially dangerous packages.
- Read dosage instructions and follow them exactly.
- Dispose of leftover medicinal fluids, pills, and household products. (Flush them down the drain or toilet.)
- Never re-use a drug you "happen to have around the house" without first checking with your doctor.
- Keep syrup of ipecac handy to induce vomiting, if necessary.

Reprinted by permission of the Closure Manufacturers Association.

The Nonprescription Drugs Manufacturers Association (NDMA) in Washington, D.C., has published a booklet called *Know What You're Taking* (November 1994). The brochure includes information from Ann Brown, chairman of the U.S. Consumer Product Safety Commission, who says, "It's important to know the difference between tamper-resistant caps (designed for one-time use to show you if the package already has been opened) and child-resistant caps (designed for repeated use to make it difficult for kids to open)." Brown also emphasizes that "if parents don't relock the cap after each use, the child-resistant device can't do its job—keeping children out!"

The NDMA recently published the following quiz on OTC drugs—"over the counter" or nonprescription medicines that the FDA has decided are safe and effective for use without a doctor's prescription. You can find OTC drugs everywhere, from drugstores to supermarkets to convenience stores. More than 450 products sold over the counter today use ingredients or doses once available only by prescription. That's why the industry "underscores the need for personal responsibility in the proper use of medicines," notes the NDMA.

## Medic Alert! Poisons

### What's Your OTC I.Q.?
1. TRUE OR FALSE: An over-the-counter (OTC) medicine is one that is regulated for safety and effectiveness by the Food and Drug Administration for use without a doctor's prescription.
2. Which of the following items is required by the FDA to appear on a nonprescription medicine label?
(A) Directions (B) Ingredients (C) Expiration date
(D) Tamper-resistant warning (E) All of the above.
3. It is possible for some OTC medicines to interact with
(A) Alcohol (B) Food (C) Other medicines
(D) All of the above.
4. When using an OTC product, you should
(A) Read the label. (B) Examine the package's tamper-resistant features before buying it. (C) Examine the medicine inside the package closely before taking it.
(D) All of the above.
5. When a pregnant woman takes medicine:
(A) She need not be concerned about the effect it may have on her unborn baby. (B) Some of the medicines can pass from the mother to the unborn baby and cause problems.
6. Child-resistant packaging is
(A) Not the same thing as tamper-resistant packaging.
(B) Designed to keep youngsters out of your medicines.
(C) Not available for use in this country. (D) Both (A) and (B). (E) None of the above.

Answers:
1. TRUE. The FDA regulates both prescription and nonprescription medicines.
2. (E) All of the above. The FDA requires each OTC label to tell consumers how to use nonprescription medicines and when to stop.
3. (D) All of the above. Potential interactions are on the OTC label.
4. (D) All of the above.
5. (B) Medicines can pass to the unborn baby and this can cause problems.

6. (D) Both (A) and (B). Tamper-resistant and child-resistant closures have different purposes, but both are there for your protection.

>Reprinted by permission of the NDMA.
>First appeared in *Reader's Digest* (November 1994).

## Poison Education

Efforts have been made on many fronts to educate both parents and children about poisonous substances. Thirty-eight national organizations, representing the government, industry, health professionals, and consumers have formed the Poison Prevention Week Council, an independent nonprofit coalition. The U.S. government designated National Poison Prevention Week in 1961 to be held annually during the third week in March. The council's activities are funded by its member organizations and via the sale of National Poison Prevention Week posters. The posters are very graphic. The tag line on the 1994 edition reads, "Children act fast . . . so do poisons—Don't let it happen to your child!" The illustration pictures Mom (or a sitter or caregiver) on the phone, back turned to a toddler busily shaking pills onto a table. The poster for 1995 shows Mom chatting with Grandma in the parlor, while a child investigates (and ingests) pills she found in Grandma's unlocked bedroom cabinet. The poster is headlined: "Everything at Grandma's Isn't Candy."

Following are three points for parents from the Poison Prevention Week Council and the Consumer Product Safety Commission:

- A growing child is curious about things that glitter, colorful pills, bottles, and containers of all kinds. To thwart a crawling infant, don't keep household products below the kitchen sink unless the cabinet is locked or secured with child safety latches.
- A child able to walk can get into bottles or boxes containing medicines or household products in a split second, in the time it takes for Mom or Dad to answer the telephone or doorbell. If you must leave the room for only an instant, put the container in a safe spot.

## Medic Alert! Poisons

- A child able to climb can find places that a parent thinks are beyond baby's reach. Find a high shelf and better yet, lock the cabinet or closet where these products are stored.

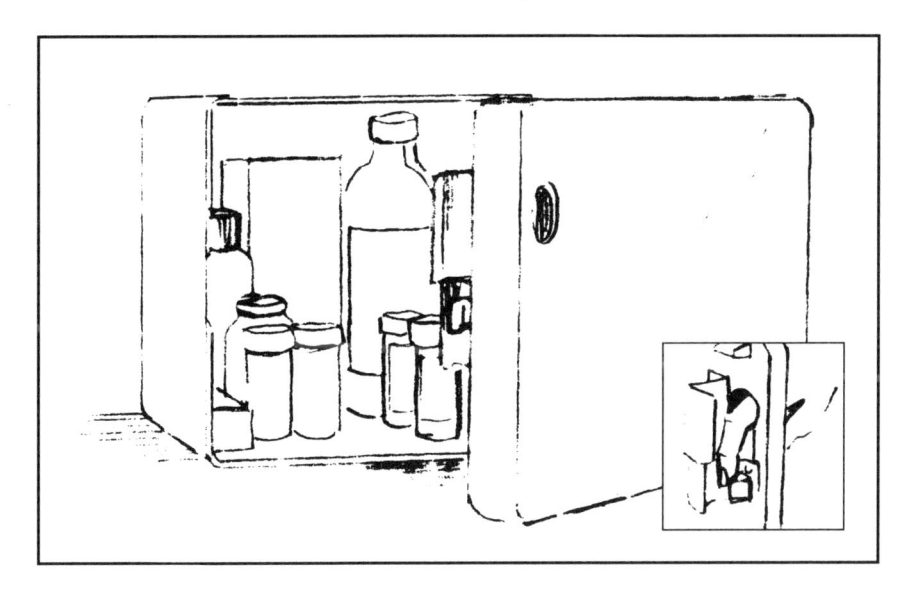

As part of The Injury Prevention Program (TIPP), the American Academy of Pediatrics (AAP) has written that parents should teach children not to drink or eat anything unless it is offered by a known adult. The academy also warns parents to "be alert for repeated poisonings. Children who swallow a poison are likely to try again within a year."

*Protecting Young Children from Poisoning* (1993), published by Macfarlan Smith Ltd. in coordination with the National Safety Council, includes advice to reduce the amount of poisonous material in your home: "Make it a point to buy products that are less toxic.... Many poisonings occur while the product is in use. Never leave products open and unattended when children are present.... Always supervise children in your home and especially when you are visiting others."

In addition, some communities use "Mr. Yuk" stickers, which are easy for children to identify. When your child learns to recognize the face on the sticker, you can put them on boxtops or containers of various "yukky" substances.

## Medic Alert! Poisons

# Poison Checklist

Is your home a haven for poison accidents waiting to happen? The U.S. Consumer Product Safety Commission (CPSC) has compiled a detailed checklist to help you create a poison-free environment.

### Kitchen:

❏ 1. Are all dangerous products in locked cabinets?
❏ 2. Are potentially harmful products out of your children's reach?
❏ 3. Are harmful products stored away from food, so that no one could possibly confuse the poison and the food?
❏ 4. Do oven cleaners, furniture polish, drain cleaners, and similar products have child-resistant caps?
❏ 5. Are potentially harmful products left in their original containers? If you have a bit of liquid furniture polish remaining and you put it in a clean cola bottle to save space, a child could drink from that bottle thinking it contained soda. In addition, the labels on original containers may give first-aid antidotes in case of accidental ingestion.

### Bathroom:

❏ 1. Do all your "harmless" medicines (i.e., aspirin) have child-resistant caps?
❏ 2. Do you hold onto out-of-date medicines? Get rid of them.
❏ 3. Do you get rid of substances such as boric acid, camphorated oil, and oil of wintergreen when they get old?
❏ 4. Do you keep prescription medicines in their original containers? The originals bear labels with prescription numbers and dates, so that in case of accidental ingestion by a child, your druggist can tell your doctor exactly what was ingested (even if the ingredients are not listed).

The original label of an over-the-counter drug is equally important. It's crucial that you know what was accidentally ingested—information you don't have, if you switched the product to a different container.

❏ 5. Finally, do you keep medicine with iron out of the reach of young children? Poison Control Center data says that iron supplements are responsible for 30 percent of pediatric poisoning deaths from medications. When consumed by a child, even a small number of iron pills can cause death. The CPSC requires iron medications (sometimes identified as ferrous sulfate, ferrous gluconate, or ferrous fumarate), prenatal medicines with iron, and vitamins with iron to be packaged with child-resistant closures. Replace caps securely every time you take one. If you discard iron pills, flush them down the toilet; don't place them in a wastebasket where children can find them.

## Diagnosing and Treating Household Poisonings

Not all medicines and household chemicals are poisonous, and not all exposures necessarily result in poisoning. If you find your child playing with a bottle of medicine or some household product, how can you tell if she has swallowed some and what should you do? Here are some diagnostic tools for determining whether a child has been poisoned:

### Poison Swallowed
—open container near child
—abnormal behavior
—stains or burns on mouth, hands, or clothes
—unusual odors from mouth, body
—drowsiness
—overstimulation
—difficult or abnormal breathing
—coughing or gagging
—abnormal pulse rate
—sweating
—abdominal pain, nausea, or vomiting
—convulsions

### Poison Inhaled
—weakness/dizziness
—unconsciousness
—headache
—disorientation
—coughing
—red or blue skin color
—shortness of breath
—nausea

### Medic Alert! Poisons

- If poisoning or drug abuse has occurred or is suspected, don't wait for symptoms to appear. Seek medical help at once.
- Do not absolutely trust labels to give you information about antidotes. Call the Poison Control Center (PCC), and they'll tell you what you can believe.
- Do not induce vomiting unless you're told to by your PCC.
- Do observe if the child is conscious or having convulsions.
- Do not forget to take the poison container, the leftover medication, or the drugs, the poisonous plant or spoiled food, or any vomited material to the emergency room so that it can be analyzed.
- If poisoning affects the eyes, flush them with lukewarm water for fifteen minutes.
- If poison affects the skin, remove contaminated clothing and wash the affected area gently with soap and cool water.

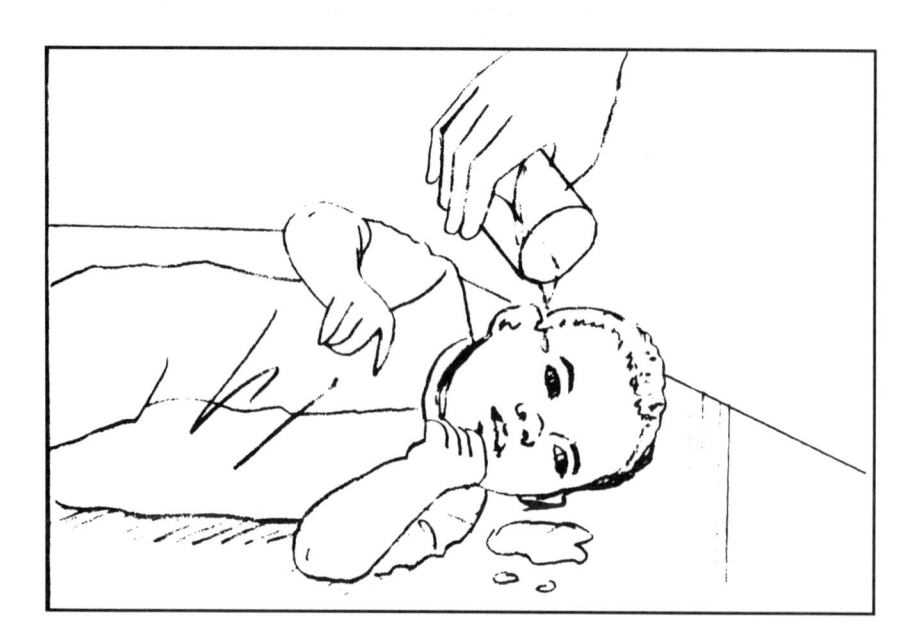

Medic Alert! Poisons

## Poison Control Centers

If you suspect your child or a family member has ingested or inhaled a poisonous substance, the best move is to call your Poison Control Center or your physician at once. If you're unable to contact either, call 911 or 0 for operator. If you can't find the number of your local Poison Control Center in your phone book, ask your doctor. Post the number along with other emergency numbers next to the phones in your home. When you call the Poison Control Center nearest you, try to stay calm and continue to reassure your child. You will need to be able to answer the following questions:

1. Was the poison swallowed, inhaled, or absorbed through skin contact, or was it splashed into the eyes?
2. What kind of poison is involved? Read the label.
3. What was the amount swallowed?
4. When was it swallowed?
5. What are the child's age and weight? Has the child any existing health conditions or problems?
6. Has the child vomited?
7. How long will it take you to reach the emergency room?

Rose Ann Soloway, administrator of the American Association of Poison Control Centers, says, "Poisons act so quickly. When a poisoning occurs, you've got to be prepared to act quickly, as well. People need to call us immediately. After all, that's why we're here. The centers are the first line in treating any kind of situation that possibly involves poisoning, providing twenty-four-hour-a-day emergency treatment advice for all kinds of poisonings—everything from medicines to household products, on through snake bites and spider bites and chemical exposures. A person who calls the poison center is immediately given the most appropriate individualized treatment and advice for the specific problem; there is also a telephone follow-up to be sure that things worked out the way they're supposed to."

Soloway says that most of the time, with a call to the poison center, a poisoning can be treated totally over the telephone. However, if someone does require medical care, the victim will be sent to the closest emergency room. The poison center will call ahead to the hospital, providing emergency treatment advice to the doctors and nurses there.

Soloway concludes by noting that in case of a possible poisoning, never wait to see what might happen; you should call right away. "Ideally, call your poison center ahead of time to get poison prevention information appropriate to your area—how far the center is from your house, for instance. And put up stickers with your center's emergency number on it."

The following is an updated listing of Poison Control Centers in the U. S.:

## Poison Control Centers

### Alabama
Alabama Poison Center, Tuscaloosa
408-A Paul Bryant Drive
Tuscaloosa, AL 35401
Emergency Phone: (800) 462-0800 (AL only) or
(205) 345-0600

Regional Poison Control Center
The Children's Hospital of Alabama
1600 7th Avenue South
Birmingham, AL 35233-1711
Emergency Phone: (205) 939-9201,
(800) 292-6678 (AL only) or (205) 933-4050

### Arizona
Arizona Poison and Drug Information Center
Arizona Health Sciences Center, Room, #3204-K
1501 N. Campbell Avenue
Tuscon, AZ 85724
Emergency Phone: (800) 362-0101 (AZ only),
(602) 626-6016

Samaritan Regional Poison Center
Good Samaritan Regional Medical Center
Ancillary-1
1111 E. McDowell Road
Phoenix, AZ 85006
Emergency Phone: (602) 253-3334

### California
Central California Regional Poison Control Center
Valley Children's Hospital
3151 N. Millbrook, IN31
Fresno, CA 93703
Emergency Phone: (800) 346-5922 (Central CA
only) or (209) 445-1222

San Diego Regional Poison Center
UCSD Medical Center
200 West Arbor Drive
San Diego, CA 92103-8295
Emergency Phone: (619) 543-6000,
(800) 876-4766 (in 619 area code only)

San Francisco Bay Area
Regional Poison Control Center
San Francisco General Hospital
1001 Potrero Avenue, Building 80, Room 230
San Francisco, CA 94110
Emergency Phone: (800) 523-2222

Santa Clara Valley Regional Poison Center
Valley Health Center, Suite 310
750 South Bascom Avenue
San Jose, CA 95128
Emergency Phone: (408) 885-6000,
(800) 662-9886 (CA only)

University of California, Davis, Medical Center
Regional Poison Control Center
2315 Stockton Boulevard
Sacramento, CA 95817
Emergency Phone: (916) 734-3692,
(800) 342-9293 (Northern California only)

## COLORADO
Rocky Mountain Poison and Drug Center
645 Bannock Street
Denver, CO 80204
Emergency Phone: (303) 629-1123

## DISTRICT OF COLUMBIA
National Capital Poison Center
3201 New Mexico Avenue, NW, Suite 310
Washington, DC, 20016
Emergency Phone: (202) 625-3333,
(202) 362-8563 (TTY)

## FLORIDA
Florida Poison Information Center-Jacksonville
University Medical Center
University of Florida Health Science Center-Jacksonville
655 West 8th Street
Jacksonville, FL 32209
Emergency Phone: (904) 549-4480,
(800) 282-3171 (FL only)

The Florida Poison Information Center and
Toxicology Resource Center
Tampa General Hospital
Post Office Box 1289
Tampa, FL 33601
Emergency Phone: (813) 253-4444 (Tampa),
(800) 282-3171 (Florida)

## GEORGIA
Georgia Poison Center
Grady Memorial Hospital
80 Butler Street S.E.
P. O. Box 26066
Atlanta, GA 30335-3801
Emergency Phone: (800) 282-5846 (GA only),
(404) 616-9000

## INDIANA
Indiana Poison Center
Methodist Hospital of Indiana
1701 N. Senate Boulevard
P. O. Box 1367
Indianapolis, IN 46206-1367
Emergency Phone: (800) 382-9097 (IN only),
(317) 929-2323

## KENTUCKY
Kentucky Regional Poison Center of Kosair
Children's Hospital
P. O. Box 35070
Louisville, KY 40232-5070
Emergency Phone: (502) 629-7275,
(800) 722-5725 (KY only)

## MARYLAND
Maryland Poison Center
20 Pine Street
Baltimore, MD 21201
Emergency Phone: (410) 528-7701,
(800) 492-2414 (MD only)

## MASSACHUSETTS
Massuchesetts Poison Control System
300 Longwood Avenue
Boston, MA 02115
Emergency Phone: (617) 232-2120,
(800) 682-9211

## MICHIGAN
Poison Control Center
Children's Hospital of Michigan
3901 Beaubien Boulevard
Detroit, MI 48201
Emergency Phone: (313) 745-5711

## MINNESOTA
Hennepin Regional Poison Center
Hennepin County Medical Center
701 Park Avenue
Minneapolis, MN 55415
Emergency Phone: (612) 347-3141,
Petline: (612) 337-7387, TDD (612) 337-7474

Minnesota Regional Poison Center
St. Paul-Ramsey Medical Center
640 Jackson Street
St. Paul, MN 55101
Emergency Phone: (612) 221-2113

## MISSOURI
Cardinal Glennon Children's Hospital Regional
Poison Center
1465 S. Grand Boulevard
St. Louis, MO 63104
Emergency Phone: (314) 772-5200,
(800) 366-8888

### Montana
Rocky Mountain Poison and Drug Center
645 Bannock Street
Denver, CO 80204
Emergency Phone: (303) 629-1123

### Nebraska
The Poison Center
8301 Dodge Street
Omaha, NE 68114
Emergency Phone: (402) 390-5555 (Omaha),
(800) 955-9119 (NE & WY)

### New Jersey
New Jersey Poison Information
and Education System
201 Lyons Avenue
Newark, NJ 07112
Emergency Phone: (800) 962-1253

### New Mexico
New Mexico Poison and Drug Information Center
University of New Mexico
Albuquerque, NM 87131-1076
Emergency Phone: (505) 843-2551,
(800) 432-6866 (NM only)

### New York
Hudson Valley Regional Poison Center
Phelps Memorial Hospital Center
701 North Broadway
North Tarrytown, NY 10591
Emergency Phone: (800) 336-6997,
(914) 366-3030

Long Island Regional Poison Control Center
Winthrop University Hospital
259 First Street
Mineola, NY 11501
Emergency Phone: (516) 542-2323, 2324, 2325, 3813

New York City Poison Control Center
NYC Department of Health
455 First Avenue, Room 123
New York, NY 10016
Emergency Phone: (212) 340-4494,
(212) P-O-I-S-O-N-S,
TDD (212) 689-9014

### North Carolina
Carolinas Poison Center
1000 Blythe Boulevard
P.O. Box 32861
Charlotte, NC 28232-2861
Emergency Phone: (704) 355-4000,
(800) 84-TOXIN (1-800-848-6946)

### Ohio
Central Ohio Poison Center
700 Children's Drive
Columbus, OH 43205-2696
Emergency Phone: (614) 228-1323,
(800) 682-7625, (614) 228-2272 (TTY),
(614) 461-2012

Cincinnati Drug & Poison Information Center and
Regional Poison Control System
231 Bethesda Avenue, M.L. 144
Cincinnati, OH 45267-0144
Emergency Phone: (513) 558-5111,
(800) 872-5111 (OH only)

### Oregon
Oregon Poison Center
Oregon Health Sciences University
3181 S.W. Sam Jackson Park Road
Portland, OR 97201
Emergency Phone: (503) 494-8968,
(800) 452-7165 (OR only)

### Pennsylvania
Central Pennsylvania Poison Center
University Hospital
Milton S. Hershey Medical Center
Hershey, PA 17033
Emergency Phone: (800) 521-6110

The Poison Control Center serving the greater
Philadelphia metropolitan area
One Children's Center
Philadelphia, PA 19104-4303
Emergency Phone: (215) 386-2100

Pittsburgh Poison Center
3705 Fifth Avenue
Pittsburgh, PA 15213
Emergency Phone: (412) 681-6669

### Rhode Island
Rhode Island Poison Center
593 Eddy Street
Providence, RI 02903
Emergency Phone: (401) 277-5727

### Texas
North Texas Poison Center
5201 Harry Hines Boulevard
P.O. Box 35926
Dallas, TX 75235
Emergency Phone: (214) 590-5000,
Texas Watts (800) 441-0040

Southeast Texas Poison Center
The University of Texas Medical Branch
Galveston, TX 77550-2780
Emergency Phone: (409) 765-1420 (Galveston),
(713) 654-1701 (Houston)

### UTAH
Utah Poison Control Center
410 Chipeta Way, Suite 230
Salt Lake City, UT 84108
Emergency Phone: (801) 581-2151,
(800) 456-7707 (UT only)

### VIRGINIA
Blue Ridge Poison Center
Box 67
Blue Ridge Hospital
Charlottesville, VA 22901
Emergency Phone: (804) 924-5543,
(800) 451-1428

National Capital Poison Center
3201 New Mexico Avenue, NW, Suite 310
Washington, DC, 20016
Emergency Phone: (202) 625-3333,
(202) 362-8563 (TTY)

### WEST VIRGINIA
West Virginia Poison Center
3110 MacCorkle Avenue S.E.
Charleston, WV 25304
Emergency Phone: (800) 642-3625 (WV only),
(304) 348-4211

### WYOMING
The Poison Center
8301 Dodge Street
Omaha, NE 68114
Emergency Phone: (402) 390-5555 (Omaha),
(800) 955-9119 (NE & WY)

Reprinted by permission of the American Association of Poison Control Centers.

# Systemic Poisoning
## Lead Poisoning

What kind of lead is poisonous? According to the American Academy of Pediatrics' guide, *Caring for Your Baby and Young Child* (Bantam, 1991), lead poisoning occurs when a child eats chips of old paint containing lead or dirt that has been contaminated by lead; it can also be ingested by breathing, or by drinking water from pipes lined or soldered with lead. Perhaps the most dangerous and hidden source of lead is the dust created as lead-based paint chalks, chips, or peels from deteriorated surfaces. Walking on small paint chips or opening and closing a painted frame window can create lead dust. You can also generate lead dust when you sand an old piece of furniture coated with lead-based paint.

Thousands of children tested in various states have been found to have a blood lead level that is too high. What is too high? The U.S. Consumer Product Safety Commission published a note in its *Consumer Product Safety Alert* stating, "The current blood lead level which defines lead poisoning is 25 micrograms of lead per deciliter of blood. However, since poisoning may occur at lower levels than previously thought, various federal agencies are considering whether this level should be lowered further so that lead poisoning prevention programs will have the latest information on testing children for lead poisoning." When a child is exposed during the first two years of life, the lead may accumulate. As low a level as 10 micrograms per deciliter of blood can interfere with a child's cognitive behavior (reading and writing) and can cause a decrease of the IQ, affecting her ability to reason and to think.

Most children suffering from lead poisoning never look sick. Early symptoms include persistent tiredness and lethargy, irritability (fussing and crying), loss of appetite, stomach discomfort, reduced attention span, insomnia, and constipation. Lead toxicity affects almost every system in the body, including the central and peripheral nervous systems, kidneys, and blood. In addition to inhibiting both prenatal and postnatal growth, lead may also affect the stomach and cause intestinal problems, or it may cause anemia or hearing loss.

Because this is the most important environmental health problem facing young children, according to the Department of Health and all home services' agencies, it is imperative to give each child at the age of one, and again at two, a blood lead screening test. "Blood lead screening should be a part of routine health supervision for children and can best be addressed by increasing children's access to health care," advises the AAP Committee on Environmental Health. This screening requires just a finger prick, and you may expect to pay about $20 per child.

In 1993, in Cincinnati, Ohio, researchers tested 245 children aged ten days to six years from an older inner-city area with high rates of childhood lead poisoning. The lead concentration in these children was tested four times a year. When the children were six, their motor development was tested. The results? Significant levels of lead caused poor coordination, poor reaction time, and poor eye-hand coordination. Even low to moderate lead levels were associated with mild difficulty in gross motor skills and considerable difficulty in fine motor skills. Small amounts of lead can damage a child's kidneys and stomach, and can affect coordination, reflexes, and other aspects of motor development. Based on these findings, the researchers recommended that efforts be redoubled to remove children from lead exposure.

If you think the study detailed above seems removed from your child and her environment, it may come as a shock to learn that lead was commonly included in house paint produced before 1977, and may be found today on walls, doorjambs, and window frames in older homes, particularly those built before 1960. Prior to the 1960s, lead paint contained as much as 50 percent lead. In 1970, the government issued a warning that decreased the amount of lead in paint to .06 percent. The threat of poisoning from paint is dismissable only if your house was built after 1978 when final federal regulations restricting the amount of lead permitted in paint took effect. It was thought that lead poisoning was a problem primarily affecting the poor, but it has now become clear that it is equally troubling for the affluent and the middle class due to renovation and reconstruction of homes. Lead, it turns out, is everywhere. City, suburban, and rural children are all at risk if they breathe in lead dust or eat lead paint, chips, and dust. There are 3.8 million homes in the U.S. with decaying or deteriorating lead paint. Two million children under the age of six live in these homes.

As paint ages in an older home, it chips, peels, and becomes dust. The busy mouths of toddlers welcome these colorful chips. And, even if they don't eat these insidious bits, the dust can get on their hands and into their food. Even if the old paint was covered up by layers of new, safe paints, the underlying paint can still chip or peel off along with the newer layers and fall into your child's hands. If you live in an older home, the best prevention is to repaint thoroughly. That means scraping off all traces of the old paint, even if it's not peeling, and repairing all ceiling and wall cracks before the new paint goes on. It's a good idea to hire trained professionals to remove the lead paint from your home. Never keep children in a house where paint removal is going on; avoid the spread of leaded dust. Move in temporarily with friends or family, and stay till the renovation is over and the house has been given a final and proper cleaning.

If you can't remove the paint, seal over surfaces covered with lead paint with paneling or plasterboard. A second and far less costly option is to investigate with your paint dealer a coating containing Bitrex® developed by companies such as Macfarlan Smith Ltd. The flavoring Bitrex is used to prevent ingestion of many poisonous household products. Its exceptionally bitter taste counteracts lead's sweet taste. Thus, if stripping all the paint off is prohibitive in cost, you can put up a barrier layer of an encapsulating product containing Bitrex.

If you can't repaint or encapsulate, avoid dust pile up and damp mop bare floors and surfaces with a high-phosphate detergent to clean up loose paint chips around windows, doors, and woodwork. Throw away all cleaning cloths. If you must keep rags or cloths used for these purposes, never wash them along with the other laundry. Place duct tape or plastic over loose paint for a temporary covering.

To remove paint chips and dust from around the outside of the house, hose off porches, sidewalks, driveways, and the sides of buildings. Scrub with a stiff brush or broom and soapy water, then rinse as clean as possible. Pick up and throw away paint chips.

If you're renting and you suspect lead levels are too high, your landlord must answer your queries with the truth. If he or she fails to respond, call your local department of health. You have legal recourse if your suspicions are well founded.

As mentioned before, lead paint is not the only source of lead. Others include:

- Dirt, such as soil near a major highway, near an industry that uses lead, or around an older home with chipping outside paint, can be contaminated by lead. Food grown in contaminated soil or stored in opened cans is suspect.
- Drinking water from plumbing with pipes lined or soldered with lead is hazardous. Many newer fixtures contain lead solder, and old water pipes are made of lead. Water supplies should be tested for lead content.
- Leaded gasoline is also a problem. According to the American Academy of Pediatrics, "Leaded gasoline has released an estimated 30 million tons of lead into the air."

- Old newspapers or comic books lying around the house are another source of lead, as they are sometimes printed with lead ink. If they are valuable collectibles, store them in safe containers. Otherwise, recycle or throw them out.
- Other sources include crystal decanters, medicines, bread wrappers, pickle wrappers (pickle leaches acid out of the wrapper leaving lead behind), some hair dyes, products from other countries (such as Mexican pottery, Chinese chalk, dyes from India), and brass faucets. Hobby items that use lead include ceramics, stained glass, fishing sinkers, and bullets.

Now that you know the sources of lead, here are some other ways to prevent poisoning:

- Prevent children from eating dirt (or any other foreign substances, for that matter).
- Avoid using lead around the home for hobbies and other purposes.
- Keep the work clothes of an adult who works in a lead industry or who uses lead for a hobby separate from clothes of the other family members. Wash those clothes separately with a phosphate cleaner.
- If you suspect that your child is exposed to lead at school, do not hesitate to ask questions. Most schools are hyperaware of the problem, and renovation and fresh painting are the rule. But, as always, it's better to query your local department of public health or Poison Control Center than to suffer the consequences. Some states have set up programs that deal exclusively with lead poisoning prevention. Check your own city sources.

It is easier to seek treatment for any illness when the symptoms are evident. One problem of lead poisoning is that some children show little or no symptoms until they are of school age and they fail to keep up with their peers in class work or show hyperactivity. The finger prick test, the most common screening, is done at clinics, doctors' offices, and hospitals. If this test result shows that a child has been exposed to too much lead, your pediatrician will perform a second and more accurate test, this time obtaining a larger sample of blood taken from a vein in the arm. Now he or she can measure the exact amount of lead in the blood.

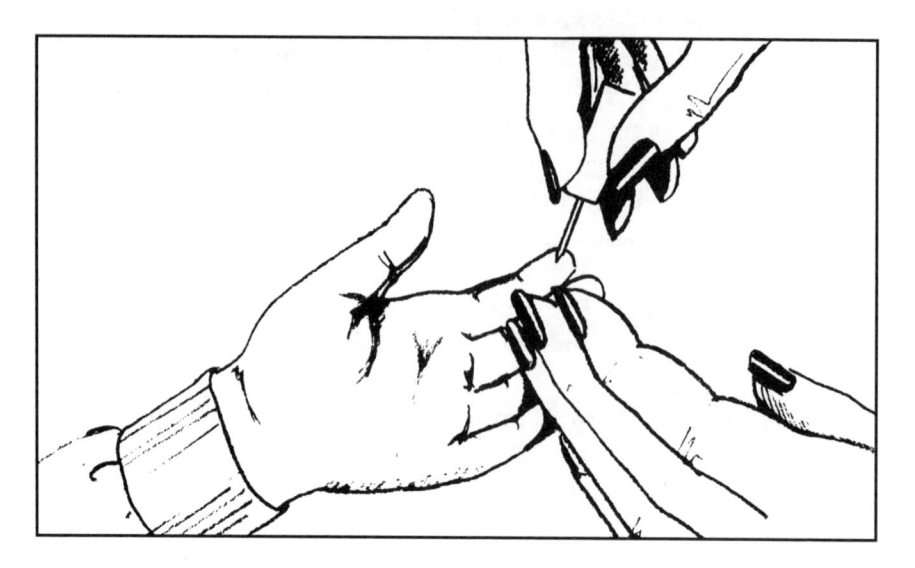

Medicines and hospitalization may be used to bind the lead in the blood and to help the body eliminate it. The amount of medicine and treatment, of course, depends on the extent of damage.

Finally, whom should you call if you suspect that your child has suffered lead poisoning? Your pediatrician, your local health department, or the nearest Poison Control Center. With proper prevention you can avoid that phone call.

## Carbon Monoxide: The Silent Killer

Carbon monoxide poisoning is called a "silent killer" because it creeps up on many of its victims, often in their sleep. And it is generally because of this stealth that approximately 1,500 Americans a year die from this gas. Infants and children are among the most susceptible. In 1990, there were 582 deaths nationally due to carbon monoxide (CO) poisoning, including no deaths under five years of age that year and thirteen deaths of children five to fourteen years of age. By 1992, in-home deaths due to CO poisoning of children four and younger were up to 301. Twenty deaths were reported for children five to fourteen years of age. Causes of poisoning ranged from cooking stoves to heating equipment to fumes from standing motor vehicles. Carbon monoxide is a gas, "a product," writes the American Lung Association, "of incomplete burning of carbon-containing materials such as natural gas or heating oil." CO is both colorless and odorless. When inhaled, it inhibits the blood's capacity to send oxygen through the body. This can eventually lead to permanent brain damage. An unconscious victim may go into cardiac arrest.

In the summer, CO can come from outside sources such as charcoal grills and gas-powered lawnmowers. Winter, however, seems to make the problem worse. CO is produced when fuels such as natural gas, propane, heating oil, kerosene, coal charcoal, gasoline, or wood burn with insufficient air. Houses with a fuel-fired furnace or space heater, a wood stove, a wood or gas fireplace, an attached garage, gas appliances, or gas water heaters are especially vulnerable. And if the chimney is clogged or cigarette smoke fills the air, the situation worsens. A booklet issued jointly by American Sensors, a firm that manufactures CO detectors, and the American Lung Association states: "In these energy-conscious times, we all want to save by weatherproofing our homes. But if your house is tightly sealed against the elements, CO polluted air becomes trapped more easily, increasing your exposure to the danger of poisoning."

Symptoms of carbon monoxide poisoning may be confused with flu: nausea, persistent severe headaches, and dizziness. There may be severe abdominal pain, chest pain when exercising, ringing in the ears, and a feeling of weakness, with difficulty moving about. You may feel ill or tired at home, but feel fine upon leaving home. You may have a rapid heartbeat or pulse. Age matters when it comes to the effects of CO poisoning. For the younger child, a lower level of CO in the system may produce serious toxicity. The level allowed is 15 percent CO in the blood for a child. In an adult, a level up to 25 percent CO in the blood is considered acceptable. In pregnant women, the level allowed is 10 percent, as it can affect the fetus.

To guard against this threat, it is a good idea to buy CO detectors and place them around your home in or near sleeping

**Medic Alert! Poisons**

areas. (Since October 1994, Chicago has required CO detectors in all homes, and many other towns and cities have similar ordinances.) CO detectors are similar to smoke detectors in that they give off an alarm if an excessive level of CO is detected. These cost between $30 and $75 and require no installation, and some models don't accumulate low levels of CO and thus are not prone to false alarms. Look for products recognized by reputable health and safety organizations, and check that the product is listed under the Underwriters Laboratories Standard UL 2034.

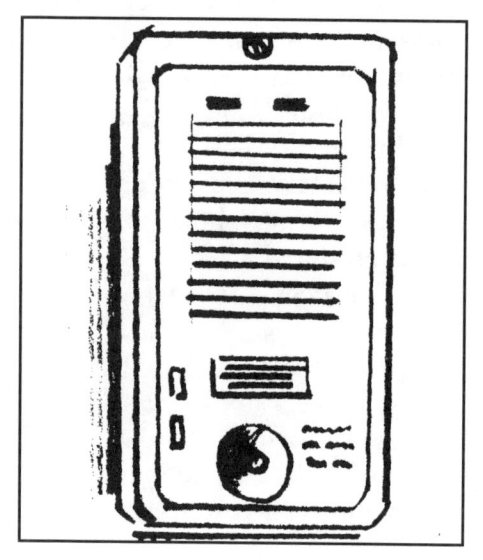

Some CO detectors have a sounding alarm. Place these near bedrooms or next to the furnace. Additional placements could include the kitchen, if your stove uses gas, and by any space heater in your home.

CO patches, another warning tool you can purchase, may not be as effective. Color change of the patch shows that CO is being admitted into the air. However, the person wearing the patch will most likely be asleep or become unconscious when exposed to CO, and therefore will not be able to check if the patch has changed color.

Ways to avoid CO poisoning:

- If you have an attached garage, keep the outside doors open when you're warming up the car (always, not only in winter). Then the carbon monoxide can escape from this enclosed space.
- Check the color of the flame from any heat source—space heater, stove, and so on. It should be blue. If it is yellow-orange, CO is present.

- Have your chimney and flue cleaned professionally.
- Have your home furnace and heating system checked by a heating specialist once a year to be sure they are working properly. Carbon monoxide can seep through areas that have rusted or corroded, and it can escape through heat exchanges with holes. Make sure your furnace has good intake of outside air.
- Make sure stoves and heaters are vented to the outdoors and exhaust systems aren't blocked and don't leak.

If you suspect CO in your home, whom should you contact for help? If someone is in immediate danger, or is seriously ill, call 911, and, of course, get the victim out into the open air at once and do basic CPR. Once the ambulance arrives, the paramedics will administer loose oxygen. Later, for further information, call your local health department or Poison Control Center.

## Other Gases and Toxic Substances

Gases other than carbon monoxide may be present in your home at any time. The following gases could cause serious health risks to your family:

- Propane is a colorless gas which is stored under pressure in a liquid state and is used as both a fuel and a refrigerant. It can leak from the tanks of propane-powered heaters, stoves, barbeques, refrigerators, furnaces, and other appliances; when it leaks, it can be very explosive. To check for such leaks, use a propane gas detector. Place it as low to the floor or ground as possible because propane gas sinks.
- Natural gas in the home can leak, too, from gas appliances such as dryers, fireplaces, heaters, stoves, furnaces, and refrigerators. Gas leaking from outside or below ground level can also seep into the home. This kind of gas is also volatile, so any spark or source of fire could cause an explosion. Because this gas is so light, it rises above the source of the leak to the ceiling. So, if you use a natural gas detector, place it near the ceiling.

## Medic Alert! Poisons

- Radon is reported to be a leading cause of lung cancer. Radon is an odorless gas given off by soil or rock with trace amounts of decomposing uranium. Radon gas from the soil leaks into your home in levels that vary daily as well as seasonally. It can enter through building cracks in the foundation or walls, drains, sumps, joints, and other openings. Water can also transport radon gas into your home. Conditions in old houses allow radon to enter: porous masonry foundations, dirt basements, crawl spaces, and even the porous concrete of cinder blocks. Radon kits approved by the Environmental Protection Agency can be purchased for fifteen to twenty-five dollars. EPA-approved professionals are qualified to seal the problem areas by caulking perimeter floor-wall joints, caulking random floor cracks, or covering crawl spaces and the sump pit with airtight material. Tuckpointing and vapor barriers will also block radon's entry. Outside soil must be treated, as well.
- Formaldehyde is a gas released from pressed-wood products such as particle board, fiberboard, plywood paneling, and some fabrics when temperatures and humidity are high. Particularly irritating to the respiratory tract, banish this gas from your home by eliminating these materials.
- Asbestos is a material of microscopic mineral fibers that is used to make roofing or flooring materials, wall and pipe insulation, and other home products. It can cause terrible lung problems. Materials containing asbestos should be covered with an airtight seal if they're exposed, or removed by professionals if they're flaking or damaged.
- Biological pollutants can enter homes via pets, plants, and even through improperly maintained air conditioners, humidifiers, and air-cleaning filters. If your child has allergies, or a sensitivity to nondisease-causing irritants such as dust mites or animal hair, it's a good idea to have a skilled professional come into your home and simply clean your vents.
- Wood smoke from fireplaces and wood-burning stoves can be toxic. Because the particulate (pollution left from incomplete burning of the wood) is easily trapped in the lungs,

wood smoke has been targeted by the EPA (though wood fuel is a much smaller part of the market than oil or coal). To reduce this risk, simply open your windows. A more costly solution is to install a masonry heater (average cost, $20,000), which stores heat behind glass doors. According to Steve Busch of Buckfield, Maine, who installs the heaters, elaborate flues separate the heat from the smoke, "storing the heat, but burning fuel at its maximum potential." Properly fired masonry heaters, Busch says, are environmentally appropriate, and safe; the surface heat is low, compared to most wood heat appliances.

- Finally, can chemicals in a substance as mundane as the local drinking water be toxic? It sounds farfetched in the final years of the twentieth century, but it has been suggested that the use of aluminum salts to purify water may lead to brain damage. It is not thought to be dangerous to children, but exposure over a lifetime is risky. It probably wouldn't hurt to check what goes on with your city's water purification process.

## Drugs

Parents who care about their children's safety think of them doing drugs the same way they think of them being caught in the middle of a roaring fire, a car crash, or a tornado. There's just one difference. While the other tragedies may be accidental, drugs seldom are; they're poisons of choice. Alcohol in particular can be a problem because society sends kids mixed signals about it. Alcoholic beverages are legal, and children may see their parents enjoying a drink at home or pouring wine for a festive occasion. According to the U.S. Department of Education's publication *Growing Up Drug Free* (1990), the result is that "4.6 million teens have a drinking problem. . . . 4% of high school seniors drink alcohol every day, and alcohol-related accidents are the leading cause of death among young people 15-24 years of age."

What can parents do? To combat drug and alcohol use by your child, first send clear no-use messages. The best way to help is to be a good listener. Let her bring problems home to you and

**Medic Alert! Poisons**

help her to confide in you by not becoming angry; anger tends to end any discussion you might share.

One of the most common agents in this battle is the low self-esteem that can push a child into doing what her friends do ("If I do it, too, they'll be my friends."). Children look to others to tell them what to do, and if the direction is wrong, the child may be sunk. That's why a parent's attention and positive feedback are so important. The building of self-esteem begins at home at a very young age. Developing a secure self-image, of course, starts with love.

Although memories do not begin, experts say, until around the age of three, that warmth, that parental atmosphere of love and approval as the child grows up, establishes the feeling that the child matters, is precious to her parents. This is the fodder that feeds her self-image. It does not follow, however, that as she begins to grow and relate with her peers, she will love herself because you love her. But it helps set the tone. And positive self-esteem, learning to value herself, is likely to help her battle feelings of self-pity, anger, and self-dislike that can crop up when she drives down an occasional bumpy road with her peers.

Many parents and child development experts say that self-esteem is only part of the picture; that building knowledge, skills, and character are equally or more important. What a child learns to do, in other words, is as important as how she feels.

In teaching your child life skills, remember that her trust is your greatest tool and most precious resource. Responding to a failure or disappointment with false praise jeopardizes that trust. Say your child is not chosen for a team. If you say, "Oh, don't pay any attention. You're the best player around," and the child knows that in all truth she's not, you have not helped at all and have, in fact, damaged the truth in the relationship. How can the child now believe anything you say?

Instead of lying, lead with your child's strengths: "You may not be the best at that, but you sure are the best at (drawing, tennis, whatever the child does excel in)." Encourage the child to work at something; praise the efforts, not just the result. Wanting to do something is the start of doing it, and as the child works hard, she deserves praise.

## Prevention Programs

A number of prevention programs, some organized on the state level, some spreading nationally, are available to help parents in this battle. It is up to parents to find out what they are; to read materials children bring home from school, to learn and to help.

### DARE

Some local police departments cooperate with state police, boards of education, and the state's department of alcoholism and substance abuse to present students with an anti-drug program called Drug Abuse Resistance Education (DARE). The concept guiding the seventeen-week program is simple: DARE to say no! DARE was first developed in Los Angeles and is now used in many parts of the country. This program, which is focused on fifth and sixth graders, teaches students what being grown-up really means: not giving in to peer pressure, making your own decisions, and learning to cope with life's problems in positive ways. It has been joined by several other fine, all-encompassing programs that accompany a child from kindergarten all the way through high school in an effort to teach her to resist drugs and alcohol.

### *Growing Up Drug Free*

Among available materials, none is better than a booklet first sent to parents in 1990 by the U.S. Department of Education called *Growing Up Drug Free*. Some of the most important points made in this publication center on communicating your sense of values to your child. If you are specific and consistent ("Our no alcohol/no drug use applies to you whether you're home, at a friend's house, or anywhere"), you're a step ahead.

### The Comprehensive Health Education Foundation

The Comprehensive Health Education Foundation (CHEF), a nonprofit health education organization based in Seattle, Washington, has produced a video titled "Monica and the Powerful Drug" (1991), as part of the third-grade package in CHEF's series, *Here's Looking At You, 2000*. The video is a fourteen-minute cartoon, deceptively simple and festooned with wit,

## Medic Alert! Poisons

color, and music. Monica is a female monkey at the zoo who follows her big brother into alcohol-related trouble. In a literal case of "monkey see, monkey do," Monica wants to drink because she sees her big brother doing it, even though he gets sick making "a human out of himself," as the video's narrator, an opossum named Opi, puts it. The opossum says: "Alcohol makes them *think* they're cool. I don't drink alcohol, and I *know* I'm cool." In the end big brother wises up, sees the kind of bad influence he is being, and turns away from the bad company that encouraged his drinking. Monica is saved, thanks to her brother's wisdom.

A second video, made for first graders, is called "Ask For It." Animals take on the tasks of teaching in this video, too, instructing kids on how to say no, as well as how to share, how to look someone in the eye and converse, and how to say please. Tackling the idea of communicating, with a parrot, a fox, and a frog at the helm showing how it's done, is a charming way to begin this ingratiating series.

CHEF director Dr. Neil Starkman states the foundation's aims: "This is a drug education program for students from K through twelfth grade. It has had several predecessors—it actually started as an alcohol education program, and it's been expanded. In 1986, it became *Here's Looking At You, 2000,* and it was revised several years after that." Starkman feels that people praise the program because "It's proven to be effective, and it's easy for teachers to use. We make use of skills—teaching kids skills on how to stay away from trouble, how to use self-control. For example, in younger grades, we teach a skill where a student learns to ask for something, instead of just taking it. And all that does is to try to reduce the risk factor of antisocial behavior. There's a lot of data to indicate that when kids are antisocial or aggressive in the early years, they're more and more aggressive for getting into trouble with a lot of things, including drugs.

"The program makes use of a lot of learning and teaching styles: books, games, audiotapes, simulations of activities that involve large groups and small groups in different projects. A parent newsletter is sent at every grade level and there are activities that students can take home and do with their parents. There are worksheets a teacher can copy, and everything in all the audio and videotapes is spelled out explicitly." The course offers particularly good instruction dealing with "refusal skills," self-control, and taking a stand on issues. Children are helped particularly with developing self-esteem.

### The Million Dollar Machine Program

Another program that sets out to prevent alcohol, tobacco, and other drug use is the excellent Million Dollar Machine Program, focusing on kindergarten through sixth grade. Produced by a New Jersey corporation called KidsLife Resources, the video and program has been experienced by more than two million students in the country, who have been learning from three robots named Foobie, Punchy, and the Caring Coach.

The "million dollar machines" are not Foobie or Punchy at all, but rather the children's own bodies. The idea is to teach kids to "keep a clean machine" and that drugs, alcohol, and other addictive substances will turn them away from their full potential.

A robot personally visits each school, introducing teachers and students to the curriculum. At a live parents' orientation, parents meet the robot, too, and understand the life skills' lessons their children learn in school. Classroom materials include more than six hundred activities and discussion topics and forty interactive worksheets, posters, and other guidelines. Different assemblies are held for kindergarten through third grade and fourth through sixth grade.

### McGruff, the Crime Dog

One of the best McGruff pamphlets is titled *Winners Don't Use Drugs* (1979). In simple but effective words, the dog named McGruff tells kids that drugs are just plain dangerous: "Alcohol can make you sick to your stomach or act in embarrassing ways. Worst of all, alcohol makes it hard for your brain to grow right."

As for illegal drugs, "Some of these illegal drugs are marijuana, PCP, LSD, cocaine, and crack. Ask your parents, school nurse, or teacher to help you find out how each of these drugs hurts your body and your mind."

McGruff talks about the kids' family members. If they want to use tobacco and alcohol, well, "adults don't always make the best choices." And, "if persons in your family are using any of these drugs, tell them you love them and you hope they will stop. Maybe you can talk to another grown-up who can help."

The good old dog also says that if kids take drugs, they'll have a hard time concentrating on the things they used to enjoy. And drugs make it hard to do well in school and sports. McGruff tells why ("marijuana stops your hands, feet, and eyes from working well together"; "smoking marijuana or cigarettes will damage your lungs and make it hard for you to breathe") and urges the kids who read this pamphlet to "Be a winner—winners don't use and users don't win."

Share all of the ideas and reasons given above with your child. If you can turn just one life away from the pain engendered by drugs, the ultimate poisons, isn't it worth thinking about and talking about and working hard to achieve?

**How to Say "No Way"**

The following worksheet from the Millon Dollar Machine Program helps kids say "no" to tobacco. There is a space at the bottom of the page for the child to write his or her name, and another space to fill in the date. Note that there is also a space for the parent to fill in his or her initials, so that the teacher can be sure that the work has had parental recognition.

The point, of course, is to aid the child in brushing up on his refusal skills.

**Medic Alert! Poisons**

# How to Say "No way!"

If someone tries to get you to do something bad, there are lots of ways to protect your Million Dollar Machine! Read this story, and then talk about the different ways to say "no" with your folks.

> PJ and some friends were playing kickball after school. Everyone was getting tired when Sal said "Hey, I have some matches. Let's start a campfire."
>
> Right away, PJ said "I don't think that's a good idea!"
>
> His friends said "Oh come on, don't be a chicken. We'll just start a small fire, OK?"

**What could PJ do then? Explain to a parent how PJ could try out each one of these ways to say "No!" in that situation.**

**1. PJ could CHANGE THE SUBJECT by:**

☐ making a joke and saying he wants to finish the ball game.

☐ reminding his friends how much trouble they could get in.

**2. If that didn't work, PJ could STAND UP FOR HIMSELF by:**

☐ acting shocked that his friends would do something so dangerous.

☐ saying "No, I'm not going to to do it. It's dumb!"

**3. If that didn't work, PJ could GET AWAY by:**

☐ making an excuse to leave like:
"I've got to get home for dinner."

☐ just walking away from the kids who are pressuring him

**4. Finally, PJ could GET HELP by:**

☐ telling an adult what happened.

☐ asking a big brother or sister to help.

PARENT'S INITIALS

Put a check next to the ways to say "no" that YOU think would work best.

Tell a story about a time you stopped a bad situation like PJ did.

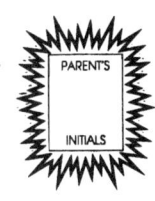

NAME _____ DATE _____

© Copyright 1990 GoWell & Kent Inc., Mt. Holly, NJ

This page is used with the permission of GoWell & Kent, Inc., Mt. Holly, New Jersey, and KidsLife Resources, Mt. Laurel, New Jersey.

111

**Medic Alert! Poisons**

# Very Important Tips

**POISON PREVENTION**

1. The most common causes of accidental poisonings are medicines (including iron pills), insect sprays, kerosene, lighter fluid, furniture polish, turpentine, paints, solvents, and products containing lye and acids.
2. Never leave poisonous substances out. Return them to a safe place, locked up and away from children, right after use.
3. Use child-resistant closures. Poison control officials nationwide stress that such containers are highly effective in preventing children from accidental poisonings. This effectiveness should not be compromised by adults who fail to take an extra moment to reclose the caps.
4. Read labels on household products and follow directions.
5. Keep all products in their original containers. Don't place kerosene, antifreeze, paints, or solvents in cups, glasses, milk or cola bottles, or other storage containers used for food or drinks. Never transfer dangerous products to a bottle without a child-resistant closure.
6. Keep foods and household products separated. You'd be surprised how many householders forget to observe this rule.
7. Pets can be victims, too. Dogs and cats rummage through garbage cans and eat from open containers in the garage and around the yard. Don't allow pets into areas where pesticides or other poisonous substances are being used.

**POISONING TREATMENTS**

1. Act immediately and follow the latest procedures issued by the National Safety Council and the American Red Cross.
2. Stay calm. Keep your child calm.
3. Look in the child's mouth. Remove any remaining pills or pieces of plant. Take these with you to the hospital (in a plastic bag).
4. If medication (or drugs) have been swallowed, do not give anything by mouth unless the poison center says to do so. If chemicals or household products are swallowed, call the PCC and ask whether you should make the patient vomit.

## Medic Alert! Poisons

# Very Important Tips

5. Keep a bottle of syrup of ipecac to induce vomiting. If you go on vacation, take it with you; have Grandma stock it (or any relative or friend your kids visit regularly). It is inexpensive (under $2 at most drugstores), so be sure to always have a bottle on hand at home.

6. Remember, prevention's the best cure. Keep all poisonous materials out of sight, under lock, or high out of a toddler's reach.

### LEAD POISONING

1. If you have remodeled or renovated the house, have you tested for lead? If you're planning on remodeling an old house, it's best for the family to leave the house until the remodeling is completed and cleaned up.

2. If you are remodeling your home, don't become involved with interior decoration until the trained professional has completed remodeling and the workspaces are properly cleaned up.

3. Control dust, paint chips, and debris; as dust spreads, lead spreads. Prevent your child from eating paint chips and dirt.

4. A family member with a lead-related job or hobby (painters, battery plant workers, pottery makers, stained glass artists, etc.), should remove work clothing before entering the home and clean up well. Even with these precautions, check young children in the family to make sure lead hasn't been brought into the house.

5. Use cold tap water to mix formula for infants; let the water run for two minutes first. The Department of Public Health further advises not to use water from the hot water tap for cooking, drinking, or preparing infant formula.

6. Was your home built prior to 1960? If yes, have lead tests done by a professional.

7. If you live in an apartment building, check to see if anyone living there has ever had lead poisoning.

**Medic Alert! Poisons**

# Very Important Tips

### MEDICINES

1. Dispose of old medications. Pour them down the drain or flush them down the toilet and rinse the container before discarding. Don't put the container with its contents into your trash basket.
2. Never call medicine "candy." Sometimes, a parent thinks it may be a good way to entice a child to take medicine, but when left alone, the child might locate the bottle and eat or drink its contents.
3. Since children tend to imitate adults, avoid taking medications in their presence. Avoid drinking medicine from the bottle.
4. Always turn on the light when giving and taking medicine, to be sure both medicine and size of dose are correct.
5. Always be wary of guests who carry medications in purses, pockets, or briefcases. Children can sometimes find and swallow them. ("Let's go look in Grandma's purse," or, "That's Uncle Joe's briefcase. Let's peek.")

# Chapter 4

# The Toyland Safety Zone

TOYLAND SHOULD BE A SAFE PLACE for all boys and girls. In the best of all possible worlds, every child would have toys to play with, the toys would be safe, and each toy would be automatically age-appropriate. However, in this real world, toys can pose great danger to children. According to a Connecticut Public Interest Research Group study, at least twenty-five children in the United States died in 1991 choking on toys, and about 130,000 were treated in hospital emergency rooms for toy-related injuries. This chapter describes precautions being taken by toy-makers and discusses what parents can do to buy playthings that are harmless and to keep them harmless.

**Toyland Safety Zone**

# Regulating the Toy Industry

On November 18, 1988, President George Bush signed into law the Labeling of Hazardous Art Materials Act, mandating that all art materials be reviewed to determine the potential for causing a chronic hazard, and that appropriate warning labels be put on those art materials found to pose a chronic hazard. The law applies to many children's toy products, such as crayons, chalk, paint sets, modeling clay, coloring books, pencils, and any other products used by children to produce a work of visual or graphic art. The result is that parents buying art materials, school supplies, and toys that fit into the "art" category, now find that these products are accompanied by the statement, "conforms to ASTM."

Though other states have now climbed aboard the bandwagon, Connecticut was the first to require the small-parts warning label. Toys for children three to seven years old may pose a hazard to children under three. Labeling items meant for the older age group combats the incorrect assumption by parents and caregivers that the age suggestions on toy packages relate only to developmental levels. They may think "Jennifer's only two and a half, but she's developmentally more advanced than a three-and-a-half-year-old, so I can buy her this toy." The problem is that in spite of her development, Jennifer may not be able to resist putting the toy's small parts in her mouth, and they are very dangerous if caught in the airway.

Toy safety is regulated by the U.S. Consumer Product Safety Commission (CPSC), which employs teams of field inspectors to monitor the marketplace for both domestically and foreign-produced toys that could pose safety hazards. Under the Federal Hazardous Substances Act and the Consumer Product Safety Act, the CPSC has set safety regulations for certain toys and other children's articles. Manufacturers must design and manufacture their products to meet these regulations. However, the industry's voluntary safety standards lead to close cooperation between the Toy Manufacturers of America (TMA) and the CPSC.

Peter Reynolds, U.S. president of the Brio Corporation, explains the toy manufacturer's responsibility under the law:

## Toyland Safety Zone

"In the U.S., the way the law currently stands, you do not have to test products to see they're safe, but if at any point you discover that they're not safe, then you have to report it to the CPSC. After they investigate, the result is anything from a 'stop sell' to a full consumer recall; whereas, in most other countries, you have to test the toys prior to them being put on the market. In most instances, as an intelligent manufacturer, we have all our toys tested on a regular basis by an independent laboratory. We test them in the factory in Sweden to ensure that they pass all international standards, and again in the United States and Europe."

According to Reynolds, safety is of top importance. In the area of physical safety, Brio follows the voluntary guidelines of the CPSC federal guidelines and standards to the letter. Reynolds also credits the toy industry for its vigilance. "You can look at it from a humanitarian perspective and say they want children to have good, safe play experiences, which I believe is the truth, or the cynical perspective, which is if you injure a child, it's not very good marketing. But they do try very hard."

Reynolds notes as examples of the impact of industry efforts the discovery that some plastics are carcinogenic, and the determination of the allowable lead content in paint. There are other safety demands in producing toys: "Take wood, for example. The American 'drop test'—to test the physical strength of a toy—is approximately twice as high and twice as long as the drop test in Europe, which essentially means that toys in the U.S. have to be twice as strong. This makes it difficult to make wooden toys for children under eighteen months old." The Brio Corporation uses an independent lab not only to conduct the drop test, according to Reynolds, "but all the paint is tested, batch by batch. Whenever a batch of paint is tested at the factory in Sweden, a sample is sent off to a testing lab. This is because the yellow paint delivered last month may have been made at a different part of the factory than the yellow paint we get delivered this month. So each batch is tested on every occasion."

Laurie Strong of Fisher-Price, Inc., a sixty-five-year-old company that has been a subsidiary of Mattel, Inc., since 1993, notes that the company does extensive testing to meet both U.S. and

**Toyland Safety Zone**

European standards as well as the company's internal standards. Strong assures product reliability, stating that Fisher-Price toys "are evaluated at the prototype stage, which is when they're just being developed. They're evaluated by watching what's going on in the play laboratory. A one-way mirror enables kids to be watched interacting with the product." This helps develop toy standards and anticipate how the product will be used and abused.

David Eagle, national sales manager of Playmobil USA, says of crib toys that many manufacturers are not using straps and cords that would hold the product across the crib, preferring things that attach, either with plastic screws or some sort of clasp, to the side of the crib. Older children need supervision, too. "Take an electric toy, like a train set. You don't want them sticking the plug in and out of the socket. Obviously, too, there should be care taken with toys that have sharp points, swords, and sticks. It's not an issue with under three-year-olds."

# Choosing Safe Toys for Your Child

## Safety Guidelines

Most toymakers will tell you that the first requirement of any toy is that it must be fun. But they are quite aware that toys must also be safe before parents will buy it. As Diane Cardinale of the Toy Manufacturers of America says: "It's important to choose safe, age-appropriate toys, and we stress the importance of proper supervision." According to Brio's Peter Reynolds, parents should always look at a toy to see that it is what it's supposed to be: "If there are pieces broken off, or pieces too small for your children to play with, then return the toy to the store. Don't ever try to fix a product. Take it back to the store and get a new one. Make sure the toy is what you're supposed to get. Even at the store, take it out and have a look at it, so you can ask for another one if anything's missing, or anything's cracked or chipped. We do it when it

## Toyland Safety Zone

comes to shoes or crockery, before we buy it, to make sure we're getting what we think we're getting."

Now that you know the ways in which the states and the national government, as well as toy manufacturers, have worked for safety, here is what you can do: Select toys carefully. Properly supervise your children at play. Supervision is the best way to be sure your kids don't suffer from toy-related injuries. In buying toys, the key to success is to *know your child*. Here are a few pointers to follow as you shop for a toy and what to do once you've brought it home.

### Selecting Toys

1. Find and follow age recommendations and look on packaging labels for any warnings or other safety messages from the manufacturer. Attend to these warnings just as you do to an expiration date on foods at the grocery store. You wouldn't buy sour milk or bad meat. Do you want to buy a toy with so many sharp points? "Nontoxic" on a toy's label only means that the toy contains no poison that could prove fatal; your child could still become sick from ingesting or inhaling material from the toy. Be sure to check out the toy and use your own judgment.

**Toyland Safety Zone**

2. Check to see if the toy has areas of danger. There may be sharp points, small parts, or pieces dangerous for infants to handle. David Eagle of Playmobil USA warns: "There are small parts in toys and then there are the pieces that pop out—say a clown face with a nose that pops out—which can become an unintended small part. So be sure with all toys for infants up to age three that everything is welded properly and attached to the product as securely as can be."
3. Look for labels denoting such safety features as "Flame retardant" or "Flame resistant" on fabrics of cloth dolls and toys.
4. Choose "Washable/Hygienic materials" when buying stuffed toys and dolls. When buying baby's first toys, look for those that can be cleaned or washed off easily. Battle against germs on these toys, because they are sure to go in your baby's mouth.

### Unwrapping and Assembling Toys

5. When a gift-wrapped toy is given to your child, exclaim at the pretty paper and ribbons, right along with him. Then dispose of the wrappings and ribbons immediately. No need to make a big fuss about this. Kids are more interested in the toy than its wrappings, anyway. However, these materials can pose the safety hazards of choking and poisoning. (Some ribbon dyes can be toxic.)
6. After removing the gift-wrapping, before you give the gift to your child, remove and throw out all manufacturer's packaging. This includes the paper, plastic, ties, and pinnings. To keep them sanitary, many toys are tied into inner wrappings—boxes within boxes—which are then covered with plastic and put into the outer box. Get rid of all of these potentially dangerous packaging materials before giving the toy to your child.
7. Use the "truncated cylinder test tube" available in retail stores to test small parts for choking dangers. Developed by

**Toyland Safety Zone**

the CPSC, the clear plastic tube determines which items are too small to give to a child under three years of age. If the item falls through, into the tube, it is a choking hazard. Marbles and small balls that come in older siblings' games will fall through. Be aware that there are children over three who can't handle items like this; parental judgment is called for.

8. When you've purchased a toy, and brought it home, DO read the instructions. Many toys must be assembled, and the directions are there for a reason: to be followed. Even something as simple as failing to align edges, because directions weren't read or followed, can result in a child's fingers being cut.

9. Battery-operated toys should not be accessible to an infant; keep them confined to big sister's room. Install batteries in a toy for an older child properly to avoid any overheating or exploding. This can happen if the ends are improperly connected.

## Infant Toys

10. Remove toys with strings from a baby's crib when baby becomes mobile. *Mobile* is the operative word here. The first crib toys hang directly over the baby, some in vivid blocks of black and white, others in vibrant jewel-like colors. Some mobiles feature little figures dangling at the ends of straps or strings. As your baby looks up, his tiny senses are stimulated. When he begins to move, and finally to sit up, reaching for the pretty mobile takes on an ominous note. (See Chapter 5 for information on another related danger, venetian blind cords that are accessible to babies.) Remove all crib toys that are strung across the crib or playpen when your child is beginning to push up on his hands and knees or is five months of age (whichever occurs first).

11. While baby is sleeping, take rattles, teethers, squeezy toys, and any other toys from the crib.

**Toyland Safety Zone**

12. Make very sure that your baby's first toys, including squeezies, rattles, and teethers, are large enough so that they can't slip down or become lodged in his throat. If you keep teethers in the freezer, try to place them in a germ-free sanitary container of their own.
13. Pacifiers should be sturdy and easy to wash. The pacifier's protective shield should be too large to fit in your baby's mouth and should have ventilation holes, in case it does get in his mouth. Don't let a pacifier deteriorate to the point that it weakens and develops holes or tears. If infection seems rampant in your house, with colds passing from sibling to sibling, occasionally boil all pacifiers for three minutes or so. It could be helpful in stopping the transfer of germs.
14. Don't pin the baby's pacifier to him with a ribbon, string, or strap, long or short.

**Toy Storage**

15. Storage for toys is important. Toys shouldn't be left around rooms, hallways, or stairs where people can stumble over them. Invest in or construct a large toy box. Be sure there is sufficient ventilation, in case an infant crawls inside.

16. Toy box lids are always a source of problems. The most important safety feature of a toy box is its hinge. Buy a spring-loaded lid-support device that can keep a lid from falling on a child's head or neck, or from closing and trapping a child playing inside the chest. The device (according to the Consumer Product Safety Commission) costs about $7.50 and should be used on all chests that store toys.
17. Show your child how to put his toys safely away on shelves and/or in his toy box. Learning to keep his room safe and neat (so people don't stumble over toys underfoot) is fun for a young child.

## Choosing Appropriate Toys

Many adults have a hard time choosing children's toys. Afraid of opening a Pandora's box, parents face the question of appropriateness. As noted, toys are the stuff of play exploration and learning fun. "It's a mistake to assume play is merely entertainment," says Dr. Richard Chase, associate professor of Psychiatry and Behavioral Sciences at The Johns Hopkins University School of Medicine, and president and CEO of the New York-based Child Growth and Development Corporation. For a child, he says, handling a toy is a process of exploration. "It starts with identification of the toy's physical characteristics, and then progresses to figuring out how the toy works. Tugging, pushing, and pulling help a child to understand what a toy can do. After this understanding is achieved, children then try to figure what they can do with the toy."

Joanne Oppenheim, editor of *Oppenheim Toy Portfolio* and co-author with Stephanie Oppenheim of the annual *The Best Toys, Books, and Videos for Kids* (HarperCollins, 1996), believes that toys are learning tools, so it's important that toys be age-appropriate. "If they don't build competence and confidence, they can be inappropriate, boring, or frustrating, like giving a two-wheeler to a toddler too young to learn to ride it." Oppenheim also points out that certain toys seem to grow naturally with a child, taking on new functions as the child's imagination and motor skills develop. Blocks, for example, are chewed or thrown by infants (a soft fabric

**Toyland Safety Zone**

is good). "In the next stage, large stackable blocks are fun for a child to tote and carry. Next, a child will manipulate the blocks and begin building with them, and, in the early school years, children begin problem-solving." While sturdy generic building blocks can fulfill each of these stages, Oppenheim also suggests Lego-style blocks, Lincoln Logs, and finally erector sets, for which play often requires following a plan.

Suppose your little one sees a toy advertised consistently on TV and, like every other child watching, wants that toy. Should you buy it for him? "Yes," says Oppenheim. She does think that toys should be geared to a child's age and readiness, but if your child wants the hottest toy advertised on TV, why not? "There's nothing wrong with a little glitz if it's not dangerous or offensive to your own value system. But there's so much junk out there, I wish parents would consider the good books and videos."

If you have children of different ages, you are certain to have toys around your home that are appropriate for each of those ages. However, the five-year-old's game is obviously not appropriate for your two-year-old's use. Even if a toy is safe, when used improperly it can cause not only injuries but death. When it comes to managing toys and siblings of different ages in your home, keep older kids' toys away from an infant, because they may contain small parts on which infants can choke. Babies are naturally curious about their older siblings' toys. Board games, building blocks, sets and structures with Lego-type pieces, even little baskets full of play makeup or play kitchen or grocery items must be kept out of baby's reach. Children should also learn to respect each other's possessions. Teach an older child that there are certain things he and baby can share; point out the ones they cannot share. An older child who has his own room away from the baby will be glad to keep his own toys in his room so baby won't get to them. If an older child shares a room with baby, he should have an area that is separate and personalized for toys, such as a higher shelf that baby can't reach, or a separate toy box.

Toys are meant to be fun, to spark a child's interest, help develop new skills, develop their imaginations, give them the chance to explore, develop hand-eye coordination, strengthen muscles, and develop physical coordination (especially in the case of outdoor toys and sports). Remember that each child is unique in his stage of development, so look not only at the toy that is marked age-appropriate for a three-year-old, but be sure your three-year-old is ready for that specific toy. If parents follow that rule, they can introduce the appropriate toys at the appropriate times for their children.

## Age-Appropriate Toys for Safe Play

### Children Three and Younger

Burton L. White, Ph.D., author of *The First Three Years of Life* (Simon & Schuster, 1985), recommends particular toys for particular ages. Again, parents should know what kind of toys are appropriate at each stage of development. The following tips should help you to introduce the right toys at the right time.

THREE TO FIVE WEEKS: A well-designed mobile hanging above the crib is the best first toy.

THREE TO NINE WEEKS: During the "looking" phase, small mirrors will amuse a baby fascinated by his own image.

TWO TO FIVE MONTHS: A crib gym will help a child reach for objects and bring them closer to explore.

TWO TO SIX MONTHS: A floor gym is appropriate, and a battery-operated swing with gentle, pacifying movements is also nice at this stage.

FOUR-AND-A-HALF MONTHS TO SEVEN-AND-A-HALF MONTHS: Babies love to bounce in a jumper at this age until about eight or nine months.

SIX MONTHS TO THREE YEARS: Bath toys with squirters and water wheels are better than those that just float passively.

EIGHT TO EIGHTEEN MONTHS: This age enjoys pop-up toys with buttons to push or handles to turn.

TEN MONTHS: Cardboard books are good, but until fifteen months, tots will mostly turn or chew the pages instead of looking at them.

**ONE TO THREE YEARS:** Building blocks appeal to this age, and a low three- or four-wheel riding toy is a reliable source of fun. Videos are fine, and the child's interest will increase from eighteen months onward. Dolls and doll purses (with objects like plastic toy combs and keys) are useful for imaginative play.
**TWELVE TO TWENTY-FOUR MONTHS:** Kids love big balls.
**FOURTEEN MONTHS TO THREE YEARS:** Give children something to scribble on and at two they'll actually start drawing. A climbing toy, like a small jungle gym, is also right for this age.
**SIXTEEN MONTHS TO THREE YEARS:** Simple puzzles offer hand-eye challenge and a feeling of success when completed.
**EIGHTEEN MONTHS TO THREE YEARS:** "Scenario" toys (play schools, stores, kitchens, parking garages) feed the imagination.
**TWO TO THREE YEARS:** Toy telephones are useful for make-believe play, while a small tricycle will be enjoyed after the second birthday.

For further recommendations, consult *The Toy Report*, published by The Canadian Toy Testing Council, a year-round guide to toys that is available in most bookstores. The Canadian Council tests and approves many fine toys, designating appropriate ages for their use. Some of their recent suggestions—a nesting toy (Nesting Farm Animals®) by Little Tikes™ and a soft cuddly Puffalump Kids® doll by Fisher-Price™—were deemed "best bets" for ages six to twenty-four months. Another "best bet" for one- to three-year-olds was Playskool's™ Baby Doll®, and, for ages five to eight, Parker's™ Monopoly Junior® was deemed another best bet.

## Children Over Three

Many of the challenges of keeping an older child safe do not arise when caring for children under three. His desire to get up and go, his ability to create, and his awareness of technology all make parents' jobs much more complex. The following tips will help you lessen the hazards of your "big kid's" toyland.

1. Junior equestrians love rocking horses, and you should check to make sure the steeds are steady. Inspect the rocker

**Toyland Safety Zone**

base; if it's made of wood, are there splinters? If there are uncovered springs, you might try the solution of Susan Whitehead, a mother of four from Menasha, Wisconsin. Susan slips the cardboard tubes from inside paper towels over the springs of the rocking horse and other rocking toys to avoid pinched fingers.

2. Any riding toy you buy for a growing child should be sturdy enough to last through several seasons and to be passed down to the next child in line. The wheels should be spread the right distance apart to be completely balanced for stability, and chrome or metal should be rust-free. Pedals and hand grips should not be slippery; be sure little hands and feet can grip well. Always find a safe resting place for a riding toy. Just as you keep your car parked in the garage, the riding toy should have a parking space, too; it should never be left in the driveway. Kids on tricycles and other riding toys are not very visible, so it's a good idea to buy a flag for a trike or small bike that will be visible to drivers.

3. Remember, first helmets are the way to start kids on the right road. That means that children must always wear helmets from tricycles to bikes, and on skates, too (particularly in-line skates).

4. When creativity strikes, art supplies are the best bet. Crafting a simple necklace or bracelet using a special bead-based jewelry set (a perfect project for an eight-year-old), affixing buttons to an inexpensive picture frame, or finger-painting can be great fun. But you must note the hazard labels to be sure that you purchase safe art supplies. Never

**Toyland Safety Zone**

be afraid to ask your salesperson what is potentially dangerous if absorbed through the skin or inhaled, and if he doesn't know, tell him to learn for the sake of other parents like you.

5. Kids should use water-based paints, not oil-based, and big brushes. Thin brushes, the kind you may use, are not only hard for little fingers to grip but go easily into little mouths. Buy jumbo crayons for the same reason.

6. Instead of clay, choose Play Doh®. Playskool™ Play Doh is safe for children of three years of age and older to use as the ingredients are nontoxic.

7. Avoid the airplane glue often used on models, and the rubber cement you keep in your desk drawer is off-limits. Children can use white glue (such as Elmer's®) or plain old school paste.

8. Provide children's scissors, and teach your child how to use them properly. Make sure he knows that scissors are not so much toys as utensils that facilitate cutting a variety of materials, from paper plates and felt to cutouts. Check that the size fits the child's hand, and be sure to buy right-handed scissors for a right-handed child and left-handed scissors for a left-handed child. Each child should have a pair of his own. Kids don't mind sharing paper, crayons, or glue, but handing scissors back and forth can be dangerous, especially if one child is in a different developmental stage than another.

9. Children like to use chalk and tend to get carried away. If you prefer your home and yard unchalked, assign an area where chalks may be used freely. Teach your child to respect the property of others, including the next-door neighbors' driveway and walk.

10. Keep easels, tables, or whatever is used for art projects—including paste, paints, crayons, brushes, and glitter—in a separate area. Pick an area that is easy to clean, near a sink, if possible, to facilitate cleanup. Place a drop cloth or an old sheet on the floor so messes don't cause parental scoldings. Tables and little chairs should be child-sized and

**Toyland Safety Zone**

easily cleaned, as well. You may want to install a cork board so that works of art may be hung and displayed. (That way, not everything has to go on the refrigerator with magnets!) Each child should have his own smock (plastic smocks are good), or you might offer old workshirts. Do not set up the creative corner near a stove, fireplace, or heater. Try the back porch, or the backyard can serve your purpose when the weather is good. If need be, make the area a temporary one, which changes according to circumstances. In that case, keep a sheet on hand to be draped across the floor and use a folding table and chairs. Finally, store all materials in boxes, bins, or little carrying baskets to keep things separate and easy to find. Impatient little fingers are less likely to get into difficulty if things are in place. Labeling boxes is a good idea too.

11. When you want to be on target with electronic toys for your older child, aim them directly at his ability. Look at the controls to see if they're well spaced and uncluttered. Is the overall weight and size right for your child? A toy meant for a nine-year-old with a small keyboard could be awkward for his finger size. Is the screen well sized and easy to read? Are the letters and numbers the size and shape that your child recognizes?

12. If the toy talks, is it understandable? Is there an auto-shut-off feature that saves the life of batteries? Does the toy offer positive reinforcement for correct answers? Can your child easily erase and correct mistakes?

## Safe Toys for Outdoor Fun

During the winter, we all tend to hibernate a little, though many of us love winter sports. But, when nice weather comes, we hasten outdoors, and that's, of course, when many injuries occur. Here are some recommendations for safe, age-appropriate outdoor play.

INFANTS TO EIGHTEEN MONTHS: At this age, exploring his immediate environment is great fun. Lay a busy blanket on the grass, or take the baby for a ride in a baby swing. Be sure it has a safety belt. Fabric toys that stimulate his senses are all recommended.

**EIGHTEEN MONTHS TO THREE YEARS:** Children love toys that offer mobility in many ways, such as ride-on toys, rocking horses, and swings. Push toys are great, too, and the push-and-pull toys that make sounds (popping, chimes, etc.) are even more exciting to the toddler. Miniature lawn mowers, shopping carts, or baby strollers provide opportunities for pretending and scenario play. Be sure all push-and-pull toys are sturdily made and evenly balanced so that they don't tip over and pull your little one down with them.

**THREE TO FIVE YEARS:** Beginner roller skates are appropriate now, and tricycles, too. Sprinklers are invigorating on a hot summer day, but keep your sprinkler's force low. Climbing on a jungle gym or zipping down slides are good for stretching muscles. It's important to remember, though, that these pieces of equipment pose special safety hazards.

**FIVE TO EIGHT YEARS:** Competitiveness comes into play at this age. This is the time toys like basketballs, baseballs, and jump ropes are perfect for children who are now more interested in what they can do than in what the toy can do. Large, rather than small, soft and colorful balls are good for practicing batting and are easier and safer for beginners.

**EIGHT TO TWELVE YEARS:** These children are ready for more sophisticated sports equipment and remote control airplanes, cars, and trucks. If your child is interested in fast-moving sports, be sure to get the helmet and wrist, elbow, and knee pads, too. Safety equipment is a necessary accessory with all sports toys.

## Unsafe Toys
### Loud Toys

The CPSC is a good source for advice on unsafe toys. One category of unsafe toys comprises those that make loud noises. Toy caps and some noisemaking guns can produce sounds at noise levels that are not only irritating to adults but can damage hearing in the child. The law requires that this label be written on boxes of caps producing noise above a certain level: ("WARNING—Do Not Fire Closer Than One Foot to the Ear—Do Not Use Indoors"). Caps producing noise that can injure a child's hearing are banned. If your child receives a gift that produces sounds at noise levels that can damage hearing, throw it out.

### Projectiles

These dangerous items are sometimes called "propelled objects." Some projectiles are very common in children's toy boxes; dart guns or bows and arrows with soft rubber cups can and will cause serious eye injuries. Of course, if the family has a dart set, the adult darts should be locked away. Avoid purchasing toys which could be capable of firing articles not intended for use in the toy, such as pencils, screws, or nails.

### Electric Toys

According to the CPSC, electric toys that are improperly constructed, wired, or misused can cause burns or electric shocks: "Electric toys must meet mandatory requirements for maximum surface temperatures, electrical construction and prominent warning labels. Electric toys with heating elements are recommended only for children over eight years old." Even then, children should be taught how to use these toys carefully and always under adult supervision.

One of the difficult aspects of electric toys is the prickliness of their power source. Batteries must be handled with great care and attention. If a battery is simply reversed (positive end where the negative end belongs), the battery can overheat and rupture. Parents should install batteries both in household appliances and children's toys. Household batteries can leak fluids that can cause chemical or acid burns. If a child swallows a battery, immediately call your local Poison Control Center as battery acid will cause internal burns and poisoning. Batteries can also be a source of lead poisoning. (See Chapter 3.)

If you try to recharge a battery not intended for recharging, the battery can overheat and rupture. If you have a rechargeable battery, be sure to use the charger meant for the size and type of battery you have. In other words, don't use an automobile battery charger to recharge flashlight batteries.

Don't use alkaline and carbon-zinc batteries together in the same appliance. Mixing old batteries with new, freshly charged ones is also dangerous. Always use a complete set of new batteries of the same type when replacing batteries.

## The Importance of Toy Maintenance

Some toys become ragged because they are loved. They're dragged around the house, and their repeated cleanups and trips into the family washer and dryer have a way of aging them. But other toys become ragtag because they are not maintained properly. At best, these toys are ignored. At worst, they cause injuries to the children meant to play with them.

All toys should be checked periodically for potential safety hazards and discarded if they are beyond repair. Has a wooden toy an edge that should be sanded to keep splinters from little fingers? Has a fabric toy come apart at the seams, enabling the baby to put the toy's stuffing in his mouth? Toys can break, and little parts do become accessible. Your baby can swallow them or stuff them in his nostrils or ears. Proper maintenance or disposal, then, is critical. If you don't let the sad old toys pile up, you'll be relieved and your child's play will be safer.

**Toyland Safety Zone**

# Very Important Tips

1. Toys should not only be fun, but safe too. If a toy is cracked or a piece has fallen off, throw it away because the edge of the crack may be sharp and could cut a finger or the broken piece may be small enough to be swallowed by an infant.

2. It's important to choose age-appropriate toys, and to choose toys that will grow with your child, such as blocks.

3. Read labels on toys carefully for safety features such as flame resistance.

4. After unwrapping any toy, immediately throw away all plastic, ribbons, and other wrappings to prevent choking or other hazards.

5. Battery-operated toys should not be accessible to infants.

6. Remove all crib toys once your infant is beginning to push up on his hands and knees.

7. Remember to put away all toys when your child is done playing with them to prevent anyone from tripping over them.

8. A few unsafe toys are loud toys (toy caps), projectiles (dart guns), electric toys (electric trains) — if the connections are faulty.

9. Suggestions for infant toys: mobiles, push/pull toys, nesting toys, mirrors, and floor gym. Toy suggestions for older kids: Pop-up toys, Legos, puzzles, dress-up clothes, cars/trucks, paints, skates, and bikes.

10. To keep toys from becoming ragged, be sure to maintain them according to their original instructions.

# Chapter 5

# The Childproofed Home

EVERY DAY, THOUSANDS OF CHILDREN SUFFER NEEDLESSLY due to avoidable household accidents. National Safety Council statistics note that not only are twenty-six million children hurt or injured annually around the home, but as many as two million require medical attention as a result of household accidents. In addition, according to former U.S. Surgeon General Antonia Novello in 1992, 100 children die every day from avoidable accidents. Illinois pediatrician Dr. Terri Merens reports that from birth to six months of age, injuries can occur out of nowhere, often due to carelessness. Rolling off a bed, for instance, may result in a bump or bruise or, at worst, death. It may also cause a head injury or long-term neurological problems.

## Childproofed Home

With these statistics in mind, the childproofing industry works to protect both young and old. Safety-proofing a home can benefit the elderly, as well as people with special needs. But especially for homes with small children, childproofing is imperative. Adults can't watch toddlers every minute of every day.

The childproofing concept originated in California in the 1970s. Today, numerous companies provide free home safety evaluations and then install any necessary safety improvements to eliminate potential dangers in the home. It's best to work with professional childproofers. In most cases, they can distinguish the reputable products from those that are simply well marketed. Proficient childproofers offer fire safety products, electronic child locators, carbon monoxide and lead testers, and a wide range of safety devices for every part of the house, including cabinet locks; electrical outlet covers; acrylic bannister guards; "cushioning" for bathtubs, tables, and hearths; nonslip bathtub and floor coatings; locks for toilet lids; safety gates; and fire retardant spray. The best childproofers also offer in-home infant CPR certification.

Pointing out commonly ignored trouble spots can wake up parents: electrical outlets, toilet bowls, under-the-sink kitchen repositories stocked with bottles and cans emblazoned with bright colors that appeal to children, and other household fixtures that parents take for granted. Children see things differently. One sees dresser drawers and thinks, "I can climb those just like a ladder"; another looks at stairway banisters and thinks, "This is a great place to play jail—I'll just stick my head through the bars." Then there's the infant who wonders what's at the bottom of Grandma's unlit basement stairs. What about the child who leaves Mom's side at Grandma's, wanders into the bedroom, and finds Grandma's medicine? Without childproofing, these seemingly innocent-looking situations can yield poisoning, shock, head injuries, broken bones, and worse, all of which could occur in just a split second. Most parents say, "I was standing right there."

Parents need to be aware of places in the home where children can find toxic materials. They need to be particularly aware of safety in the kitchen and around plants that babies might be tempted to eat. A baby might be burned accidentally by a parent's

## Childproofed Home

hot coffee or tea. And toddlers who touch light bulbs or radiators may receive second-degree burns. In addition, falls are particularly hazardous, including those from the high chair. High-chair straps left carelessly unfastened may have been the cause. Taking those three extra seconds to fasten them is well worth the effort.

Between six months to two years, a child learns to crawl, walk, and run. Childproofing will give you some peace of mind during that active period; you won't be lunging constantly to save your child's life. Of course, it's equally important to say no and to teach your child that some things in the house she must not touch. Both saying no, to help you through the "terrible twos," and childproofing can make life easier for you and your child.

The following section will familiarize you with household childproofing products for kitchens, bathrooms, living rooms, dining rooms, bedrooms, stairs and banisters, and exercise equipment. Keep your day-care center in mind as well and check to see if it is as properly childproofed as your home.

# Some Basic Childproofing Equipment

## Safety Latches

The importance of safety latches for drawers and cabinets cannot be overemphasized. Three fine safety latches are the Kindergard®/Mace Security International® cabinet latch, the Gerber® drawer latch, and the Rev-A-Shelf Tot Lock®. Beware of locks made from an inferior plastic or with an inadequate locking design; they give you a false sense of security.

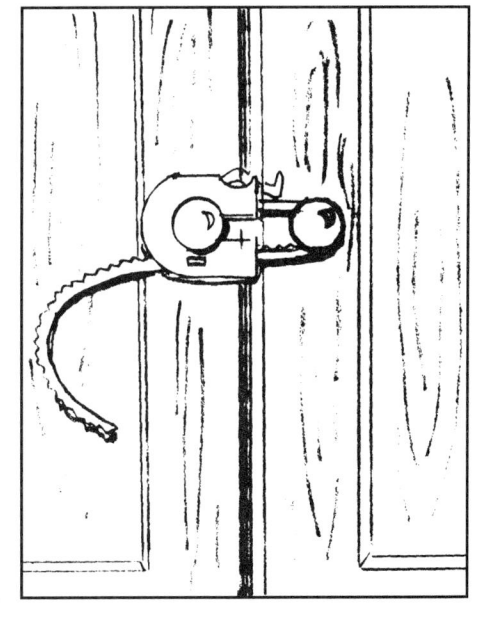

## Room Monitors

Room monitors really do seem to give parents peace of mind. Place one in your baby's room while she sleeps and keep the other with you. Monitors allow you to sleep with doors closed during the night for fire safety. There are many brands available.

## Fire Ladders

Use a fire ladder when you can't get to a first-floor exit. There are two types: one has flat plastic steps and ropes on the sides, which makes it easy to climb down but bulky to store; the second has metal rods to step on and chains to hold onto, making it lighter in weight and easier to store and use.

To use the ladder, unfold it and place it on a windowsill, attaching it with the ladder's two large hooks. Release or unravel the rest of the ladder outside the window. Then climb out the window and down the ladder. Most fire departments recommend that you not test a ladder because it's easy to fall off. If possible, wait until the firefighter can bring his or her ladder to you.

## Doorstops

Make sure to use one-piece doorstops. Children playing with a doorstop that prevents the door from hitting the wall may pull the tip off the end and choke on it.

Take the following house tour to see how your home might be better childproofed.

# The Kitchen
### General Hazards

Kitchens are the number-one breeding ground for germs in the house. Both *E. coli* and salmonella get their start there, living on sponges, dishrags, and especially cutting boards. Change sponges often, wash dishrags, and clean all cutting boards and food preparation surfaces thoroughly with detergent and warm water.

## Childproofed Home

Kitchens contain any number of other potential hazards. To help your children avoid these hazards, lock up dangerous items such as poisons, knives, food processor blades, tinfoil or plastic wrap boxes with serrated edges, and breakable objects. Never leave loose kitchen knives unattended on counter or table. Knives stored in butcher blocks on the counter should always be pushed as far back as possible. Better yet, store them in a locked drawer. Plastic sandwich bags should also be placed in a locked drawer for they may cause suffocation if accidentally placed over a baby's face and head.

Place all utensils in the dishwasher pointed down. Toddlers want to imitate Mom or Dad, and Mom and Dad reach into the dishwasher all the time, so your child will too. Once you've put the dishes away, lock utensils in a drawer or cabinet with a childproof latch.

Placemats, tablecloths, and towels can cause problems, as a child tugging at the edge of one hanging off a table or counter might pull something heavy and hot onto herself. Or the child could even topple the table and cause a serious injury. Whether it is a hot cup of coffee, a sharp knife, or a heavy pot, place nothing at the edge of a table or counter, especially on a tablecloth or other hanging fabric.

Garbage cans hide poisons, germs, and items that could suffocate or choke a child. Small toy parts, food, and plastic bags can cause suffocation. If the child can get to the garbage can, do not use a plastic bag in it. Better yet, try to find kitchen garbage cans that have virtually childproof tops. Some are better than others.

Vertical blinds can be dangerous if attached at the bottom with chains or cords that can cause strangulation. Make sure to tie the cord up and out of the child's reach by shortening it or using a cleat on the window or door frame. (See Bedrooms, page 154, for a more thorough discussion of venetian blind cords.) Magnets on refrigerators can be choking hazards; use them only near the top of the fridge. If one falls off, check its back to be sure a piece of the magnet isn't missing for a crawling child to find and swallow.

## Childproofed Home

## Poisons

Some people like to use poison stickers like "Mr. Yuk," available from Poison Control Centers in some parts of the country. If used properly, these scowling poison green faces should discourage a child away from items on which they appear. On the other hand, some safety experts believe Mr. Yuk can actually induce children to investigate; the National Safety Council does not promote their use.

Everyone agrees, however, that it is important to keep poisonous, chemical, or petroleum products in their original containers. But be aware that, to children, certain containers may look good to drink from—Mr. Clean®, for instance, looks like apple juice, and Sparkle® looks like grape juice. If poisoning does occur, you'll need to give the identity of the liquid or powder—obvious from the original container—when you call Poison Control.

Even if you move poisons from below the sink to a higher shelf, you will need to clean up the bottom of the cabinet, as any spilled product or residue can still poison a child. That's why it's best to put a lock on cabinets under the sink and always lock a pantry. (See Chapter 3 for more information on poisons.)

## Furniture and Appliances

On major appliances with large openings, such as the household washer or dryer, you may wish to use an appliance lock so a child can't climb in.

Be sure to keep high chairs far enough away from a table, wall, or counter to prevent your child from pushing off that surface and tumbling over. If the high chair does go over, with the child strapped in it, her head will be exposed to a hard fall.

The edges of some kitchen tables are just the right height to meet a toddler's head. Cover edges that have sharp corners with padding. OFNA™ Baby Products' Toddler Shield® protects children from table edges. Made of PVC vinyl, it expands to fit various-sized tables, cushioning edges.

Since children can easily open bi-fold doors from the bottom, you may wish to use locks on them; these can often close off pantries, cleaning closets, and washer-dryer cupboards.

## Childproofed Home

Stove shields block burners, thus keeping a child from heat and pot handles. When cooking, always make sure you use the back burners. If you need to use the front burners, turn the handles of cooking pots and pans inward and backward. This helps to prevent a child from pulling over boiling water or sizzling foods and risking serious burns. If you have stove knobs, consider knob covers or remove stove knobs.

If you are getting rid of an old refrigerator, most states require you to take off the door before throwing it away to keep children from climbing in and suffocating. If you store an old refrigerator in your garage, be sure to remove the door. In general, beware of any type of container with no inside handle that a child might crawl into and close so that it is airtight.

### Electrical Concerns

Telephone and answering machine cords often hang too low; keep them out of the baby's reach. Always unplug appliances before you clean or repair them and after you've finished using them. Only adults should handle appliances, but make sure you

## CHILDPROOFED HOME

unplug the toaster just in case your curious baby tries to discover how to pry out the toast. Dry your own hands before you touch any part of anything that's plugged in, including the cord. Make sure, too, that the kitchen floor beneath you is dry.

Do you have a kitchen desk topped by a computer? To guard against shocks, install ground fault circuit interrupter (GFC) outlets in the kitchen and on computers throughout the house. Call your electrician or your local hardware dealer to find out more about these outlets for any type of shock prevention.

Avoid using an extension cord with a high-energy appliance, but if you must, read the instruction manual carefully and be sure to use a heavy-duty cord; never bypass the three-pronged plug; and *never* let a child near an extension cord. Never put a child on top of a counter, where she might investigate wall outlets. (For more on outlet covers, see page 147.)

Be sure to cover dangerous kitchen switches with switch locks. Cover the disposal switch in the sink area to keep little fingers out of trouble.

## The Dining Room

Look at the undersides of your table and chairs. You may be amazed at what you see: nails, bolts, staples, splintered wood, and more. The tracks on which the dining room table expands are sharp enough to cause cuts to the head and hands. When you take a look at the underside of things from a child's point of view, you can understand the need for childproofing.

Some armoires, etageres, or dining room breakfronts light up to make china, crystal, and glasswear glitter and gleam like shiny new toys. Such a display can tempt a curious child in her terrible twos to climb up on a dining room chair, and pull the whole thing over. Turn off the lights on the breakfront and replace the best crystal with unbreakables that aren't quite so sparkly.

Fine china and flatware should be placed behind closed doors in locked cabinets or buffets. Blocking off the entire room is an option, too. Outlets, window cords, and poisonous plants can be other dining room dangers.

## Stairways
### Gates

If you have a small child, block all stairways at the top and bottom as soon as she can crawl, usually around six months—sooner for some children, later for others. Generally, it's wise to keep the gates up until she's at least two, depending upon her agility, dexterity, and strength. At the top of a stairway, the gate must be mounted with screws into a wall or banister so it isn't removable. A pressure gate is not suitable at the top of the stairs, because a child can push through the gate, and both child and gate can fall down the stairs. However, it's fine to use at the bottom of the stairs, in a hallway, or in a doorway when you wish to block a child's access to another room or area.

Children *want* to know how to navigate stair steps, so they will listen if you teach them carefully. Be patient; be repetitious; some children have more strength and agility than others. Take a gate down if the child tries to climb over it. If she succeeds, not only has the gate outlasted its usefulness, but it becomes a safety hazard in itself. Usually, children start to climb around the age of two. Some kids will never climb over a gate, and you can use it until they're three or four. Even with gates, you should never leave a little one unattended on a stairway. After you have taken the gates down, always accompany a child going up and down stairs, particularly if they're steep.

Andrew Churgin, business division manager at Denver-based Gerry Baby Products Company, notes that all of his company's safety gates are made according to the voluntary standards set by the JPMA, and they conform "to the minimum of those standards, for example, height, in terms of a small child not being able to climb the gates, and the amount of force they can take, and the holding power in opening. Over and above that, we look for any other potential safety conditions, concerns, or hazards from the use of the product—being able to pinch one's finger, or a toe, or a catch point, something a piece of clothing could get hung on—all are concerns you pay attention to in working with juvenile products." Some issues arise from the use of different products by different

## CHILDPROOFED HOME

ages. "Suppose an older brother or sister is around. Let's say it's a product used for a six-month-old baby, and there's a two-year-old who's much more mobile. In the case of the safety gates, you think about who is climbing. Is there holding power in the doorway, and are there no catch points or pinch points?" says Churgin.

### Banisters and Posts

Banister posts should not be more than four inches apart, although building codes allow between four and six inches. However, six-inch spaces between the posts are wide enough for a child to get her head stuck or fall through, injuring her neck, head, or spine. Commercial netting can be tied onto the railing but if improperly installed—easy enough to do—a child can pull the netting up or down between the ties and push a leg, an arm, or even a head through. Netting does not adequately prevent injuries.

If the stairway posts are horizontal or of ornate wrought iron, the netting will not prevent a child from getting a toehold that can be used for climbing. Instead of using netting, a good childproofing company will customize clear sheets of acrylic to tie along the posts with strong nylon ties, creating a solid, clear barrier the length of the railing. Holes are drilled in the acrylic, and the barriers cannot be taken down by children but can be cut off by an adult. Alternatively, a new plastic guard product now on the market comes in two different-sized plastic panels with a series of holes and nylon ties, so that they can be adapted to a wide range of banister styles. Although not as attractive as custom work, these panels are effective and a little less expensive.

## Stair Steps

Keep clutter off the stairs. Many falls occur when things collect on the stairs—from laundry baskets to piles of magazines. When people try to get around these obstacles, they often fall. Also, adjust the lighting to illuminate the steps and anything on them properly.

Check that the steps are the proper height and depth and that they are all the same. A half-inch difference from one step to the next can cause a fall because when steps are out of synch, you may not put your weight on your foot in the proper place. Although this is probably the last thing people think about when they're buying a house, it shouldn't be.

# The Family Room
## Furniture

Cocktail and end tables with sharp (or even rounded) edges can cause serious head injuries. Pad them with a Toddler Shield® like the one OFNA carries. Manufacturers may tout "nonbreakable" glass tables, but such tables can cause severe injuries.

It's probably prudent to put away anything taller than it is wide. Consider lamps, dressers, sculpture, plants, and so on. Try to avoid putting anything unsteady on something taller than it is wide, such as a picture frame at the edge of a tall bookshelf.

**Childproofed Home**

A climbing child can fall down and bring the frame down on her head. Use L-brackets on top of the bookshelf or screws through the back of the unit when bolting bookshelves, baker's racks, and entertainment centers to the walls. Make sure you screw into a stud to ensure that you properly secure the unit. Built-ins can be safer than separate pieces of furniture, such as an etagere, unless the latter is bolted to the wall. Beware of glass; it will not support a child's weight. If you have a glass shelf unit, take away the bottom shelf to prevent the child from climbing. This can apply to bookshelves, as well.

### Gun Cabinets

Do you store guns in your family room? *Guns kill 2,000 children a year.* Children who shoot each other or themselves get the guns from their parents' unlocked cabinets, drawers, or household boxes. Guns should always be unloaded and kept under lock and key. Look into purchasing trigger-locking devices.

### Appliances

Televisions on high viewing stands or carts are more common in classrooms than homes, but it is worth noting that rolling such a stand over a threshold or other low barrier can cause the TV to pitch forward and fall. Place TVs on lower furniture, as far back as possible.

A VCR lock protects curious little fingers and prevents damage to the VCR. Or, leave a tape inside so the VCR can't be opened. Always lock up bar areas to prevent children from getting into alcohol or breakable glassware.

Most family rooms have telephones; post emergency phone numbers nearby. Ideally, you should post them at every phone in the house so you won't be running from one floor to another in an emergency.

The downstairs family room (or the kitchen) may be the right place to keep first-aid kits and medical books: essentials for a safe home. A first-aid kit for infants and toddlers with smaller-sized bandages and a specialized first-aid booklet is recommended. More comprehensive emergency medical treatment booklets for infants, children, and adults contain sections that refer to each possible type of injury, including severe bleeding, head injury, neck injury, and severe vomiting, giving the reader simple step-by-step emergency instructions. A good childproofing firm should carry these books.

## Electrical Cords and Outlets

Electrical cords can trip, strangle (if kids become tangled up playing in them), severely burn and scar little faces (if the cords are chewed through), or worse, even cause electrocution. In family rooms, where there are likely to be TV sets, VCRs, all kinds of audio equipment, and often computers and other electronics, be sure that electrical cords don't cross traffic areas, where they can be tripped over. Cover all cords with plastic tubing; use cord shorteners if the item is close to the outlet and the cord will be gathered in one spot. Cord organizers prevent a crawling child from chewing on cords. These nylon ties band groups of cords together labeled with colored dots to identify which cord goes to what and covered with a tube. Also, hide extension cords, but not under a carpet, which may start a fire.

Look for products designed to attach hanging lamp cords to the back or underside of a table. Push the TV back against the wall so that a child can't get behind it; use cord tubing and cord shorteners here. To keep a child from chewing or playing with TV cords, use a TV stand with a back to it, so the child can't reach through the stand to the cords behind it.

Cover outlets around the house with safety plates or covers. Outlet plugs or caps are not recommended, as kids learn how to pull them out and may choke on them. And if you are using an outlet (say, with a lamp cord), the child need only pull the cord out to reveal an open outlet to play with. Several types of outlet plates that keep the holes covered at all times are on the market. The best type of outlet plate has doors that twist or slide back and forth and, if a child pulls the plug out, the door snaps back into place, closing off the holes. With lamps, clocks, or TVs that are always plugged in, use a dome-style outlet cover that locks the plug into place. You can choose between two types: one that opens and one that screws into place. Both work.

## Fireplaces

Another potential hazard commonly found in the family room is the fireplace hearth. Hearths are usually made of brick, slate, or cement. Some form an overhang that protrudes into the room. Block this off or pad it.

Never leave a child alone with a blazing fire. And, don't ever place a space heater within reach of a child.

Store wood, matches, fireplace gas keys, and pokers up high, or put them away in locked or latched lower cabinets. To a toddler, it may look like a good fort, and you can be sure she'll put wood or ashes in her mouth. Fireplace gas jets pose dangers as well, and wood and paper when burned can emit toxic fumes. Fake wood contains toxic chemicals that shouldn't be ingested. (For more on fireplace hazards, see Chapter 1.)

## Sliding Glass Doors

If you have a sliding glass door leading to the terrace or patio, keep it closed and locked, if necessary, to prevent your children from wandering outdoors unsupervised. Or, keep the patio door opened no more than four inches. This admits air, but keeps the child inside. Place stickers on these sliding doors at the child's eye level to alert her to the presence of glass.

## Bathrooms
### Tubs, Showers, and Toilets

Children drown in buckets, diaper pails, toilets, and bathtubs every year. Never let any amount of water stand in the tub. A child can drown in under two inches of water in less than thirty seconds. When she's in the tub, always keep your hand near your child's back and never leave her unattended. A child sitting in a ring in the tub can drown if you leave the room and the ring tips over. The ring is just a device to help you bathe the child; it is not intended to keep the child from drowning. Some parents use infant tubs with nonskid tape on the bottoms. A small tub is, in many ways, better for bathing a baby than the large tub, but she must still be supervised every second.

## Childproofed Home

Always keep the toilet lid down and use a toilet lock. It takes an adult only a second to learn to use it, and it assures a peace of mind most parents rave about. The Fisher Price Lid Lock® and Gerber Toilet Lock® are recommended.

To make taking a bath safe for a child, turn the hot water down to 120°F or below on your hot-water heater to lessen the chance of accidental burns. Install scald-safe devices to shut off water automatically at 114°F, well below the 120°F burn threshold. Scald-safe devices fit on the sink, shower, or tub spout; install them yourself or call your childproofer or a plumber.

Check the bathtub edges. Soaps, shampoos, and other items can harm infants' digestive systems. Keep such supplies on a high shelf or rack that hangs from the shower spout, or set up floor-to-ceiling poles with shelves.

Many injuries occur climbing in and out of the tub. When the baby has graduated from her smaller tub and is ready to use the big tub, place a nonslip mat or stickers in the tub. If you use stickers, make sure they're not more than two inches apart, because a little foot can slip on a narrow slick surface. Also, pad the spout; ask your childproofer or inquire at a baby furniture store, or consult a baby products catalog about the many types of spout pads available.

Pad the side of the tub as well to help lessen the blow to the head if she falls. Commercial padding like Polliwog® fits snugly over the tub's top edge. Shorter versions accommodate shower doors.

## Electrical Appliances

Keep all electrical devices away from tubs, showers, open toilets, and wet sinks, and make sure your hands are dry before plugging in or turning on any electrical appliance. If you're drying a child's hair with a plugged-in hair dryer, don't use it on a damp floor and never in the shower. Put the toilet lid down before using an electrical appliance in the bathroom, and never set a radio, phone, or any other electrical device on the edge of a tub or sink. If you want music in the bathroom, find a battery-operated radio meant for use near water.

## Floors

If you are installing a new floor in a bathroom, look for a rougher type of surface; the more shiny, the more slippery. There's also a way to put a nonslip surface on your existing bathroom floor. When using a nonslip chemical in the tub or on the floor, read the instructions before use. Because of its potent smell and toxicity, keep your child away and ventilate the room while you're doing it. Use bath rugs with nonskid bottoms and make sure kids wear nonskid socks when in the bathroom.

Many newer homes have spa-type bathtubs with a step, usually of marble or tile. Childproofers receive many calls about head injuries caused by falling on this step, so they recommend that it be professionally padded.

## Medicine Cabinets

The more bathrooms you have in your home, usually the more medicine cabinets. In any bathroom, get rid of old medicines, of course, and outdated prescriptions. Sometimes, children sit in the sink and play in the medicine cabinet, easily making the ascent from the floor to the toilet to the sink top. All poisons, including vitamins and iron supplements (the number-one cause of poisoning in the home), cleaning supplies, makeup, shaving supplies, medicines, and so on, should be stored high out of the reach of kids and locked up. Locks for medicine cabinets tend to be inadequate. They all use tape, not sturdy enough to lock securely. Consider using a child safe for medicine instead of medicine cabinets. Only an adult finger can reach its latch through a hole in the front. These may be used elsewhere in the house, as well, for dangerous items.

Make sure that all the medicines you buy, from aspirins to cough medicines, have child-resistant closures and caps. These help to prevent more poisonings than most other measures. Adults should remember to close caps tightly after *every* use.

## Bedrooms
### Children's Rooms

FURNITURE STANDARDS. These days, furniture doesn't get shipped to stores and end up in your child's bedroom without a good deal of inspection. According to Deborah Albert, spokesperson for the Juvenile Products Manufacturers' Association, the "JPMA has a certification program to reduce injuries and deaths, and to give parents added assurance that a product is safe to buy if it bears a certain logo. The voluntary certification program started twenty years ago with the development of a standard for high chairs." The standards were written by the American Society for Testing and Materials (ASTM), a Philadelphia-based nonprofit organization, and are currently developed in cooperation with industry members, consumer groups, staff from CPSC, and any other interested party. To become JPMA-certified, the product is tested independently for compliance with the standards, and, if it passes the test, the manufacturer may apply the JPMA certification logo.

Even though many products comply with stringent standards, it's a good idea to inspect furniture thoroughly before using it in your home. Cutting accident risks more than compensates for the time you spend investigating.

**CRIBS.** According to JPMA spokesperson Albert: "Do not buy an older used crib because it could have missing or loose hardware or have corner posts that could become hazardous—they shouldn't be higher than one-sixteenth of an inch above the end panel, crib slats no more than two and three-eighths inches apart, with none loose or missing." If the posts are more than two and three-eighths inches apart, a baby could get her arm or leg stuck between them. Also, if the corner posts stick up past the height of the rest of the railing, then these posts might catch clothing and hang the child. Cut off the tops of posts such as this and sand them well. To be safe, discard older cribs. And don't buy a crib with a decorative cutout in the headboard or footboard. Babies have been known to trap their heads in such a cutout.

Tighten all nuts, bolts, and screws periodically. Whenever the crib is moved, secure all mattress support hangers. Check the hooks that lower and raise the height of the mattress regularly to be sure none are broken or bent. Open hooks may allow the mattress to fall. Use a crib that meets Federal Safety Standards and Industry Voluntary Standards for cribs.

Be sure your crib has a firm, tight-fitting mattress. A crib mattress should be nonallergenic, stain-resistant, nonabsorbent, and antistatic. It should fit snugly, with no more than two fingers' width between its edge and the crib. In a wider space, a child can get stuck between the crib side and the mattress and suffocate. Always keep the drop side up when the baby is in the crib. Install crib attachments only on the wall side of the crib. Otherwise, the baby might use them to climb up and out of the crib. Experts recommend moving the baby into a toddler or regular bed when she's two years old (or thirty-five inches long).

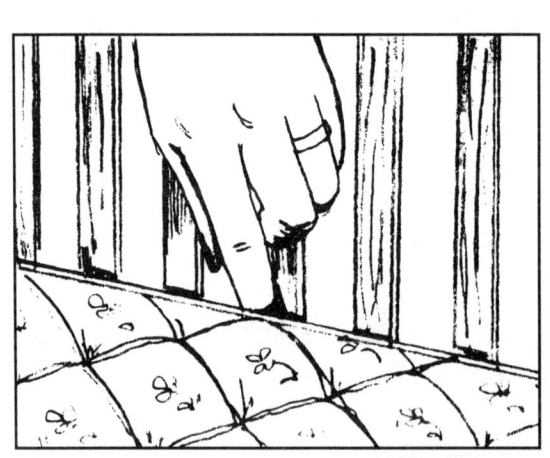

**Childproofed Home**

Infants under one year shouldn't be left on adult or youth beds. They can suffocate while sleeping if they become trapped between the mattress and bedframe or a wall, if they become wedged between an adult and the mattress, or if they sink into a waterbed while on their stomachs.

Suffocation can also occur if a child is left on a soft blanket or comforter. Do not leave pillows or stuffed animals in the crib with a very young child.

**OTHER BEDS.** The Consumer Product Safety Commission (CPSC) warns that bunk beds with tubular metal frames have been known to collapse during use. Inspect all eight mattress support "fin" tabs and pockets on such beds for breaks or cracks in the metal and welds. It's probably best to use both beds on the floor, rather than stacking them, unless you've found them to be in perfect shape.

Use bed rails not only to prevent the child from falling out, but also to help her feel more secure while making the transition to an adult bed. You can place bed rails on both sides, but remember, with too much space between the wall and the bed, a child can get caught or injured.

**OTHER FURNITURE AND ROOM DECOR.** Falls from the changing table might be the earliest accident a baby experiences when she suddenly begins to roll over at around four months. Until then, you become used to walking away from the baby to get whatever you need, and suddenly she cannot be left alone any more. Learn not to walk farther away than your hand can reach. If your changing table does not have straps to prevent the baby from falling, purchase your own safety strap for separate installation or place baby on the floor.

Never leave a baby in a mesh playpen with the drop side down. The holes in the netting of a mesh playpen should be no larger than a quarter of an inch.

Keep wall hangings and pictures in frames away from the crib (and out of a child's reach elsewhere in the house). Wall hangings are sometimes heavy. They may have strings on them (most weavings do), and all are attached to the wall with nails.

**Childproofed Home**

Venetian blind cords can strangle children, in many cases, if a crib is too near the window. Or perhaps furniture under the window gives the child a way to climb up and play with the venetian blind cord. The same thing can happen with vertical blinds and drapes that have continuous cords. Look for a product called the Break-Thru Safety Tassel® made by Hunter-Douglas (or varieties by Gerber and other companies). To install, cut the current cord at the bottom into two pieces and attach the Safety Tassel. With traditional cords, if a child's head becomes entangled in the loop, she could strangle. The Break-Thru Tassel breaks apart under less than two pounds of pressure and causes the cords to separate.

Use line cleats with venetian blinds and all other cords or window dressings so that you can hang the cord up and out of the reach of the child. (Incidentally, drawstrings on clothes can also be a factor in the strangulation of children. If they catch on something, such as a banister pole, a railing finial, the end of a chair, or play equipment, they can create a noose. Clothes with a string or a hood should not be used during active playtime.)

## All Bedrooms

FURNISHINGS. Watch out for throw rugs with ends that curl up, or older carpet that's not tacked down properly. Tape or tack them down because they often cause children to fall. Many products can make a throw rug nonskid: tape, rubber mesh, or nonskid glue applied to the underside of the rug.

Old bedroom furniture (or any furniture) can have splinters. And watch out for lead paint. If you have antique or vintage furniture or you live in an older home, do test your paint; a variety of lead testing kits make it possible to test in your own home. (See Chapter 3 for information on lead poisoning.) Even a little undetectable lead dust can cause disorders such as learning disabilities, poor coordination, and more. These can be prevented, if you'll undertake the effort to test for lead.

Try not to stack furniture too high, because children like to climb. A dresser with a hutch on top, or two flat dressers on top of each other can be hazardous. Kids also try to climb bookshelves that look like a ladder.

## Childproofed Home

Sometimes toddlers try to move furniture or open and close drawers on dressers. Pulling all the drawers out, and then pushing them all back in makes a good game. But, sometimes, when the drawers are all pulled out, the dresser can fall over on the child. The Consumer Product Safety Commission found this type of accident associated with two thousand hospital emergency room visits each year from 1982 through 1986, including six deaths. (Bookcase tip-overs accounted for an additional 580 hospital visits and one death.) Also, children pinch fingers when closing them in drawers.

Remember that picture frames can fall off tall dressers and bookshelves. Watch the placement of knickknacks and other items that can land on a child's head.

Children have been known to pull up in-floor vents, exposing edges of the ductwork that can inflict severe cuts. These can be rusty, too, and thus doubly dangerous. Either screw down or partially line the bottom of the vent with double-sided foam tape to prevent the child from pulling it up.

**WINDOWS.** The Consumer Product Safety Commission estimates that about seventy deaths occur annually in falls from windows, 25 percent among children ten years of age and younger. Never put furniture under a window. A screen will not keep a child from falling out of the window. Use a vent lock, which allows you to open a window only four inches, enough to ventilate the room, but too small for a child to fit through. Or, if your local fire codes permit window guards, install them in the lower half of your windows to prevent falls. In New York City, for example, the health department requires the use of window guards in multi-family housing. Window bars are another option; there are many types on the market. (Down the road, you can always fill in the holes made by the window bars or guards, and your windows will look just as they did before.) Some gate manufacturers recommend using their gates for window guards. Finally, the CPSC recommends opening windows from the top, not the bottom.

**LOOSE OBJECTS.** Items pulled out of pockets at the end of the day can become choking hazards. These include coins, paper clips,

**Childproofed Home**

and keys, which need to be put up high in a container the child can't reach. Keep pocket items in a closed box or a small container in a top drawer of a dresser, or at least organized in a bowl at the back of the dresser top.

Parents often leave dry-cleaned clothes wrapped in plastic on the bed within children's reach. It's wise to take the plastic off clothes before you come into the house. Put it in the garbage, tied in a knot. If you leave it outside, the child can't get at it. If you must keep clothes in these plastic bags, put them directly into a locked closet. In many closets with double wardrobe poles, the dry cleaning can go up high. But dresses and gowns need space and even though placed up high, the plastic still hangs low enough to be easy to grab and therefore dangerous. So lock the closet, or remove the plastic.

Many children are injured when a toy chest lid falls on their heads and necks. Check the lid to be sure a proper locking hinge supports it.

## Basements and Exercise Rooms

Basement doors should have automatic closing devices on them. Sometimes, when someone goes through the basement door the child will follow immediately, crawl to the open door, and fall down the steps.

Whether you keep exercise equipment in your basement, your bedroom, or elsewhere, remember safety measures. A child should not climb on these machines; if she puts her weight on one of them, she could fall. Store free weights on the floor, never on a shelf, from which they could fall.

Many of the larger pieces of equipment are electrical, so always keep them unplugged. Some of the older equipment, such as treadmills, may have only one switch; but some of the newer pieces of equipment have two, including an automatic safety switch. Nevertheless, it's still a good idea to keep your child from "experimenting" with this expensive and dangerous equipment. Some parents place a playyard around their machine(s); others use

**Childproofed Home**

hook-and-eye door locks or other types of locks on the door. (If the older kids want to exercise, and you can't be there to supervise, send them out in the sunlight to the backyard or the nearest playground.)

## The Garage

Many children are injured or killed when they become trapped under garage doors. Install an automatic garage door stopping device, which aims a beam of light across the opening about a foot, up and off the ground. If the beam is broken by a child getting in the way, for instance, the garage door stops immediately. It's a good investment.

Garages conceal many dangers, including chemicals and mechanical tools such as saws, lawn mowers, and more. Store all devices properly and make sure none of them can be turned on. Lock up all chemicals or store them up high, away from children.

## Outdoors

Children do leave their homes without parents knowing. All doors with access to the outside should be equipped with some sort of alarm that sounds when the door opens. Save a Child's Life Door Alert® is one of several such alarms on the market.

Finally, remind children that wires, electrical equipment substations, and transformer boxes are all dangerous and off limits. Make sure they don't climb power poles or play in trees with power lines running through them.

Keep all power tools, electric lawn-care tools, and plugged-in radios at least ten feet away from sprinklers, pools, and puddles. They should never be used outside in wet weather or on wet grass, trees, or bushes. Look for the Underwriter's Laboratory mark on power tools, which means they've been tested for safety, but be firm about making electrical tools off limits to children. Above all, instruct your child to seek shelter during a thunderstorm—but never under a tree. If she's indoors, tell her to keep clear of windows and turn off and unplug the TV and other appliances until the storm passes.

## Childproofed Home
# Very *Important* Tips

1. Childproofing your home helps you and your child avoid injuries and other hazards. A few childproofing basics include cabinet and drawer latches, room monitors, and fire ladders.

2. Lock kitchen cabinets containing poisons, knives, tin foil, and plastic wrap. Clean up any spilled residue from poisons in cabinets.

3. Don't leave a cup of hot coffee on the table if the tablecloth extends beyond the sides. Baby may pull herself up by the cloth and spill the hot liquid on herself.

4. Don't leave electrical appliances plugged in and the cords dangling.

5. Sand any splintered wood and remove any nails that stick out of furniture.

6. Install gates, but not pressure gates, at the top of any stairs once your child is crawling. Also, keep stairs free of toys and other objects to prevent falls.

7. If banister poles on your stairs are more than four inches apart, apply a clear plastic covering along the stairway to prevent children from falling through or from getting their heads or limbs stuck.

8. Bolt to the wall bookcases, entertainment centers, and any other furniture that is taller than it is wide. This prevents small children from climbing and pulling furniture over on themselves.

9. Lock away all guns in a box, cabinet, or drawer at all times and keep the key out of children's reach.

10. Cover all electrical outlets to prevent children from getting shocked or burned.

11. Keep children away from fireplaces and any open fires. Keep fireplaces free of wood, ashes, matches, and utensils. If your fireplace is gas-powered, hide the key from children.

12. Lock sliding glass doors to prevent children from wandering outside. Use door alarms to alert you that a child has opened these doors.

## Childproofed Home
# Very Important Tips

13. Use toilet locks to prevent children from drowning in toilets. When bathing a child, never leave her unattended, even for an instant.

14. Keep any bathroom hazards such as electrical appliances, razors, soaps, and shampoos out of children's reach. Lock all medicine cabinets.

15. Use nonslip bath mats or treat your bathtub with a non-slip surface to prevent falls in the bathroom.

16. Check beds and cribs for a JPMA certification label, which means it has met industry safety standards. Check furniture for any hazardous pieces, such as nails, screws, or posts, that stick out and could harm children.

17. Never place a changing table or crib next to a window. Children can pull themselves up and fall out the window, or they can strangle on venetian blind cords. In general, tie up all cords and place them out of reach, and make sure that there are working locks on windows in children's rooms.

18. Place children's toys in the bottom drawer of furniture or the bottom of closets to prevent climbing falls.

19. Lock doors to basements, exercise rooms, and garages so children won't go exploring.

20. Discuss with children potential outdoor hazards and what precautions to take to prevent accidents outside.

## Chapter 6

# Oh, What Fun It Is To Ride!: Planes, Trains, Automobiles, and Other Conveyances

WHEN IT COMES TO VEHICLE SAFETY, the good old scout motto applies: Be Prepared. That means not only using a car seat for your child, but, even more important, using it correctly. This chapter covers all aspects of car safety, including being a good pedestrian, as well as safety on trains, boats, buses, and planes. (See Chapter 7 for information on stroller, bicycle, tricycle, and in-line skating safety.)

## Automobile Safety

Car travel can be fun for kids, but it can also be potentially dangerous. Motor vehicle accidents still remain the number one killer of children under five years of age. Each year, more than 40,000 children under five are injured in cars. Misuse of car seats is a major contributor in these horrifying injuries and deaths, though, of course, nonuse is an even greater factor. It should be noted, as well, that overall, according to the National Safety Council, motor vehicle accidents are the leading cause of unintentional-injury deaths for children and persons ages one through thirty-seven years. This is important and relevant, even though the primary concern here is with children one to twelve years old. And, although it is true that accidental motor vehicle deaths do increase markedly among teenagers, learning more about safety measures when they are children may help adults to change those unfortunate statistics.

### Buckling Up Kids: The Statistics

Kids thrown from cars are four times more likely to be killed and thirteen times more likely to be seriously injured. Another fact is that seven out of every ten car crashes occur within twenty-five miles of home. (How often do we hear "I don't need my seat belt; I'm just going to be driving around town"?) Even (or perhaps *especially*) the new mother leaving the hospital with her newborn baby should remember to buckle up—herself *and* her baby.

In l993, all motor vehicle accidents involving children under age four led to 1,000 deaths, a decrease of 800 from 1992. That same year, collisions between motor vehicles caused the deaths of 400 children in that age group. Six hundred children ages five to fourteen died.

Three years before that, in l990, the National Highway Traffic Safety Administration and the Law Enforcement Travel Network (LETN) also reported the fact that 222 children four years old and younger were protected by child restraints. An estimated 1,546 lives were saved from 1982 through l990, and the figure continues to climb.

**Planes, Trains, Autos**

The types of motor vehicles in accidents may vary, just as causes of accidents do. According to the National Safety Council, collisions occur between cars and trains and between buses and pedestrians, as well as between motorcycles and bikes. Many truck accidents are alcohol-related.

Statistics have a lot to tell us. For instance, LETN statistics reveal that a 20-pound child would be thrown with more than 200 pounds of force at an impact speed of only ten miles per hour. (And, not incidentally, if that child's 180-pound father was not wearing a seat belt, he would slam into the dashboard with a force greater than 3,600 pounds at thirty-five miles per hour.)

Airbags are designed to supplement the seat belt, not to be counted on alone. Nearly 42,000 lives were lost to traffic crashes in the year 1993, almost as many as in ten years of war in Vietnam. Further, Americans bore the brunt of over $167.3 billion in financial costs arising from these accidents.

**Planes, Trains, Autos**

## Child Safety Seats

The laws of many states mandate that children up to four years of age must be placed in child safety seats. Most states require that children four to six years of age wear seat belts and, in time, all states will decree that car safety seats be built into cars. It is recommended that all parents buy, properly install, and always use a federally approved car seat.

And even if laws didn't require safety seats, there are compelling reasons for their use. Children have softer bones, weaker neck muscles, larger and heavier heads (in proportion to their bodies), and more fragile bodies than adults. Because children are light, they can be easily thrown upon impact. Most injuries to children are the result of being thrown into a windshield or dashboard, crushed (by an adult), or thrown from the car. The child safety seat is designed to hold the child securely and protect him from hitting something inside the car or from being thrown out of the car. The seat also absorbs the force of a sudden stop or swerve, spreads the force of a car's impact, and prevents crushing of the child by other passengers.

*Infant* seats are used from birth to six to twelve months of age, or eighteen to twenty pounds in weight. These seats face the rear; the safest place to install yours is in the middle of the backseat. Infant seats have wide, sturdy bases, and the padded sides support the neck and head. Never place a rear-facing infant seat in the forward position, and never place a rear-facing infant seat in the front seat of a car with airbags. A bag inflating in a crash could push the baby against the passenger seat, causing injury.

*Convertible* and *toddler* seats accommodate children who weigh between twenty and forty pounds; they face forward. Convertible seats may be used for infants from birth (if the baby is about seven pounds) to toddlers of twenty pounds between one and four. Convert the seat to a forward-facing position and place it upright in the back seat of the car when the child reaches about twenty pounds and can sit up unsupported. (It is then sometimes called a toddler seat.) Five-point harness seats are also approved. A five-point harness system refers to the straps on the car seat itself—two straps go over the child's shoulders, two go over the hips, and one strap sits between the legs.

*Booster* seats may be used for children who weigh between thirty and sixty pounds. These face forward and have no backs, but have a partial shield.

Be sure you have chosen a safety seat that elevates your toddler or preschooler so that he can see the sights out the window: cars and trucks, signs and people, country and city. Children enjoy having sights pointed out to them. Sometimes you can make a game of it, and you'll have fun sharpening your own powers of observation.

It should be obvious, but just placing baby in the seat isn't enough; always be sure to buckle the car-seat restraints securely. Refer to your auto owner's manual for proper installation and look for any mention of an extra clip for the seat belt to secure the car seat. These clips are free of charge, but your auto dealer may not mention them. Ask and read your owner's manual carefully. Meanwhile, here are some additional tips regarding car travel with kids:

**BIRTH TO NINE MONTHS:** As you've found, newborns are not exempt from accidents. It bears repeating: Always use a car seat no matter how young your child. Pad the seat at the sides and crotch if needed to support the baby's head and neck, as well as to keep baby from sliding forward. Always use the seat properly, and always use the strap. Be sure to purchase only a federally approved car seat. Check the label for the statement: "Meets federal safety standards 213. Certified for use in motor vehicles and aircraft."

Baby does best traveling in clothing with legs; secure the car-seat straps snugly between his legs. Don't wrap him in a blanket before putting him in the car seat. The harness straps won't stay snug and high on his shoulders. When you put baby in the seat, place his bottom and back flat against the seat. If you leave a gap, you may not be able to adjust the harness straps properly. When baby's in a rear-facing position, you may want to secure the car seat at an angle by placing a rolled-up towel between baby's car seat (at the bend of the seat) and the vehicle's seat.

**NINE TO TWENTY-FOUR MONTHS:** Bring toys, music, and books to entertain your child in case he gets restless in the car seat. Make sure the car seat is appropriate for the child's age and weight.

**TWENTY-FOUR TO FORTY-EIGHT MONTHS (TWO- TO FOUR-YEAR-OLDS):** Children this age should always use car seats. Teach your child never to yell and distract the driver, which may cause accidents.

Finally, there will probably come a time when your child may try to get out of his safety seat. Don't panic. If this happens, stop the car as soon as possible. Be firm and serious. You must convey the message that you mean business, no matter how many times you must rebuckle, or how many trips it takes for him to get the picture. Be patient. If you're consistent and firm, you'll get the message across.

Don't forget, however, that there's no rule that says you can't be comforting, as well. The contented child feels that he is loved, and isn't that what using a child safety seat is all about?

**Planes, Trains, Autos**

## Seat Safety

Can you answer all of the following statements with a "yes"? Read on to determine whether your family's car safety quotient is 100 percent.

### General Use

❑ 1. When I get in a car, I automatically put on my safety belt and encourage anyone riding with me to do the same.

❑ 2. When placing my child in a car seat, I check that the car seat and my car are compatible. When I buckle my child's belt or harness, I make certain that it is securely fastened and fits snugly.

❑ 3. I check my child's seat belt to make sure it is fitted properly. (Always check the fit of the child safety seat in your car so you know your child is comfortable in it, not too tight and not too loose. Adjust the harness around seasonal clothing to leave about an inch of slack so your child can move.)

## Planes, Trains, Autos

❏ 4. Even though my car has airbags, I still use my safety belt. (If you don't use your seat and shoulder belt, you'll roll under or over the airbag and go right through the windshield; children usually go under airbags if they are passengers in the front seat. Airbags do not work in secondary impacts, rollovers, or rear or side impacts. Manufacturers who make cars with passenger-side airbags recommend not using safety seats in the rear-facing infant position at that location. Read your car manual for more information.)

### Infant Seats

❏ 5. I never place infant seats on a front passenger seat with airbags or an automatic seat belt. (The airbag could severely injure a baby.) Always place infant seats in the back seat, and always face the seat backward until the child is at least six months old and weighs at least eighteen pounds.)

### Toddler Seats

❏ 6. When my child is at least six months old and weighs at least eighteen pounds, I will place him or her in a toddler seat in the back seat in a forward-facing position.

**Planes, Trains, Autos**

## Booster Seats

❑ 7. I know that booster seats face forward and are designed to be used by children weighing from thirty to sixty pounds.

Note: For a specially designed safety seat for a "special needs" child, who may not be able to fit properly in a conventional child safety seat, contact the National Easter Seal Society at 312-726-6200.

## Seat Belt Use

Parents who teach children to buckle up help them form safety habits that will stay with them into adulthood. Parents set examples for their children, so they should always buckle up as well. There is a greater likelihood of injury to the parent if the parent is unrestrained. Parents themselves must remember to buckle up every time, so children will imitate them, and everyone will ride safely. Further, by teaching children regular use of safety seats and, when they are old enough, safety belts, parents promote safer and happier driving on every trip, whether long or short.

What happens when your child refuses to buckle up? You can do several things. If parents start early with infant seats and make using seat belts a part of the proper procedure for riding in a car, there will be little need for explanation. Always be consistent. A child will also respond to a parent who tells him, "I'm buckling you up because I love you."

When your child has graduated from a child safety seat to a lap-shoulder belt, remind him that buckling up is adult behavior and praise the child for each use of the seat belt when entering the car. In hot weather, be sure that seat belts are cool before they touch your child. (This also applies to car seat parts. Use a cloth cover on the car seat to block out the sun's rays.)

Be sure that older children using lap-shoulder belts keep the shoulder strap snug. An eight-year-old who weighs seventy pounds uses this type of belt, but he still may be too small for it. If the shoulder belt crosses face or throat, place it behind and wear only the lap belt. Never wear a shoulder belt under the arm; in a crash, ribs could be broken. Older children using a lap belt should wear it snug and buckled low on the hips.

It has been reported that many older children (five to nine years old) wear seat belts incorrectly. Some graduate to seat belts when they weigh forty pounds and are about forty inches in height. Because they're so much smaller than the adults for whom the belts were intended, the shoulder belt does indeed cross the neck and face instead of fitting snugly across the chest. As for that snug lap belt, kids may think it should fit across the stomach, when it *should* cross the pelvic bone. Because these misapprehensions are uncomfortable, kids may throw their seat belts aside. Some car manufacturers are indeed addressing the problem. General Motors, for example, offers seat belts with clips that reposition the shoulder belt away from the face and neck. Another innovation is a device called the SafeFit, a padded nylon sleeve through which you thread the shoulder belt, thus repositioning it. Still another is the Child-Saver, a two-foot-long slotted plastic bar that also repositions and secures the lap and shoulder belt. The SafeFit is under $16; the Child-Saver is about $13.

A word about car pools: If it's your turn to drive, make sure you have enough belts to accommodate every child. If another parent is driving, ask if his or her car has enough belts for all of the riders.

Finally, older kids may tell you that wearing a safety belt isn't cool. Tell them the coolest kids buckle up, as do astronauts, jet pilots, and race car drivers.

**Planes, Trains, Autos**

### A Short Safety Seat and Seat Belt True or False Quiz

1. You're going only two blocks from home, but you're driving because of bad weather, rather than walking. You don't have to use a car seat for your ten-month-old, do you? Your two-year-old? Four-year-old?
2. Your eight-year-old doesn't need to wear his seat belt going to school, only on the way home.
3. If you are driving a very slow five miles per hour, your one year old doesn't need to be in a car seat.
4. It's okay to bring your newborn home from the hospital in your arms.
5. You may keep an infant from sliding forward in a car seat by placing a rolled towel between the bar and the crotch strap.

Answers: 1. False, false, false. 2., 3., 4. All false. 5. True.

A word about number four: Even if you suspect it can't apply to a newborn, it does. The most dangerous place for a child to be while traveling is in an adult's arms. It's called the "child-crusher position" because in an accident, a child will be thrown from the adult's arms, and if the adult is not restrained, the child will act as a "cushion" between the adult's body and the dashboard and/or windshield and can be crushed to death.

### Other Auto Safety Tips

No parent needs to be reminded of the feeling of responsibility one has behind the wheel. It's part of the territory that comes with parenting to do everything you can to assure a safe ride. Here are a few additional tips to make each ride a safe one:

1. Never leave children in a car alone, even if the doors are locked.
2. Before or after a car trip, when children are in the driveway, watch for them at *all* times.
3. When a car is in motion, children should stay in their seats. There are many things you can do to occupy them so that they don't become restless and begin moving about. Music tapes, books, and activities are but a few preoccupations.

### Planes, Trains, Autos

4. Always use strap and harness, no matter if an infant or an older child is in a car seat.
5. Your lap is *never* the safest place in a motor vehicle for a child.
6. The Midas Project Safe Baby Campaign, developed with the assistance of the National Highway Traffic Safety Administration, issued the good advice that you should never try to tend to a crying baby while driving. Find a safe place to stop if you plan to take baby from the car seat to comfort him.
7. Be sure to secure any items in the car that can "fly" loose in case the car must be stopped suddenly, such as a tissue box, loose toys or books, or groceries. Once you've made it a habit to be sure that such items are securely in place when you get into the car, it will become second nature, and you'll all ride more safely.
8. Keep the car in good working order and winterize annually. Change the oil and filters when necessary (about every 3,000 miles); check the tires, the battery, the car's electrical system, and the horn; take a look at the headlights and taillights—do the turn signals and flashers work perfectly? Do you have a spare tire, just in case? Do you need to change the windshield wiper blades (often a must after a hard long winter)? Are the door locks in working order?
9. Check the car's safety features. Does your car have an antilock braking system to help prevent wheel lock, improve control when braking, and decrease stopping distances when roads are slippery and icy? If it does, don't expect that the antilock braking system can do everything; you still must be a careful driver. Learn how to make the system work correctly. Don't pump the pedal; that neutralizes the system. Instead, step firmly on the brake and hold it down. You may then feel a vibration in the brake pedal that shows the system is working. In addition, four-wheel drive has been a great aid to drivers. Four wheels, not just two, pull in the same direction, thus increasing traction. Still, four-wheel drive is an aid to, not a substitute for, careful driving on icy or slippery roads. Even though you can accelerate faster, decelerating or stopping a four-wheel-drive vehicle takes just as long as in a two-wheel-drive vehicle.

**Planes, Trains, Autos**

10. How to change a tire should be on every parent's must-know list. Maneuver your vehicle to the right side of the road's shoulder and put on your emergency flashers. If the area is unsafe, ignore the warning not to drive on a flat tire and head for a place where the tire can be replaced in safety. Is it better to stay in the car than to go hunting for help if the car breaks down? This may be good reason to own a car phone. If you don't have a car phone, experts advise remaining in the car, doors locked, until the highway patrol or a tow truck spots you. If someone offers help, again, be aware of the area, and use caution. Generally, it is advised that you lower the window only enough to pass coins out to the passer-by, asking him or her to call the police from the next phone booth and report your position.

11. If you've grown lax in obeying the rules of the road, it's a good time to refresh your memory. Every state driver's license bureau prints the road rules; be sure you're up-to-date.

12. Drive defensively, keep your eyes on other drivers, and forget your dreams of auto racing.

13. Obviously, never drink and drive, and avoid driving in impossibly bad weather.

14. If you skid, turn your steering wheel gently in the direction the rear wheels skidded to straighten out your course.

15. In case of emergencies on the road, every car should be equipped with certain essentials. Check with your auto mechanic or garage on the appropriate tools for your car. Flares and flashlights (with fresh batteries), in addition to year-round emergency tools, are a good start. Some drivers stash dried foods for energy (dried fruit, raisins, fruit-grain mix), a CB radio (or a mobile phone), shovel, basic hand tools (including an open-end wrench, socket wrench, a Phillips and a straight-head screwdriver, pliers, wire cutters), a jug of antifreeze and water solution, electrical tape (to repair a leaky radiator hose), a large plastic bottle of drinking water, emergency tire inflator, windshield washer solution, and first-aid kit.

16. Never allow children of any age to ride in the open bed of a pickup truck or in the back of a camper or motor home. The

cargo area of a station wagon or van is also unsafe. In short, never let a child ride in a vehicle in which there are no restraints available, whether it is in a pickup truck bed or an automobile.
17. Finally, it's important for moms and dads to know a few aids for staying awake on the road. Of course there is only one solution to fatigue, and that is rest or sleep. Whatever you do should only continue until you can pull off the traveled part of the roadway and stop. If you're not tired or ready to stop for the night, it is still advisable to take a break every two hours or every hundred miles. Leave the expressway and pull into a brightly lit restaurant or oasis. Get out of the car and get a cup of coffee. If you're not near an oasis, open the car windows enough so that air can circulate freely. Turn on the radio; not loud, but jarring (hard rock rather than Handel). Intersperse the music with traffic reports (some stations specialize in news and traffic reports); such information can save you time on detours and keep you alert.

## Pedestrian Safety

*Ped(i)* is the Latin word for foot, so, logically, the *pedestrian* is one who walks on foot. The art of being a good pedestrian means being careful where you put your feet. Annually, in the United States, more than 90,000 pedestrians are injured in traffic accidents, and many of these are children. The National Safe Kids Campaign lists five major types of child pedestrian accidents:

1. The case of a child darting into the street, whether it's in midblock or at the corner;
2. The case of a child hidden by a bus and the car driver behind the bus doesn't stop;
3. The case of a vehicle turning into the path of a pedestrian;
4. The case of a vehicle backing up in the roadway, or out of a driveway or parking lot; and
5. The case of a walking child hidden by a truck.

Drivers who are turning right on a red light, or completing a late left-hand turn when a traffic light changes, are often to blame.

But children as well as adults bound into the street without looking. "Walk" and "Don't Walk" signs are too often ignored, and children must be taught to respect them.

Tell your child that a flashing "Don't Walk" sign means "do not enter the street." If you're already in the street, or you're in the intersection, there should be enough time to walk quickly to the other side of the street. Children need to be taught how to cross the street safely at mid-block in quiet residential areas by stopping at the curb, the edge of the road, or at the outer edge of parked vehicles, looking left, right, and left again, and then listening, waiting for all traffic to pass, and then proceeding while still watching for vehicles. Kids should never run or dash into the street, and they should be alert while walking.

In Europe, some countries are experimenting with "Wait for Signal" signs that build in the need for caution in crossing the street before the light changes. Others are trying infrared motion sensors, monitoring the pedestrian after he or she pushes the button to get a signal to cross, and gets a "Walk" signal. The sensors stop traffic until the pedestrian reaches the far curb, a help to those who walk slowly, such as the elderly. These tactics work best in low-traffic areas.

The Safe Kids Campaign offers guidelines for parents of elementary school children, "Myths and Facts About Pedestrian Safety," which sum up safe pedestrian rules.

Myth 1. A green light means it is safe to walk across the street.
*Fact:* The green light is your signal to stop and search for cars; look left-right-left. If safe, cross and keep on looking as you cross. Be alert for vehicles making a right turn on red.

Myth 2. You're safe in a crosswalk.
*Fact:* You may cross at a crosswalk, but you must stop at the curb. Look left-right-left, and when clear, cross and keep looking.

Myth 3. If you see the driver, the driver sees you.
*Fact:* The driver may not see you. Eye contact does not mean the driver sees you. Look for other signs of recognition, or wait. Be sure the car has come to a complete stop.

**Planes, Trains, Autos**

Myth 4: The driver will stop if you are in a crosswalk or at a green light.
*Fact:* The driver's view may be blocked. Or he or she may run a traffic light illegally, or turn without looking out for pedestrians. Time for you to be on your guard.

Myth 5: Wearing white at night makes you visible to drivers.
*Fact:* It won't; drivers will still have a hard time seeing you. To increase your visibility, wear retroreflective clothing and carry a flashlight. Retroreflective materials reflect light, and some reflect headlights directly back at cars. Strips of these materials can be sewn on clothes. There is also a material that glimmers; tape these patches to backpacks and shoes. (Look for these products in fabric, sporting goods, or hardware stores.) Last, but not least, walk facing traffic.

**Planes, Trains, Autos**

The National Association for the Education of Young Children (with funding from the United States Department of Transportation, the National Highway Traffic Safety Administration) has put out a booklet for parents of preschoolers on pedestrian traffic education. The WITS (Walk in Traffic Safely) program is an excellent source for parents, as well as teachers, in helping to reduce the chance of preschool pedestrian accidents.

The facts are that most children are injured near home, often on their own streets, and that most of the injured are boys. (Almost twice as many boys as girls are injured.) It's also thought that most accidents happen in late afternoon on sunny days, and that most victims weren't properly supervised.

## Train Safety

The sound of a train whistle has always been alluring to kids (and sometimes to their parents). Train tracks in your neighborhood may be less romantic, however, and it's a good idea to teach your child to respect them.

Trains may travel railroad tracks at any time, day or night; therefore, children should never be on, around, or close to those tracks. Parents should know that if a car stalls on a grade crossing, the only thing to do is to get out fast and run away from the tracks.

Thousands of people are seriously injured and hundreds killed in nearly 6,000 rail-highway grade crossing crashes every year. Although a rail-highway grade crossing presents a unique traffic environment for motorists, many drivers don't cross railroad tracks often enough to be familiar with the warning devices designed for their safety. Often they're unaware that trains can't stop as quickly as motor vehicles to avoid a collision. Others simply ignore all warning signs because they're "in a hurry," and would rather play "beat the train" than wait. Driver ignorance and impatience are the most common factors contributing to motor vehicle/train collisions at rail-highway grade crossings.

Some of the worst accidents involve commuter trains bound for suburban areas. According to the National Safety Council, in 1993 ten children under the age of four and thirty children between the ages of five and fourteen died in collisions of motor vehicles (moving or stalled) and railroad vehicles at either public or private grade crossings. Of the 10,000 accidents between motor vehicles and trains in that year, 500 involved fatalities and another 2,000 involved injuries.

Memorize this motto and teach it to your children: *The train is always faster.* Stop, look, and listen.

Representatives from a national campaign mounted by Operation Lifesaver, a national rail safety organization, often visit stations to hand out literature. Operation Lifesaver was established in 1972 in Idaho after Union Pacific Railroad and Idaho community leaders banded together to fight the growing number of rail-highway grade crossing crashes, injuries, and fatalities with a public education program. Other states that have established their own Operation Lifesaver programs all report fatalities reduced at grade crossings at rates of 28 percent to 100 percent a year.

**Planes, Trains, Autos**

## Bus Safety

There will be times when you're not at the wheel. Most often, this might involve your child's trip to school on the school bus. Believe it or not, crossing the road to and from the bus is the most dangerous part of the bus trip. On the bus, young children need to know everything from how to use exits to what to do in case of a bus emergency. States have different policies for drivers' stop, drop-off, and pick-up procedures, so no one rule will work for everyone.

For many kids, school bus rides are as inevitable as breathing, and the older the child, the more experienced he becomes. Young children, however, need to know a good deal more about the how-tos and what-fors than they might be taught by older siblings.

Begin by setting up a safe routine for getting on the bus. Your child should be dressed correctly for the weather. In winter, boots with rubber soles are best for gripping snowy, icy streets, when slipping under the bus is a danger. Ideally, it's best if your child doesn't have to hurry; he should be at the bus stop five minutes before the bus arrives. Be sure younger siblings or pets don't follow your child to the bus stop. A sturdy backpack or book bag is helpful in transporting school items back and forth and assures a more comfortable trip. If your child must make bus trips after dark, it's good to have him wear a day-glow light strip or similar reflective material on some item of clothing.

If the bus does not stop outside your door, it may be necessary for your child to cross the street to board the bus. The most important rule to learn: Look both ways before crossing.

Children should wait until the bus comes to a full stop before boarding. They should line up in single file, use the handrails, and not push or shove. Everyone should choose a seat and sit down right away before the bus starts on its way. All kids must stay in their seats while the bus is moving. Arms and legs belong inside the windows. Items are *never* thrown from the bus. Aisles are no place for belongings, such as lunch boxes and other items. Books are best kept in book bags on laps or under seats.

**Planes, Trains, Autos**

It's hard for kids to keep emotions in check, but the school bus is no place to scream and shout. Tell your child that the driver needs to listen for emergency vehicle sirens and the sound of trains when the bus approaches railroad tracks, and while it's not necessary to be silent, children should moderate their voices.

Learning how to exit the bus is just as important as knowing how to climb aboard. Kids should use the handrails, step down carefully, and move straight away from the bus, waiting for it to pull away in a safe spot, where the driver can see them.

Because buses are so big and dangerous, tell your child that if he drops a book bag from a window or as he gets on or off the bus and it is lying on the ground near or under the bus, he shouldn't try to pick it up until he tells the driver. Your child must tell the driver first because he or she may not be able to see your child as he moves around the bus.

Your child needs to know that the bus emergency exit is not used except for emergencies. Tell him to follow the driver's instructions in case of emergency, and if it is necessary to leave the bus, to leave in an orderly manner. The child should stay in a group away from traffic.

Discuss the danger zones around the outside of the bus with your child. They are at the front of the bus on both sides, and at the back on the right side. Children should know that car and truck drivers must stop for school buses loading or letting off students, and that some drivers *don't* stop. Yellow flashing lights on the bus mean *caution, get ready to stop*. Flashing red lights mean *stop*.

## Boat Safety

Children and boats *are* compatible, but unless you take certain safety measures, you might as well sell that boat. You can become a conscientious boater, says Lyndsay Green, author of *Babies Aboard* (International Marine, 1990), by preparing adequately and taking the proper precautions.

### Planes, Trains, Autos

One way to prepare is to take courses offered by the United States Power Squadrons. The United States Power Squadrons belong to a private organization of boaters (both power and sail), whose national headquarters is in Raleigh, North Carolina. There are different squadrons all over the world; Americans even have a squadron in Japan.

If you are a boater, you may already have taken a Power Squadron course; if so, you'll have a certificate of accomplishment. Or you may have passed the United States Coast Guard course. All states now require a powerboat operator's certificate for kids ages eleven or twelve to eighteen. If they take the Power Squadron course and earn a certificate, it will qualify them to receive the state certificate.

Boat handling and elementary seamanship are important for every child aboard a boat to know. Kids must understand how to operate a boat with caution and care to help prevent accidents and injury. They need to be familiar with navigation, weather, the required equipment, safety regulations, and safety operations. What is basic navigation? What are the charts and aids to navigation? In piloting, how do you chart a course? What is dead reckoning? How do you operate a marine radio? Can you identify boat types and understand nautical terms? Kids can enjoy learning all of this, just as Mom and Dad have. As each state has different regulations, it is a good idea to check what's necessary for everyone in the family to know. Everyone should know about the five types of personal floatation devices (PFDs), sometimes called *life preservers*.

Types I, II, and III are wearable PFDs. Types I and II are designed to turn an unconscious person in the water from a face downward position to a vertical or slightly backward position.

Type I, an offshore PFD used in coastal waters, oceans, and the Great Lakes, floats the best and helps the person stay faceup for a long time.

Type II, the near-shore PFD, comes in a variety of sizes for children. It may not offer quite as much buoyancy as Type I and doesn't have a crotch strap. It's best to wear for inshore boating and fishing.

A Type III PFD is designed to keep a conscious person in a vertical and slightly backward position, is very comfortable, and is often used for water sports. Although not required to turn an unconscious person to a faceup position in the water, Type III will maintain a stable faceup attitude once a person assumes that position. Type III PFDs come as specialty floatation-style vests and jackets, and they are best used when a rescue can be effected quickly.

The Type IV PFD is not designed to be worn, but rather thrown to a person in the water to hang on to until rescue. This type of PFD is commonly a ring or horseshoe buoy.

Type V PFD (ski vests and other vests) are PFDs approved for restricted use and may be substituted for Types I, II, or III only during the activity for which they are approved. They inflate when you enter the water, and they are now being made for children. Ski belts, however, are not approved by the U.S. Coast Guard.

When you visit your nearest marine outlet to purchase your family PFDs, consult with knowledgeable sales staffers on which are best for your children. In the store, check to see that the fit is perfect and not too loose. Have the salesperson show you and the child how it works, how it goes over the head, and then how to fasten and tighten all straps. Most important, look for PFDs that are legibly marked with the U.S. Coast Guard approval number. Don't buy one without this label.

**Planes, Trains, Autos**

Overall, it's best to be prepared. Of course your child should put on his PFD if a storm threatens, but, in fact, it's a good idea for kids to wear them all the time in the boat, even when accompanied by adults. In addition, a child should learn about the *lifelines,* which run around the boat from bow to stern to help keep everyone on board. People who cruise often use netting between these lines for added security. Adults and children should use harnesses in rough weather; they should clip to a solid stanchion or standing rigging.

Here are a few more tips, courtesy of Dave Rodelius of Evanston, Illinois, who teaches Evanston Power Squadron courses for adults and children:

1. Your child should always remain in the cockpit of a powerboat, and not walk around on the gunnel or walkways; he could easily slip through railings and lifelines. No child should sit on the bow. A jarring wave will make him fall off or lose his grip. In big seas, the child can be submerged as soon as the boat hits a wave. So, no bow!
2. When you're locking through (going through locks, which you do in all canals), never let a child off the boat.
3. Keep children from climbing around.
4. Do kids need any further equipment? You can attach both a whistle (kids love whistles) and a light on the child's PFD. Some lights will go on automatically if the child falls into the water.
5. Eighty-five percent of boating deaths are caused by the lack of a PFD. And in 80 percent of those cases, the PFD was right there in the boat, but the child didn't have it on, for whatever reason, and it floated away. Motorboats can go so fast! Always wear a PFD, and always place one on your child.

Check to see if your state has a Boat Registration and Safety Act, and if it offers a boat safety course. You can be sure that your state requires most watercraft to be both registered and titled. Your state department of conservation or natural resources probably publishes a guide to registration, boat titling, and safety acts, which covers such regulations as where your boat's registration

**Planes, Trains, Autos**

numbers are to be displayed. There are many other requirements for safety's sake. For instance, did you know that on board your motorboat you're required to keep a mouth, hand, or power-operated whistle capable of producing a blast that lasts at least two seconds and can be heard for at least a half-mile? Every boat with an internal combustion engine must have a U.S. Coast Guard–approved fire extinguisher readily accessible.

Did you know that you're required to have at least two competent persons in the boat when towing a person on water skis, aquaplane, or a similar device? You're also breaking the law in some states if you water-ski a half-hour after sunset or a half-hour before sunrise.

What other regulations should you know? You can't operate a vessel within 150 feet of a diving flat (unless your craft is associated with the diving activity), and you can't under any circumstances operate a watercraft when under the influence of alcohol or drugs.

When can your child operate a motorboat? Only after he reaches ten years of age, and then, if he's under twelve, only when he's accompanied on the motorboat and under the direct control of Mom, Dad, or a guardian, or a person at least eighteen years old designated by that parent or guardian. If he's at least twelve but under eighteen, he may operate a motorboat only if he's (1) accompanied on the motorboat and under the direct control of a parent or guardian, or (2) accompanied by a person at least eighteen years old designated by a parent or guardian, or (3) earned a Boating Safety Certificate issued by the Office of Law Enforcement, or a valid certificate issued by the United States Coast Guard Auxiliary or the United States Power Squadron. No wonder so many teenagers are signing up for Power Squadron courses. Check to find out where your nearest courses are given.

A final bit of information: All boating accidents or collisions resulting in death or injury, or that cause property damage of $500, must be reported. Check with your local conservation department for the timeframe within which such accidents must be reported, and let's hope you never have to do so. If boating pleasure is the target, make safety your aim.

**Planes, Trains, Autos**

# Plane Safety

Flying with a child, you're very sensitive about the feelings of those (adults) around you, whom (you could swear) had never been, or had, a child, so it's easier if you're prepared for the flight. You should know, first of all, that the Federal Aviation Administration (FAA) recommends that infants be restrained in car seats during plane flights. If you're planning to fly with your child and to bring along his car seat, be sure to call the airline and ask if it will work in their plane seats. Additionally, you should know that as of July 1995, the Federal Aviation Administration has banned two types of seats on planes: backless booster seats and torso harnesses.

If you're flying with a child under two years of age, baby may fly free, but if you don't purchase a seat for him, you take the chance of holding him on your lap the entire time. (Some people are fortunate enough to find an empty seat next to them.)

It is an excellent idea to have baby use a pacifier as the plane ascends and descends; the sucking motion definitely keeps tiny ears from "popping." If he doesn't use a pacifier, try a bottle (juice, water, or milk) with a nipple to encourage the sucking action, or the good old thumb, if your child uses it.

Airlines usually ask seated passengers to keep their seat belts fastened even if the seat belt sign has been turned off. However, older children don't always respond to the ever-present seat belt, and they should be permitted a quiet walk or two in the aisle when Mom or Dad wants to stretch their legs, too. Parents, though, should be firm about no playing in the aisle, and under no circumstances should toys wind up in the aisle.

Just as is advised in car travel, it's a good idea to bring a surprise box or bag full of toys and books for the flight (particularly a longer flight); fun things have a way of keeping a bored child in his seat. Pack a beloved old book or toy animal along with a few new carefully chosen surprises. Always fit puzzles and games to the child's age, and don't offer anything that is likely to frustrate him. (You wouldn't do this at home, either.) If you bring crayons aboard, keep them to a minimum and in a sturdy container. Often a child can be lulled to sleep with a favorite storybook.

**Planes, Trains, Autos**

(Don't forget to keep your voice down, as a courtesy to the passenger next to you who may be trying to work.)

Whether to book a flight during nap time is problematical. Some children nap through many a flight, and others simply grow more cranky because they haven't napped, and are darned if they will do it now. Perhaps the best time to fly, if you have a choice, is bright and early in the morning, so that the child is at his best. If your child goes to sleep at night without a murmur, he may follow his regular habit and sleep through a late-night flight. But, can you count on it? No.

Joe Crawley, spokesman for American Airlines based at American's Fort Worth headquarters, advises parents that American has a policy for kids flying alone. It's best to get to the airport about an hour early. Because the airport itself can be a very scary place, escort the child right to the gate, don't just drop him off at the front door, no matter how small the airport is: "The child is checked in and a packet (a plastic pouch) goes around the child's neck advising where he's going and who's going to pick him up, as well as any special instructions (such as a dietary problem, or if he doesn't speak English)." Crawley says it is particularly important for parents to identify clearly who will pick up the child. American will not turn over a child to anyone without the appropriate picture identification (such as a driver's license).

One important detail sometimes forgotten is that the flight attendant aboard the plane is in essence the baby-sitter, the child's sponsor on board. "She or he should be notified if anything strange happens," advises Crawley. "If any stranger says something to the child that makes him uncomfortable in any way, he should immediately find the flight attendant. Children don't feel they have the authority to do that, so it's important parents give them permission." Crawley observes that most flight attendants these days are mothers and fathers, so "their maternalistic and paternalistic attitude toward children" traveling alone is a natural, sensitive response to the child.

What about children who've never been on an airplane? "Part of safety is knowledge, having a sense of comfort, and knowing what to do. The strangeness is a handicap to the child, everything is brand-new and he's never seen anything and he

## Planes, Trains, Autos

doesn't know what's going on. So it's very helpful to bring the child to the airport an hour ahead of time or on an off-date, not even the day he's traveling, and have him look inside an airplane.

"Ask a flight attendant or a desk agent if there is a plane you can take your child aboard to familiarize him with going down the ramp and through the door of the plane, so that he has some sense of comfort. It's very intimidating to the first-time flyer, adults as well as children." This process is recommended for a nervous child or one who is easily upset. "For other children with less excitable temperaments," says Crawley, "this wouldn't be appropriate."

Swissair makes long-distance flights—which are hard enough on adults, but twice the trauma for children—a breeze. A great deal of what you do, of course, depends on the cooperation of airline personnel. Mark Ellinger, Swissair's director of Public Relations and Market Communications, noted several ways his airline makes the trip safer and more comfortable.

"Most important is that upfront, at the time of booking, parents give us all the information, either directly or via their travel agent," says Ellinger. "Then we can make all the necessary arrangements, such as proper seating."

Swissair provides a baby basket for infants under eight months affixed to the front (bulkhead) row, or hung from the overhead rack, where baby can be safely placed at no charge to parents. There are a few specific seats where the basket can be placed, and there's a demand for them, so availability is based on a first come-first served basis. The basket comes with linen, pillow, and blanket.

Children who fly alone are called "unaccompanied minors" (UMs). "They're generally from five to twelve, but we'll accept them to age seventeen on the UM program upon request from parent or guardian," notes Ellinger. With advance notice parents may also hire from Swissair a special flight attendant to serve as an escort for the child flying alone. The child's fare may cost 50 percent less than an adult fare. The actual cost depends on the date, time, and destination to which the child is traveling.

Finally, Swissair will accommodate a car seat for the child, providing you have purchased a separate airline seat. The seat may face front for toddlers, but remember infants should be facing the rear.

## Very Important Tips

### Planes, Trains, Autos

**AUTO AND PEDESTRIAN SAFETY**

1. Teach your older child how to unlock the back door of the car in case he gets locked in alone.
2. Consult your physician, the National Safety Council, or the National Highway Traffic Safety Administration (NHTSA) for information on car seats for premature babies. You may wish to check for an infant car bed at juvenile furniture stores. For more information on car safety, call the NHTSA in Washington, D.C., your state department of transportation, and the National Safety Council (also in Washington, D.C.). (You'll find the addresses for these agencies in this book's appendix.)
3. Check to see if any local auto service company is offering a special deal selling car seats.
4. Check to see if your state mandates safety seats. If it hasn't, encourage your lawmakers to get to work.
5. Teach your child that when crossing a street on foot, he should always stop at the curb and recognize other street boundaries as well.
6. Though you're there to protect and supervise, encourage your child to use his own safety skills. Let him decide what to do so he will know how to do it when he's on his own.
7. Use a safety vocabulary with your child, such as *stop, crosswalk,* and *traffic.*
8. Provide toys and ideas for children to use in teaching them about play and safety. For example, they can use toy cars and trucks, dolls, or small boxes or milk cartons to build a street scene and demonstrate safety. Give them art materials so they can draw what they've learned.
9. If your child is traveling after dark for any reason, make sure he carries a flashlight and wears retroreflective material on his clothes.
10. Practice what you preach. Make sure your children see you use your seat belt and cross streets safely. With children, plan, walk, and talk together about which streets are safe to cross. The safest route may not be the shortest.

**Planes, Trains, Autos**

# Very Important Tips

### Train Safety
1. Flashing red lights mean you should stop, look, and listen.
2. *Never* go around lowered gates.
3. Railroad yards are not a playground and should never be used as a shortcut.
4. Never use a tunnel as a shortcut.
5. Never use a bridge as a shortcut.

### Bus Safety
1. Make sure your child leaves home in time to arrive at the bus stop. Walk the route to the bus with your child until it becomes second nature and you both know the time it takes to get there.
2. Every child should stand in single file while waiting to board the bus. Don't push or shove and hold onto the rail.
3. Remind your child that once aboard the bus, he should sit quietly and not shout or throw things.
4. Children should get off the bus carefully, stepping down and moving out of the danger zones.
5. Children should walk where the driver can see them and they can see the driver when they get off the bus.
6. If a child drops something on the ground, he shouldn't try to pick it up. He should tell the bus driver. Or if he left something aboard the bus, he should tell someone as soon as he gets home.
7. Children should respect the bus driver. If the driver issues instructions, children should follow them. Remember, it's their safety that is on the driver's mind.

**Planes, Trains, Autos**

# Very Important Tips

**BOAT SAFETY**

1. All children should wear a PFD when on a boat.
2. Teach children boating language and the parts of the boat. Being more knowledgeable always leads to a safer boating excursion.
3. Children under twelve must be accompanied by a parent in order to operate a boat.

**AIRLINE SAFETY**

1. Airlines recommend that infants travel in a car seat, as opposed to a parent's lap.
2. Remember, infants face backward in the car seat.
3. It's a good idea for babies to suck on a bottle or pacifier during take off and landing to help keep ears from popping.
4. It's a good idea for kids to get out of their seats and stretch briefly like adults, but no running and playing in the aisles.

## Chapter 7

# Oh, What Fun It Is to Ride!: Strollers, Bicycles, and Skates

WHEELS ARE A MOST INGENIOUS INVENTION. From childhood through adulthood, the human race has spent a good many of its waking hours dealing with that invention. But planes, trains, and automobiles are only part of the story; adults and children also use wheels for both utility (strollers) and leisure-time fun (cycling and in-line skating). This chapter details safety measures for each of these conveyances.

**Strollers, Bicycles**

## Stroller Safety

To go from 747s to strollers is quite a stretch, but you'll probably spend more time around the latter. When deciding which stroller to buy, go to your favorite children's furnishings' supplier and try them all. Push a few around the floor; see how they feel in your hands. It may be hard to select the model you want, but perhaps a "test drive" will help.

Check to make sure the stroller has a certification label from the Juvenile Products Manufacturers' Association (JPMA). That way, you know for sure that the stroller you like has been tested by an independent laboratory, and that it meets all necessary safety standards. Of course, the stroller's safety features add up to much more than how it looks. Be on the lookout for several things. Start by examining the brake. Is it comfortable to use and does it lock the wheels securely? Brakes on two wheels offer the most security. Use the brakes whenever you stop, whether the stroller is on flat land or a hill. In any case, you don't want the stroller rolling away from you.

Check the stroller's restraints. Seat belt and crotch straps should be in good working order and easy for you to fasten. Nothing is more aggravating than trying to secure the belt of a wriggling child and finding that it's hard to work. You should *always* use these straps, so be sure they do the job. If you're buying or borrowing a secondhand stroller, or if you're re-using a stroller purchased a few years ago for an older child, check that the brakes and restraints are still working well.

Be sure the stroller locks securely into the open position and that it is sturdy enough to keep its balance. The base should be wide enough to keep the stroller from tipping over if baby leans to one side. (Some wee ones are, after all, heftier than others.) If you are toting a basket for shopping, keep the stroller well balanced. Place the basket low on the back of the stroller or directly over the rear wheels. At certain seasons and in some climates, it may be a good idea to carry a small folding umbrella for Mom or Dad, in case of showers. The stroller's awning brim should be firm and protective, shielding the child from the elements.

# Bicycle Safety

## Injury Statistics

Each year, thousands of children are seriously injured in falls from bikes and crashes that could have been prevented. Head injuries are the most common, and the most vulnerable children range between six and twelve years old.

Statistics show that bicycle accidents are too frequent. According to the National Safety Council, in 1994, twenty children four and younger died riding their bikes. For ages five through fourteen, 270 deaths occurred in accidents between motor vehicles and pedacycles on private driveways, streets, parking lots, and highways.

In 1992, injuries resulting from accidents between motor vehicles and pedacycles numbered 1,900 for children under four, and 17,500 for children between five and fourteen, the largest age group for any bicycle injuries. For 1991, even more detailed statistics are available. Hospitals treated 492,000 injuries among riders up to twenty-four years old. Of these, 1,750 were head injuries to children under four, and 70,150 five- to fourteen-year-olds were hurt.

Since 1992, the figures have been rising. Today, an estimated 300,000 to 500,000 Americans visit emergency rooms thanks to bicycle accidents. Some 1,000 of these die; many suffer brain damage. Children younger than sixteen account for half of these deaths.

## Younger Riders

Bikes and babies first get together when baby is about a year old (weighing up to forty-five pounds), and the baby seat appears on Dad's or Mom's bike. The baby seat has a high back and a handle to grab in front. But even though you obey all traffic and safety laws and your baby wears a helmet while riding on the back of your bike, remember that she is still at risk. The best helmet and baby seat won't keep a motor vehicle from hitting you or prevent you from encountering a pothole in the road. Both circumstances could cause serious head injuries to your child.

**Strollers, Bicycles**

As for older children, one of the most important facts to stress when talking about bicycles is that they are not toys. They are vehicles, just like cars and trucks, and kids are "drivers" when they are in the street. The truth is that when you give your young child a tricycle, a wagon, a scooter, or a Big Wheel®, you are giving her the kind of responsibility her college-age brother has with the family car. At three years of age, children may begin to use a tricycle, which is fun and helps motor coordination and development. But watch out! According to the Consumer Products Safety Commission, each year more than 12,000 tricycle-related injuries occur that are serious enough for emergency trips to hospitals. Hands or feet can get caught in moving parts, and kids may be unable to stop. (Tricycles usually don't have brakes.) Or they may tip over making too sharp a turn. Safety in the 1990s depends on more than hand signals and helmets. (Some little ones may wear knee and elbow pads, too.) Teaching your children "bicycle smarts" helps.

**Strollers, Bicycles**

Types of tricycles include the Big Wheel, which has a low seat and is close to the ground making it more stable than traditional metal tricycles because most of the weight rides on the rear wheel; the Tough Trike®, which is easier to ride than the low-slung Big Wheel; and the traditional metal or plastic tricycle. A new tricycle from West Germany, the Safety Cycle®, actually has a hand brake to help prevent falls. The pedals only move forward and a hand-held bar enables a parent to guide the child while riding, or to use the tricycle as a stroller.

No matter what trike your child rides, be aware that she is very low to the ground and not easy for the driver of a car to see. Mount a bright-colored flag on a tall flexible pole on the back of the tricycle to make the child more visible to drivers. Also, instruct your child never to leave the tricycle in the driveway. Find or make a special place to keep the tricycle, and teach the child to store the tricycle in that place when she isn't riding it.

When your child is about two-and-a-half to three years old, it is a good time to start using training wheels. The bicycle already has the training wheels attached when you first purchase the bike and sometime between ages four and six, she'll be ready to remove the training wheels. By the time children are six or seven years of age, most are ready to ride without training wheels. Until this age, always supervise your child. Abilities vary because all children develop at different rates; don't push her to ride a two-wheel bike if she isn't quite ready.

That's why you must be sure your child's first bike is right for her. Don't assume that what one child rides is best for another. If you're puzzled about what skills are needed to ride a bike, consider these:
- the child must be able to start, stop, steer, and turn, and
- the child must be able to do all of the above without losing her balance.

When choosing a bike for a child under eight, be sure to buy one with coaster or foot brakes; most young children are not ready to operate hand brakes yet. Children under ten should be riding

**Strollers, Bicycles**

single-brake bicycles. Finally, wheels with lots of spokes (about twenty-eight) are safer. Be sure foot pedals have a good grip.

When your child has her own bike, she will find that part of the fun of "driving" is the fun of knowing how to do it the right way. The National Association for the Education of Young Children (NAEYC) has issued some great guidelines on the subject in a booklet written by Bess-Gene Holt, sent home to parents as part of the association's Children Riding On Sidewalks Safety (CROSS) program.

1. Choose play vehicles appropriate for your child's age. Toddlers can usually move a kiddie car or ride-on animal, but they may not be able to watch where they are going much before the age of three or four years. Preschoolers can ride three-wheelers, wagons, scooters, carts, and carriages. A few may roller-skate. Play vehicles such as two-wheel bicycles and skateboards are more appropriate for older children.
2. Spend time showing your child how the new toy works. How does she make it go where it's supposed to go?
3. Help your child focus on where the vehicle is supposed to go. Help her notice traffic out in the street and discuss why she must stay away from there. Help her spot other hazards (driveways, etc.).
4. Help the child understand that drivers of motor vehicles can't see her sitting on a play vehicle.
5. Attach a bike flag to the child's vehicle to make it easier to spot.
6. Start good habits now: Have your child wear a helmet; they do come in small sizes.

What's safe for bicyclists in the street applies to tiny ones riding vehicles on sidewalks, as the NAEYC informs us. Keep to the right side of the walk; ride single file; give pedestrians the right of way; pass on the left only after your warning noise lets the person walking or riding ahead of you know that you're coming; and follow traffic signs and signals. Parents should always remember to keep their children under close supervision at all times.

**Strollers, Bicycles**

Many towns and cities across America sponsor local programs, such as an annual spring bike maze, where students learn to ride carefully and use hand signals. They may be part of a school schedule or programs evolved by local government or civic sources. All are dedicated to helping kids learn to use bicycles correctly.

## Older Riders

Older riders are more aware of how to maintain their bikes and of what can happen to someone who doesn't ride safely. Today's kids register and care for their bikes. They learn that most accidents result when they don't obey lights and signs. And how can they keep their bikes from being stolen? Bicycles are stolen more often from homes than from schools. Third graders and up learn to lock their bikes properly and not to leave them on the lawn, but to put them away in the garage. (It may be the same place where that original tricycle was first stored, so putting it away is now a habit.)

Here are a few more tips for helping older children ride safely:

1. Teach your child how to make safety checks to assure that her bicycle will look its best and ride well. Continue to instill the "rules of the road" and remind your older child, just as you did when she was younger: Bikes aren't toys, and that along with the fun come the responsibilities.
2. Schedule regular vision checks for your child.
3. Periodically remind your child how best to move in traffic and discuss with her common road hazards (such as loose gravel, sewer gratings, manhole covers, and potholes), and how to handle bicycle field trips.
4. Older kids should be reminded to ride single file, and never carry passengers or tote packages that block vision and restrict control.
5. Teach your older child to bike defensively and always watch out for the other guy.
6. She should be alert for doors of parked cars opening suddenly and for cars pulling into traffic.

7. Finally, she should *never* hitch a ride with any other vehicle, and she can teach her younger brothers and sisters never to do it either.

## Using Helmets

According to the National Head Injury Foundation, about 50,000 bicyclists annually suffer head injuries serious enough to be disabled permanently. Most serious bicycle accidents, especially those involving young children, occur on quiet neighborhood streets. Bike helmets can't stop children from falling off their bikes, but they can help reduce the chances of serious brain injury.

Helmet, helmet, helmet! If your child still thinks wearing one isn't cool or is too much hassle, tell her she'd better get used to the fact that she won't be allowed to ride her bike without one. Make it the family law, if it's not yet your state law. If you, the parent, also wear a helmet, your child is likely to imitate you. And as for cool, not many kids would think that suddenly being confined to a wheelchair or going to the funeral of a friend who didn't wear a helmet was cool.

Many state legislators are currently sponsoring bills that require children under sixteen years of age to wear improved bicycle helmets. Physicians have testified that a majority of head injuries from bicycle accidents would be prevented with the use of helmets, and their urgings are being heeded. The medical journal *Pediatrics* advises that wearing a helmet would reduce the risk of head injury by 85 percent.

Let's examine two states with youth-helmet laws. Do the kids comply? In New Jersey, young cyclists (under fourteen is law) were up to nearly 70 percent compliant in the first year. Before legislation, it was estimated that no more than 5 to 10 percent of young New Jerseyites wore helmets. In Seattle, Washington, where head injuries accounted for three-quarters of the deaths and two-thirds of hospitalizations in bike accidents, the Washington Children's Bike Helmet Coalition increased awareness and taught children just how cool it was to wear helmets. Thanks to the coalition, the

**Strollers, Bicycles**

number of children wearing helmets went from 1 percent to 33 percent immediately. It is likely that the figure has risen since the first result was reported.

Good bike helmets cost between $40 and $60. To some this may be expensive, but you can't put a price tag on your own child's life; she is *priceless*. The Bicycle Helmet Safety Institute (BHSI) is the helmet advocacy program of the Washington Area Bicyclist Association, with headquarters in Arlington, Virginia. It has published a booklet that addresses how to buy a helmet.

1. Check for the Snell or other safety sticker.
2. Make sure the helmet has adequate vents for your child's riding habits.
3. Adjust the straps so they are comfortably snug. Have the child try to tear the helmet off forward, backward, and sideways. It should remain level on the head and not tilt more than an inch or two in any direction.

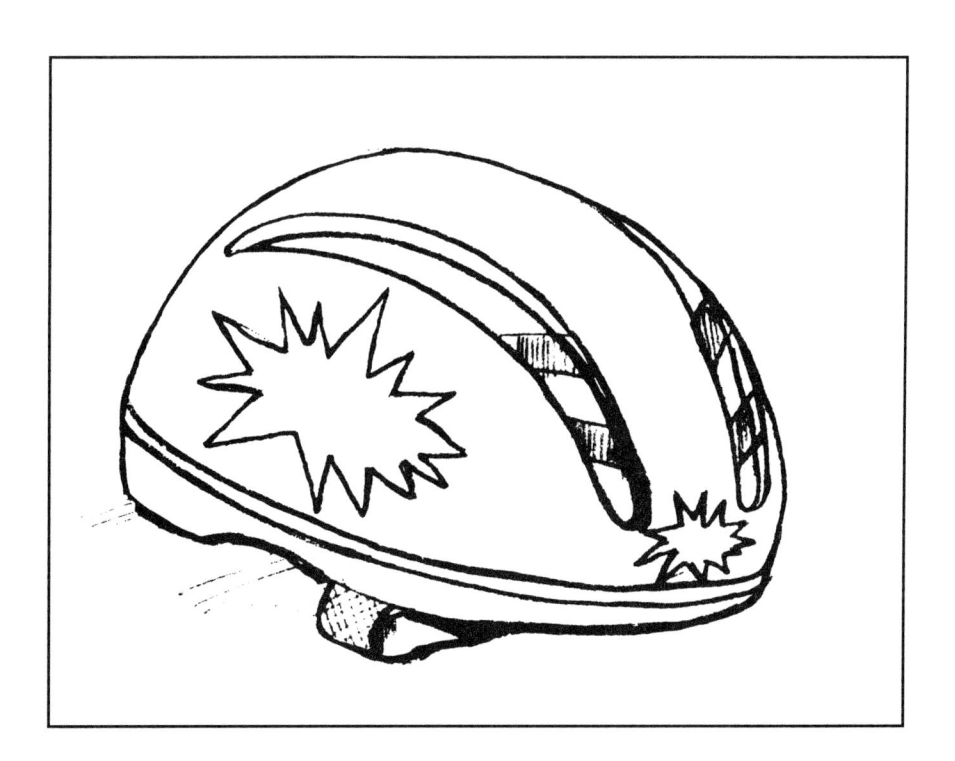

## Strollers, Bicycles

Here are more tips for wearing a helmet:
1. It should fit snugly and not rock from side to side. A properly fitted helmet hugs the head without moving forward, sideways, or backwards. The sides should cover the ears, and the back should cover the little bump at the base of the skull. Be sure the child's forehead is covered.
2. It should come with sizing pads to adjust the fit as the child grows.
3. Straps should be adjustable, so they clear the ears along the jawline and fit snugly under the chin. The child should be able to talk comfortably without choking.
4. The clasp on the straps must be easy to use. Children under eight may need help manipulating the clasp. Older children should be able to work it on their own.
5. Use a lined hard-plastic shell helmet for children older than two. For younger children, choose a foam helmet. (Hardshell helmets are too heavy for young children's neck muscles to support.) Make sure it has a fabric covering to allow the helmet to slide in case of a fall. Foam can stick to the road's surface. Most helmets are made of lightweight polystyrene and have a foam interior. Helmets weigh less than a half-pound. The smaller the polystyrene bead, the better the quality and the lighter the helmet's weight.
6. Some good helmets for children are ventilated to keep the head cool. The helmet's ventilation depends on front-to-back air flow.
7. Helmets come in all colors. Look for those with retroreflective material so that if your child must be out after dusk, she'll be visible. Older kids should also consider carrying a flashlight in their backpacks. But, more important, your child should be visible to drivers. Have her travel with a working headlight, and wear retroreflective material on her helmet and gear or clothing. Bright colors, such as hot pink, neon green, or orange, help during the day. She should also mount reflectors on the wheels, pedals, and back of her bike, and if she is riding in bad weather or

## Strollers, Bicycles

when lighting is poor (dawn, dusk, or night), she needs a working light in addition to the headlight on the bike's rear and/or side. (Leg lights work just as well.) A flashing Vistalite® attached to the helmet provides increased visibility. Look for retroreflective clothing, too.

8. Use only warm soap and water to clean helmets; some cleaning solvents may cause invisible damage.
9. If ever a child's helmet should be involved in an impact accident, be sure to replace it. Damage may not be visible, but the accident may have weakened the helmet's ability to protect the child. Replace a buckle if it cracks or any piece of it breaks off.
10. Measure your child's head for the correct helmet size if she cannot shop for it with you.
11. Your child's bicycle helmet should be rated. Look on the inside of the helmet for a green or blue Snell sticker; this means that the helmet has passed the Snell Foundation's safety test, which establishes the most stringent U.S. standard. Or, look for the seal of the American Society for Testing and Materials (ASTM). This new certification is just as good as Snell. Less stringent is the American National Standards Institute (ANSI) that many helmets carry.
12. Be sure your child is wearing a helmet when she rides in a seat on the back of your bicycle. In case of an accident, it's very easy for her to fly off, and she *must* be protected. Infant-sized helmets of the soft-shell variety are light and easy to wear for children whose necks may not yet be strong enough to support the hard-shell helmet. Because babies under a year have relatively weak neck structures, neither helmets nor bike travel is recommended for them, notes the American Academy of Pediatrics.

Finally, if you're not the only parent on the block insisting on a helmet, you're halfway there. But if other parents want to be careless, that's their prerogative. Stick to your principles. There are many grieving parents who would give anything to be able to insist on that helmet once more. Tell your child you're making this a family rule because you love her and value her and respect her intelligence in wearing a helmet. Of course the best inducement, always, is to wear a helmet yourself whenever you ride your own bike.

## Rules for Safe Cycling

Other than wearing a helmet, how can you and your child prevent bike injuries? Here are a few rules, which you should practice and review with your children:

1. Bikes should be kept in good shape, just like Mom and Dad keep the family car. Be sure to test brakes before leaving home.
2. Restrict cycling to sidewalks, paths, and driveways until a child can demonstrate her knowledge of the basic rules of the road, bicycle maintenance, and riding skills (usually around age nine).
3. Stop before riding out into traffic from a driveway, sidewalk, alley, or parking lot. Do the good old left-right-left look. Then, when there's no traffic, enter the roadway.
4. Ride on the side with, not against, traffic.
5. Obey all red lights and traffic signs.
6. Use hand signals to let drivers know when you are turning.
7. Kids under thirteen should walk, not ride, their bikes through busy intersections.
8. Wear close-fitting protective clothing and proper footwear. Put retroreflective material on the bike, helmet, knapsack, and/or outerwear to increase visibility.

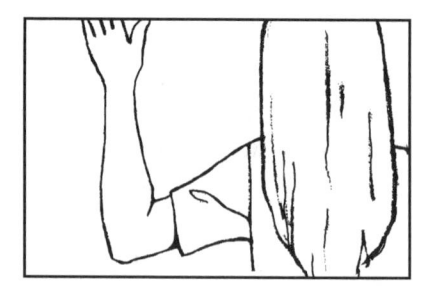

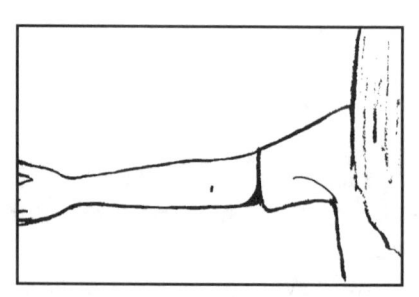

**Strollers, Bicycles**

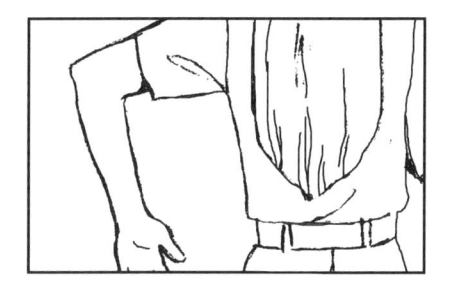

What if your child is not prepared for night riding and she's visiting a friend until after dark? Tell her to call you to drive her home. She can leave her bike at her friend's house, and everyone will feel better for it. Remind her that sometimes all it takes is a little common sense and thought to prevent problems. There'll be plenty of time when she's older to ride her bike home.

## Selecting and Inspecting a Bike

Parents may wonder when their child is ready for a bike. That depends on the child's size, balance skills (which begin at about three years of age), and comprehension of the use of brakes.

An excellent booklet called *Safe Bicycling* (1994) is available from the city of Chicago. Author Dave Glowacz says, "Your bike's most important safety feature is you. If you're not comfortable, you're more likely to ride badly and hit something." That's why you should spend some time talking to a bike dealer when you're ready to buy; a good dealer will consider your child's size and riding style. This applies to adults as well. A child whose bike frame is too tall, too short, or too long is going to ride uncomfortably. Glowacz recommends these tips for selecting the right bike for any age:

1. To check the height, stand with the bike between your legs. Measure the space between the highest part of the top tube and your crotch. For city riding, one to three inches of space is safest. If you feel overly stretched, or have pain in your neck, shoulders, or back, the bike frame might be too long for you. Try moving the seat and handlebars closer together.
2. A seat that's too low will strain the knees, while a seat that's too high will make it hard for you to pedal and put your foot down. Sit on the bike and push one pedal all the way down. Put the ball of your foot on the pedal. If your

seat's high enough, your knee should be slightly bent. If your hips rock from side to side when you pedal, your seat's too high. Don't raise your seat so high that less than two inches of your seat post extends into the frame.
3. Next, set your handlebars so you feel comfortable.

Glowacz recommends quick maintenance checks for bicyclists of any age. To be sure you're on the right track, always check the following:

1. Air. If you have no tire gauge, push each tire hard against a curb. If you can flatten it, add air.
2. Chain. A dry chain can lock up or break suddenly. If your chain squeaks when you pedal or it hangs up when you pedal backward, lubricate it. Keep a good lubricant on hand to squeeze or spray onto the chain. (First remove surface grime.)
3. Wheel Spin. Lift each wheel up and give it a slow spin. Spin the back wheel forward so the pedals don't move. If the wheel won't spin by itself or stops suddenly, see whether it's rubbing against the brake pads, frame, or something else. If the wheel's not rubbing, the problem might be inside the axle.
4. Tires. Turn each wheel very slowly and look for big bulges, bubbles, or places where you can see the inner casing. If you spot any, replace the tire. Remove glass or other debris. If the valve stem doesn't point straight at the middle of the wheel, the rim might cut it; let the air out and straighten the valve.
5. Shifting. If the bike has gears, try them all, shifting each lever from high to low. Any sticking? Have your bike shop check for "worn or dirty cables or a derailleur that needs cleaning or adjustment."
6. Handlebars. Hold the front tire between your legs and try to turn the handlebars. If they're loose, tighten the stem bolt.
7. Brakes. Adjust or replace brake cables or pads if, when you apply the brake on each wheel, one or both brake pads

## Strollers, Bicycles

don't touch the rim; you can squeeze the brake lever all the way to the handlebars and/or, on each wheel, the brake can't stop the tire from moving on dry, clean pavement.
8. Loose parts. Pick up the bike and shake it hard. Check and fix anything that rattles.
9. Check all headlights, reflectors, mirrors, and any special equipment that may be required by the state.
10. Finally, check to be sure every bicycle in the family is in good working order.

When you combine the art of being a good, safe driver with the intelligence of wearing a helmet, you can't imagine how much fun you'll have.

1. Saddle. Is it tight? Is the height comfortable for you?
2. Reflectors. Check your state or local regulations for mandatory use. Do you keep all your reflectors clean?
3. Tires. Do they feel firm? Are they cut or wearing out?
4. Toe Clips
5. Crank
6. Pedals. Are they wearing out? Do they have proper reflectors?
7. Forks. Do the wheels wobble or rub on the forks?
8. Handlebars. Are they tight? Is the height comfortable for you?
9. Spokes. Are any bent or broken?
10. Tire Valve. Is it straight? Does it leak?
11. Mirror
12. Headlights and Taillights. Check your state or local regulations for mandatory use. Can they be seen from 500 feet away?
13. Horn or Bell. Does it sound loudly and clearly?
14. Chain. Is it snug? Are there any broken or damaged links?
15. Brakes (coaster or hand). Do they stop the bike quickly and smoothly?
16. Wheels. Do they wobble or rub the forks?

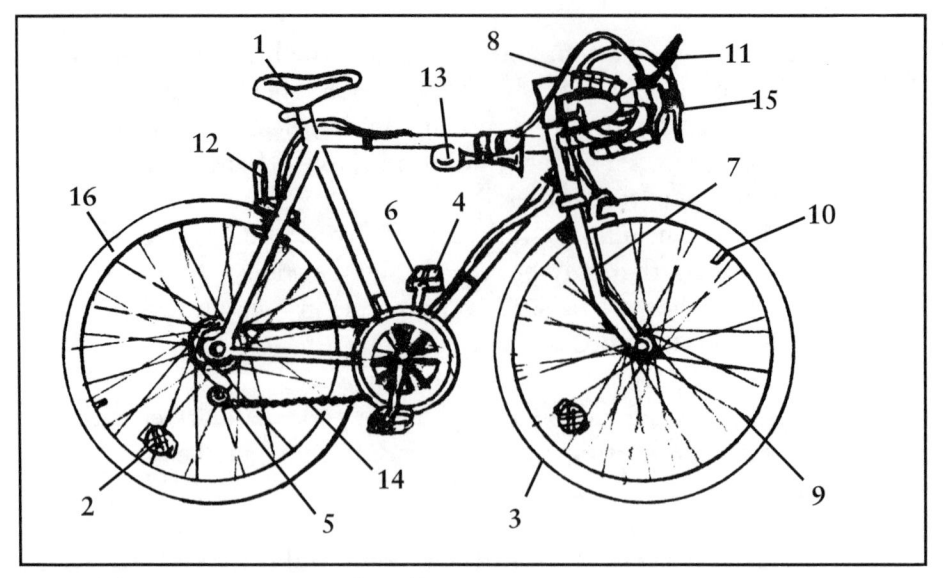

Used by permission of Bell Sports, Inc.

## Skating Safety

From 1989 to 1993, there was a 500 percent increase in the number of people using in-line skates, according to the International In-line Skating Association (IISA) in 1994. In 1992, *American Sports Data, Inc.* said, "In-line skating is the fastest growing sport in America with more than 37% of new skaters now under the age of 12."

With the popularity of in-line skating growing among young children (as well as their teen- and college-aged brothers and sisters), the need for instruction in safety measures for skaters has become terribly important. In no uncertain terms: It means the difference between having fun or being injured. In 1994, the Consumer Product Safety Commission wrote, "In-line skating injuries that require emergency room care will double to 83,000 this year, with most of the bruises and broken limbs being suffered by children under the age of fifteen."

What is the difference between *rollerblading* and *in-line skating?* In-line skating describes the sport, and Rollerblade is the name of a manufacturer. Other manufacturers of in-line skates are

**Strollers, Bicycles**

Bauer (who makes hockey skates, too), Ultra Wheels, Roces, and even Playskool. (The wheels of Playskool skates move, so they can be converted from in-line to out-line.) On out-line skates—like old-fashioned roller skates—the wheels are set up parallel to each other in two lines, like car wheels. In-line skate wheels are literally in a single line.

Gail Shrawder, an IISA Certified Instructor, has written the script for a video called *Skating Safe for Kids*. Notes Shrawder, "Once children understand the basic skills for in-line skating, they can safely enjoy a fun sport that will help to develop motor skills, muscle coordination, and balance for their active future."

How can a parent equip a child for safety in this sport? Shrawder discusses what a child needs to be safe: "(1) A helmet, which needs to fit snugly, not too loose. It can be the same helmet worn for bicycling and sledding, and your child should put it on *first*. Before she puts on skates, she should put on (2) knee pads, and then (3) the skates. Make them snug, so feet don't slip. Lift the foot in, make sure it feels comfortable, then lace or buckle the skate snugly, tight on top but not so tight on the toe part. Then, (4) add elbow pads that fit snugly; and (5) wrist guards, with Velcro® around the wrist and a stiff spine to provide support. (The splint on the side of the arm helps the wearer to slide after a fall; skin doesn't slide!)"

Skates can be a size or two large, but they must fit around the ankle and not slip. Generally, they should be fit the way one fits ice skates or ski boots. If a skate doesn't fit well, it's a hazard. Clothing too should fit close to the body (loose shorts are a no-no) and should provide protection; think T-shirt rather than tank top. A good rule is to cover the parts of the body most likely to hit the ground.

To learn how to keep her balance, have your child stand up on the grass with a little bend at the knees, keeping weight forward and skates parallel. Her shins should push against the tongues of the skates. If she bends her knees enough, she won't be able to see her skates when she looks down.

**Strollers, Bicycles**

Begin in the ready position, which is a basic athletic stance, not stiff, skates about shoulder-width apart. With ankles, knees, and hips slightly bent, arms and hands extended in front of the body so she can see them, she should bend the knees and practice moving up and down.

Scissoring comes next. From the ready position, skates parallel, have your child push down on her skates, moving one skate forward, then the other, and shifting her weight back and forth.

Still on the grass, practice the duckwalk by standing with skates in a V. Push off with the inside edge of the wheel, and glide on the center edge. It's always good to get a feel for the different edges of the skates. Once your child is confident, move from the grass to a quiet safe place with a smooth surface and no cars or bikes. She should hold her skates next to each other, keep the wheels straight, and coast to a stop.

Push off by swizzling. Shrawder advises: "Start by rolling forward just a little, both feet pointed out. Now press into the ground and lean into the inside edges, while bending your knees, skates shoulder-width apart. Now, pull those skates back together and straighten your body. Then, just repeat this motion: in, out, up, down, and you're moving."

It's most important to learn braking. The heel stop is the easiest way to brake. Skates should have one or even two. (If your child's skates are not equipped with a brake, have one added.) Have your child practice on the grass and use her stronger leg for braking.

For turning, coast slowly with skates wide and on the inside edge. The body is in an A-shape, so it's called the A-frame turn. Lean on the right skate to turn left, lean on the left skate to turn right. Keep both skates on the ground, a wide slow turn to help change direction or even slow down to get more control.

Shrawder concludes: "When a skater makes a turn, that's edging. The center edge is perpendicular to the ground. You're standing straight. For an inside edge, you lean skates in toward each other and in outside edging, you lean skates away from each other. Again, edging is used for turning, controlling speed, and learning crossovers eventually."

**Strollers, Bicycles**

Once kids learn to move, they may find they're not yet able to stop. Says Shrawder, "Grass and bushes are a good way to stop as a last resort. Better to dive into the bushes than hit the sidewalk hard."

To get the most enjoyment safely from in-line skating, kids need to learn the basic skills, practice, and get in touch with their own skill level.

# Strollers, Bicycles
# Very Important Tips

**STROLLERS**
1. Be sure the stroller has a label certifying its approval by the Juvenile Products Manufacturers' Association (JPMA) to guarantee it meets all safety standards.
2. Check brakes for security. Brakes on two wheels are best. Always use brakes whenever you stop.
3. Be sure the seat belt and crotch straps are in perfect working order. Use them at all times.

**BICYCLES**
1. Follow lane markings on every street.
2. Obey traffic signals and signs, just as car drivers must.
3. Learn and use hand signals.
4. Watch for pedestrians on sidewalks and bike paths.
5. Watch out for cars backing out of private driveways and parking lots.
6. Lock your bike when not using it.
7. Be sure your bike is well equipped: headlight, bell or horn, front light and/or taillight (some cities require both), mirror, and reflectors. These last may include a red rear reflector, a white front reflector, a red or colorless spoke reflector on the rear wheel, an amber or colorless spoke reflector on the front wheel, and pedal reflectors. A basket and/or bike bag is compulsory for most riders.
8. Wear retroreflective clothing of some sort for night riding and a bright color in daylight to stand out.
9. Don't ride double. One person to a bike is the rule.
10. Ride defensively. Look out for road hazards.
11. Ride a proper bike—one that fits your size, age, and ability.
12. Ride single file.

## Strollers, Bicycles

# Very Important Tips

**13.** Register your bike with the local police department.
**14.** Don't leave bikes outside overnight. Moisture can cause rust to develop and metal parts may weaken.
**15.** Always wear a helmet.

SKATING
**1.** Always wear a certified, correct-fitting helmet.
**2.** Do everything you can to increase your conspicuousness to drivers.
**3.** Know and follow the rules of the road just as motor vehicle drivers do.
**4.** Constantly work at increasing your skills just as you do on bicycles.
**5.** Always skate defensively.
**6.** Be aware of road hazards. Be on the lookout for sidewalk cracks, sand, holes, and so on. Scan the surface ahead.
**7.** Obey traffic regulations. Read all signs and do what they say.

**8.** Stay out of heavy traffic. Avoid areas full of congestion and go for places that are quiet and close to home.
**9.** Always yield to pedestrians. Stop to let them cross.
**10.** Master the basics. You can't become a good and safe skater without them.

# Chapter 8
# Outdoor Safety: Playgrounds and Pools

ON LAND OR IN WATER, children seem to have an abundance of what parents covet: energy. "I wanna go outside," is the universal cry, and it's good, when warm weather finally arrives, to encourage kids to run, play games, socialize, and expend that seemingly endless vigor by enjoying the outdoors and splashing about in the water. These pleasures on land or "sea" appeal to parents who aren't crazy about kids spending too many hours in front of the TV set; when summer comes, the doors open.

Parents may feel lulled into a sense that the playground or the pool is safe territory for kids. And while it's normal to be glad that they're occupied, it's important to keep an eye on where and how kids are playing and know how pools and playgrounds are being maintained for safety. This chapter is devoted to the ins and outs of playground and water safety, including some preventative tips, as well as what to do in case of an accident.

## Playground Safety

Swings that float tots through the air, jungle gyms that lift children to exciting new views of familiar places, and slides that whiz even the youngest kids down slippery slopes offer many motion-happy moments to treasure. Whether at a child-care center, school, park, or neighborhood backyard, a playground offers children a place to run and expand their imaginations, and trips to playgrounds should be a regular part of every child's schedule. The traditional play equipment—a metal swing set, a slide, a seesaw, and a merry-go-round—has given way to more creative and complicated structures of wood and rope, but the basic safety rules still apply.

**Playgrounds & Pools**

Combining active children and playground equipment usually means some type of scrape or fall, but unfortunately injuries aren't limited to the occasional skinned knee or scraped elbow. The American Academy of Pediatrics found that in just one year "about 200,000 children 15 years of age or younger—more than 500 every day—were treated in emergency rooms for injuries suffered while using playground equipment," and that "between 10 and 20 youngsters die each year from injuries involving playground equipment." The majority of injuries occur when a child falls from play equipment onto hard and unforgiving surfaces. Fatal injuries involve not only falls, but entanglement of clothing or other items on equipment such as slides, entanglement in ropes, head entrapment in openings, impact from equipment tipover or structural failure, and the impact of moving swings.

Attention to the installation, maintenance, and surfacing under the play equipment (along with proper supervision, of course) can make all the difference—and keep kids safer on the playgrounds. In short, you can prevent some playground injuries from occurring. Whether you are planning your own playground, or bringing your children to a community play center, "planning it safe" is the best way to help your kids enjoy being active when outdoors.

## Safety in Your Own Backyard

### Playground Placement

Planning, building, and maintaining a safe playground in your own backyard or nearby area is no small undertaking, but when done with knowledge and care, your child will enjoy hours of fresh air and opportunities to develop muscles, coordination, and social skills. Your own easily accessible playground is a wonderful convenience and allows you control over its safety. One good resource is the U.S. Consumer Product Safety Commission's *Handbook for Public Playground Safety* (1991), which can provide you with guidelines.

**Playgrounds & Pools**

In planning any playground, give careful consideration to the site. The ideal place is a location away from streets, traffic, and noise. If such a place is not available, a barrier or fence that surrounds the playground is recommended to prevent children from inadvertently running into a street. Consider positioning the playground where you can see it from the house, preferably from a room where you usually are, such as a family room or kitchen, so that you can easily observe what your child is doing. Lush grass, hilly knolls, and plenty of tree shade are also ideal. Ensure easy access to bathrooms, telephones, and drinking water.

Organize your playground into separate areas to prevent injuries caused by different activities and children running between activities. For example, areas where kids are actively swinging or sliding should be separated from more passive or quiet "story-time" areas.

### The Fall Surface

A child who falls on his head from a height of just one foot could sustain a fatal injury. A fall onto concrete or asphalt from only two inches can cause life-threatening head impact injuries. A four-foot fall onto packed earth or grass can also cause serious injury or death, says the American Academy of Pediatrics. Thus it is extremely important to cover the ground under your playground equipment with the proper materials. Sand, shredded cedar wood chips (which should be replaced and maintained regularly), pea gravel, and rubber mats are all currently recommended.

If you're using wood chips or something similar, you need to be selective. Sometimes utility companies or tree services offer free wood chips, but Gerry Slater, president of the Wisconsin-based Playworks, Inc., an outdoor environments company, points out that during summer and peak growing seasons, most of what gets chopped up is branches, which could be hazardous. "You can end up with some pretty long, sharp pieces of branches. Find out exactly what you are getting or tell the supplier that you would like some of it, but that you want something from bigger sections of trees." Such chips are less likely to be sharp enough to pierce the skin. Or you may want to investigate buying higher quality wood chips.

**Playgrounds & Pools**

How much loose-fill is needed? In general, a ground covering of sand or wood chips should be about twelve inches deep under each piece of equipment where falls are likely. And, the cushioning materials should extend six feet out from all sides of the equipment to accommodate a fall. A general rule of thumb: the taller the equipment, the deeper or thicker the surface cushioning and the wider the fall zones. Rake all loose-fill surfacing materials regularly to pull out trash, then fluff it up and replenish it when it tracks out or breaks down.

## Equipment

GENERAL INFORMATION. When buying equipment, carefully consider the ages of your children, or of the children who will use the playground. Decide what features on a play structure are age- and developmentally appropriate for them, suggests Gerry Slater. The National Safety Council (NSC) recommends buying "sturdy equipment that will grow and change as your children become older. Consider modular equipment that can be bought, installed, replaced or upgraded in phases." Always assemble, arrange, and anchor equipment according to manufacturer's specifications. Avoid or securely close open-ended hooks, particularly S-hooks, that can catch a child's clothing and result in strangulation.

Here are some general rules about equipment placement and installation:
1. Allow for ample room between equipment areas and play areas.
2. Be sure you and your installer understand all the safety requirements for each piece of equipment.
3. Playground equipment must be firmly anchored on the ground on a level surface.
4. As cuts from sharp edges account for a good portion of reported injuries, check equipment and wooden fences to make sure they're free of pinch points, splinters, protruding nails, or screws. All corners, metal and wood, should be rounded. All metal edges should be rolled or have a rounded capping. Check for rotor rust periodically.

## Playgrounds & Pools

5. Equipment should not exceed eight feet in height. If you plan to build some of your own equipment with wood, be careful not to buy wood that is saturated with toxic preservatives (such as creosote) that can be harmful to children. Slater recommends being "selective about the lumber you use. Sand all exposed surfaces and preferably use a router or similar machine to round over any of the sharp edges because that seems to be where most of the splintering is and the sharp edges are."

SWING SETS. Kids love swings. For safety's sake, keep swings away from fences, walls, and other equipment. Don't place more than two swings in the same section. "Swings need a wide berth," says the National Association for the Education of Young Children, which recommends extending the fall zone to at least double the length of the entire swing chain and adding two to three extra inches for greater safety. Move support beams out of the swing's range. It's also important to minimize traffic around the swings; give swings a separate area. For example, you don't want kids to run through the swing area on their way to zip down the slide or hang from the jungle gym.

Though you're likely to encounter hard wooden swings in some park areas, if you have a choice at home, select swings made of soft materials such as rubber, plastic, or canvas. If you do decide to hang a tire, be sure it cannot swing within thirty inches of any structure surrounding it. Be sure to wash it thoroughly first.

As far as safety on the swing is concerned, one good rule is simple: only one child per seat. As for babies, the NSC believes the risk of injury is too great for whatever satisfaction a six-month-old baby would get from a swing. There are some home models of infant seats sold, but they should be approved by the Consumer Product Safety Commission for that age group. Infant seats need bars and crotch straps, and an adult must supervise at all times. Be sure that the swing seat provides support on all sides.

Children should be taught to walk well around and behind the person on the swing, never in front. Children can be injured not only falling from, but also by being hit by swings. Routinely check for worn swing hangers and chains; also watch for missing, damaged, or loose swing seats.

SLIDES. It is recommended that slides have a slope of no more than thirty degrees, with four inches in height along both sides of the entire length of the sliding surface. They should also have an extended exit surface parallel to the ground so children can regain their balance and be in an upright posture at the bottom of the slide.

Guardrails or protective barriers should surround a slide. Slater, who is also a certified playground safety inspector, notes: "I think the most significant thing I've seen with some of the homemade structures are railings around raised platforms that are just horizontals [bars]. From our experience, and I think the commercial guidelines support this now, horizontal rails become ladders, so if you have a raised platform at four feet and you put two or three horizontal railings on it, the kids climb up those railings, and you get them up to six feet with nowhere to go. Our position for a long time has been to use vertical rails, more like a barrier."

**Playgrounds & Pools**

When the temperature soars, a metal slide can become as hot as a cooking skillet. Check for hot surfaces on all metal playground equipment—stairs, decks, or slides—before allowing children to play on it. Serious injuries can occur in just seconds, and children suffer second- and third-degree burns to their hands, legs, and buttocks. Younger children are at greater risk because they respond less quickly to a hot surface than older children. Consider using an alternative material, such as plastic or wood, to avoid this problem.

Check for loose footings or missing rungs on slide access platforms. Teach your child to use the ladder to climb up and not to climb the slide itself. Tell the child to wait his turn: only one child should slide down at a time, and children should learn to go down on their seats, not on their stomachs or face first. Infants who cannot sit up on their own should not be on slides. If a child is held by an adult, the adult's weight could cause serious injury to the child. Make sure that objects, debris, or other children are not in the way of a child's safe landing at the bottom of the slide.

SEESAWS. Using a seesaw is not recommended for preschool-aged children. The reason? The child's coordination must be developed enough to control lifting and landing. To balance properly, children sharing the seesaw should be of similar weights. Consider using partially buried car tires or other shock-absorbing material underneath seesaw seats. This will reduce the chance of limbs being crushed between the seat and the ground.

SANDBOXES. Keep sandboxes covered when not in use so animals don't use them as litter boxes. Occasionally clean play box sand by spraying it with water. Adults should supervise the younger set so they don't eat the sand, which could contain all manner of bacteria.

ADDITIONAL THOUGHTS. Make sure you haven't left any stray tools, stakes, or bottles and cans of chemicals lying around. Store barbecue and gardening equipment away from the play area. Cover ponds or holes that may become puddles—and potential drowning hazards—after a rainfall.

## Playground Safety Away from Home

While many playgrounds are being updated, there's still a phenomenal age range of equipment around. As with the home playground, one of the main concerns is the fall surface. Perhaps you remember hanging by your toes from the monkey bars over asphalt, a hard and dangerous surface. When visiting a public playground, check to make sure that wood chips or another material isn't simply thrown down on top of asphalt. Older slides, with open stairways and not much railing around the top, are also dangerous.

Merry-go-rounds may represent a physical hazard to three- to five-year-olds. If they do not have control over the equipment or muscle coordination is not yet developed enough, the fast motion may be dangerous. All children should be aboard before putting the merry-go-round in motion. Be sure hand grips are available. Watch out for the older hexagonal-shaped merry-go-rounds; a corner can come around quickly and clip a child. An adult should supervise.

Children have the uncanny ability to find the smallest and sometimes most dangerous objects in their play areas. Double-check the area for bottles, broken glass, aluminum cans, nails, sharp metal objects, plant or tree branches or sticks, and any other object you deem potentially hazardous. Educate your child never to touch any of these items while away from home.

**Playgrounds & Pools**

# A Public Playground Safety Checklist

Below is the National Safety Council's general checklist for safe playgrounds. If any of your answers are No, work to correct the problem immediately.

|  | YES | NO |
|---|---|---|
| 1. Is the site clean and well maintained? | ☐ | ☐ |
| 2. Can the playground be reached safely by bicycle or on foot (unobstructed pathways, stop signs, warning sign to drivers, or traffic lights)? | ☐ | ☐ |
| 3. Are all areas visible to supervising parents and motoring law enforcement officers? | ☐ | ☐ |
| 4. Do the restrooms have a security-conscious design (for instance, an open design that allows for sight lines under the structure and prevents use as an overnight shelter)? | ☐ | ☐ |
| 5. Is the barrier fencing (installed to prevent children from running into the street) in good condition, with no gap three inches or greater between the fence and the surfacing? | ☐ | ☐ |
| 6. Are automobile parking and driving areas separated from pedestrian and waiting zones by guard rails, fences, or curbing? | ☐ | ☐ |
| 7. Are safety signs both graphic and written? | | |
| 8. Is the use of pesticides/herbicides avoided in play areas? | ☐ | ☐ |
| 9. Is the play area free of vandalism? Does the park discourage vandalism with special lighting and good visibility? | ☐ | ☐ |
| 10. Are trees free from cracked limbs or pointed snags? | ☐ | ☐ |

For more information, or to report faulty playground equipment, contact your local parks and recreation department, the Consumer Federation of America, or the Consumer Product Safety Commission.

*Used per permission of the National Safety Council.*

**Playgrounds & Pools**

## Supervision Away from Home

One key ingredient for child safety is watching children carefully. Always accompany them to the local playground, or be sure a child-care provider is there to supervise. Save the hottest bestseller, in-depth conversations, and other activities for another time, because children can be expected to (and will) use equipment in unintended and unanticipated ways.

Parents and caregivers need to be aware of both a child's age and his abilities. A two- or three-year-old might have the motor skills to climb up a very high slide, but can he handle it when he gets to the top? Probably not. Similarly, children under three should be held by a parent or caregiver on the swing set or merry-go-round. According to California pediatrician Dr. Vivian Hernandez, "A two- or three-year-old doesn't necessarily understand the idea that swings are something you have to stop. A child just decides that he wants off and he just jumps." And younger children often imitate older children. "An older child might jump on the merry-go-round as it's going really fast. A younger child might not fare as well." Knowing what children are capable of understanding at a given age is of critical importance.

**Playgrounds & Pools**

## Treating Head Injuries

What do you do if your child does take a tumble and lands on his head, or takes any serious fall? "Most kids with minor head injuries get up, they cry, they're fine, and there's really not much else you need to do for them," says Dr. Mark Mannenbach, assistant professor of Pediatrics at the Medical College of Wisconsin and full-time emergency room physician. "They need to be observed, and if certain symptoms show up, parents should seek medical care by talking to their doctor at once and telling him or her what's happening or if they don't have ongoing medical care by going to the emergency room."

Most children with minor head injuries will get better quickly. However, if your child is at home after an injury, you should watch him carefully for these symptoms in the next forty-eight hours:

1. Excessive drowsiness. Your child may be sleepy and tired after a head injury. However, you should be able to wake him as you would normally from a deep sleep.
2. Incessant vomiting. Sometimes a child may vomit one or two times after a head injury. However, the vomiting should not continue or start again later. Do not give your child anything to eat for about two hours after a head injury. Begin by giving your child sips of liquids. If he doesn't vomit after the liquids, start regular foods.
3. Unsteady balance or movement. Watch your child sit, walk, and move. Be sure that your child moves equally on the right and left sides of his body.
4. Headache. Many children complain of a headache after a head injury. The headache should not get worse.
5. Confusion, disorientation, or other changes in behavior.
6. Seizures or convulsions. If your child should have a seizure, do not panic. Place him on one side where he cannot fall and be sure that he is breathing freely. Call your child's doctor or go to the emergency room immediately.

Maintaining a safe public playground environment for your child may seem to be a daunting task. However, preventative tactics can help save a child from injury or even save his life.

# Pool Safety

Children of all ages love to splash about in water in anything from a bathtub to a backyard pool, a river, or a lake, and if you're lucky enough, the ocean, too. And everyone enjoys a break from scorching temperatures on hot summer days. However, attention to water safety is crucial; it's shocking how quickly a drowning can occur. The Consumer Product Safety Commission reports that there are 300 drowning deaths yearly, and 2,350 injuries treated in emergency rooms.

Statistics from the National Safe Kids Campaign (NSKC) show that drowning is the third leading cause of accidental death among children ages fourteen and under. And the American Academy of Pediatrics has said that drowning is the second leading cause of death nationally among children ages one through four. Many children die within a few feet of safety. Babies are especially at risk. A baby can drown in just an inch of water in the time it takes to check on dinner or answer the phone. Children drown when their faces are submerged. A child's natural responses are to stop breathing, panic, or hold his breath. When the child does take a breath, he may take in water, suffocate, and drown.

Preschoolers are more than twice as likely as older children to drown, and obviously, where there's more water, chances of drowning increase. For example, the NSKC points out that in California, Arizona, and Florida—which are either close to bodies of water or are places where many people own pools—drowning is the leading cause of injury and death among preschoolers.

According to the NSKC, "Swimming pools present the greatest water hazard to toddlers (accounting for 90 percent of drowning deaths among children ages 1–3)." Often a child will be resuscitated but may be left with permanent brain damage. The NSKC estimates medical costs for near-drownings at $2,000 for each child who recovers quickly and $80,000 for each child who sustains permanent brain damage. Total direct care costs for children who suffer severe, permanent disability reach $200 million annually.

## Safety in the Home Pool

### Adult Supervision

According to the NSKC, more than half of preschool drownings occur in the home pool and another third happen at others' homes. With more than 6.5 million residential swimming pools in the United States today (and according to the National Safety Council, the number is growing), knowing how to maintain a safe pool environment is a must.

Here's a heartbreaking, but all too common scenario: A two-year-old is on the patio, which opens out onto the pool. The phone rings; Mom runs inside. She's not gone two minutes; she comes back, and can't find the toddler. Where is he? She looks on the patio, throughout the house. Finally, it dawns on her: in the pool. There she finds him, face down, near death.

**Playgrounds & Pools**

Preventable? In most cases, yes. Poolside supervision is essential for youngsters at all times. Don't leave, not even for a minute. Watch them diligently. Make sure an adult capable of rescuing and resuscitating a child is always present.

Take a class in cardiopulmonary resuscitation (CPR) and urge others to do so; you could save your child's life. Dr. Mannenbach notes that the sooner you resuscitate a child after drowning, the more likely he is to survive. "Don't just wait for the paramedics. That's too late. Parents who have pools should know CPR; older kids in the house should know CPR; babysitters should know CPR," he urges. (See Chapter 2 for instructions on CPR and check with your local chapter of the American Red Cross, community center, or doctor to find out how you can learn CPR.)

### Children's Swimming Lessons

Learning to swim provides a valuable skill and lifelong pleasure to children. It's important to show your child how much fun the water can be—and swimming is a wonderful exercise, not to mention a superb way to cool off—while at the same time giving him a healthy respect for the water. The American Academy of Pediatrics does not recommend lessons for children younger than four (although the right age will vary from one child to another), as they may swallow too much water. Very young children may develop water intoxication resulting in shock, convulsions, even death. Enroll your child at four years of age in swimming lessons at the park district, YMCA/YWCA, American Red Cross, camp, or health club. But swimming lessons do not make your child "drown proof." And even if a child has had a swimming lesson, he may panic if he falls into the pool, so never leave him alone.

### Poolside Precautions and Rules

1. "In above-ground pools, always flip up the pool ladders," says pool installer Joseph Esser. "With that one act you make sure nobody can easily get into the pool."
2. The National Safety Council recommends keeping a strong, lightweight pole (ten to twelve feet long) and a ring buoy with line attached near the pool and easily accessible.

3. Immediate access to a phone plus any emergency numbers should be available at all times.
4. Check to be sure that drain grates are not broken, as suction from the drain may disable a child and could even cause death.
5. Keep the pool area cleared of toys; if a child reaches for a toy, he may fall in the water.
6. Never allow electrical appliances near the water.
7. Post signs prohibiting diving into above-ground pools and designating diving areas (if available) in in-ground pools.
8. Do not permit glassware on the deck; only paper and plastic plates and cups should be used.
9. Keep the pool deck area free of objects that can trip people. (Unintentional water entry is responsible for more than 50 percent of all drownings.)
10. Pool depths should be marked or posted clearly. Use a safety line to designate shallow and deep-water areas.
11. Water quality (ph and chlorine levels) should be maintained carefully, according to recommended standards. Pool chemicals should be stored away from the kids' reach.
12. The pool's electrical equipment must be properly cared for.
13. Limit the number of people who can be in the pool at any one time.
14. Establish pool rules early on and stick to them. Make sure you post them and explain them clearly to both your children and guests. Some good pool rules might be:
    - Never swim alone. Children must always be accompanied by an adult who can swim.
    - Dive in permitted areas only.
    - No running, pushing, or roughhousing.
    - No electric devices on the pool deck.
    - No swimming at night and never during thunderstorms.
    - Always cover the pool and latch the gate before leaving.
15. *Never* leave the gate leading to the pool area unlocked.

### Pool Fences and Gates

One of the biggest concerns about pool safety has to do with who enters the pool area. Many children drown when they wander out of the house and fall into a pool that is not enclosed. All swimming pools should be surrounded by a fence or another barrier at least four feet in height with a self-closing, self-latching gate. Some communities request that it be higher, so check with your municipality. Be sure there are no pieces of furniture or other equipment that could aid your child or a neighbor's in "hopping" the fence. Don't rely on the side of the house to act as a wall, especially if there is an adjacent window or door.

The Consumer Product Safety Commission says that a fence and a gate can cost about $350 per linear foot. If the fence perimeter is 300 feet, the price could be about $1,050.

### Pool Covers

In addition to fences, pool covers help keep kids out of the pool when you're not around. There are several types available, including automatic pool covers. Check to see that rainwater or snow doesn't collect on top of the cover and present a drowning hazard.

Always remove pool covers completely before allowing anyone to swim. Be sure to remove any solar blankets that you use to warm the pool. A pool cover should not be considered a substitute for a fence between the house and the pool. Be aware that even when a pool is covered, a child may attempt to walk out on the cover and fall through.

### Pool Alarms

Consider installing a gate alarm that is triggered when someone opens the pool gate. Other alarms include movement-sensitive devices. Again, don't rely on a pool alarm to alert you that someone's in the pool. Nothing can take the place of adequate fencing.

### Flotation Devices

Never rely on floating toys or water wings to help keep your child from drowning. "One of the worst things people can do with their kids is use mini-inner tubes to help a baby float," says Esser.

The baby could easily float over to the deep end and flip over, or become dislodged, and drown. Even older children are at risk. "If kids can't swim, floating lounge 'chairs' give them a false sense of security." The only reliable flotation device is the life vest or life jacket approved by the U.S. Coast Guard. (See Chapter 6 for more information.)

### Kiddie Pools

"Little plastic pools filled with water are a hazard; there is no way to kid-proof them," says Esser. Never leave a child alone in a wading pool. Always empty and store kiddie wading pools after each use.

### Diving Boards and Slides

The National Safety Council notes: "Swimming accidents cause hundreds of spinal injuries each year, many resulting in permanent paralysis for the victim.... The most serious injuries, about 95 percent, result from dives into water less than five feet deep." Injuries are the result of improper diving: diving headfirst, or diving into objects, barriers, or even other swimmers. According to Esser,

"A diving board puts you four, five feet up in the air. The extra lift is like a slingshot. It could even fling you to the shallow end."

Check for proper water depth in your pool. Most home swimming pools do not have adequate space and depth of water to have a diving board. Rules about when and where to use a slide or to dive off the pool's side or a diving board can mean life or death. Children often dive and slide into water without first knowing the water depth, which can result in a life-changing head or neck injury. Always check the water depth before diving or sliding. Establish good rules about using the slide: (1) one child at a time; (2) go down on your seat; (3) always wait for your turn.

## Swimming in Public Pools and Other Bodies of Water

Away from home, basic pool rules still apply. There should always be adult supervision (by someone capable of rescuing and resuscitating a child), and each child should always swim with a buddy, no matter what the age or swimming ability.

Check out the lifeguarding facilities first. Keep an eye on your children to be sure that they don't get into a depth they can't handle.

Don't let young children and children who can't swim use inflatable toys or mattresses in water that is above the waist.

In addition, the National Safety Council provides these suggestions:

1. Seek swimming instruction from a qualified instructor for you and your children. Many water-related accidents occur when people are mistakenly confident about their swimming ability.
2. Never swim alone; always use the buddy system. Confine water activity, when possible, to areas supervised by lifeguards.
3. Children must be supervised constantly by a responsible adult whenever they are in or around water.

## Playgrounds & Pools

4. Obey posted safety rules.
5. Know and do not try to exceed your swimming limitations. Kids love to imitate, and daredevil parents in pools set dangerous examples.
6. Avoid swiftly moving water, especially rivers or unknown waters. If caught in a current, swim in the same direction as the current and angle toward the shore until you reach safety.
7. Stay out of the water during thunderstorms and other extreme weather conditions. If lightning starts, get out of (or off) the water (and any form of water skis) and seek shelter away from metal objects, large trees, and open areas.
8. Know exactly how capable you are of rescuing a swimmer. Only experienced, properly trained swimmers should themselves attempt to rescue someone in trouble.
9. Learn and practice the basic lifesaving techniques, including first aid and cardiopulmonary resuscitation. Know how to throw a line or ring buoy to a swimmer in trouble. In an emergency, you can use anything that floats.
10. If you are a poor swimmer, do not rely on inner tubes or other inflatable objects for protection. The only reliable device is a personal flotation device (PFD), also called a life jacket, approved by the U.S. Coast Guard. PFDs should be worn at all times. Nonswimmers should be supervised and should wear comfortable, properly fitting life vests when in or near the water.
11. Always check water depth before diving. Enter feet first if you are not sure of the depth. Always enter the water with your arms extended firmly over the head and keep your hands together to protect your head.
12. Avoid the use of alcohol or other drugs when you are around water. (This should go without saying.)
13. Do not permit children to walk or play on frozen ponds, lakes, or other bodies of water during winter months.

**Playgrounds & Pools**

## What to Do in Case of Submersion or Drowning

What should you do if you see a child, unmoving and face down in the water? Remove the unconscious child from the water immediately and begin CPR. If more than one person is present, send the other to call 911 for emergency medical help, and continue CPR until help arrives or until the child is breathing. If the child vomits, choking can be avoided by turning his head to one side. If you think the child has suffered head or neck injuries, try to immobilize these areas. If the child is revived before help arrives, be sure a complete exam is given to check for respiratory or nervous system damage.

*The Children's Emergency Handbook* (1993) issued by Edward Hospital, Naperville, Illinois, offers excellent instructions in case a drowning accident should occur:

- Call for emergency medical attention.
- Keep child's neck immobilized as you remove him from the water.
- Restore breathing and circulation first.
- If the child is unconscious or you suspect neck injuries, *do not bend or turn neck* while restoring breathing.
- Give artificial respiration if the child is not breathing but has a pulse. Breathe forcefully enough to blow air through water in the airway. *Do not* try to empty water from child's lungs.
- *Do not give up.* Continue CPR until the child is revived, until medical help arrives, or until exhaustion stops you.

**Symptoms:** (One or all may be present.)
unconsciousness
no visible or audible breath
no pulse
blue skin color
lips, tongue and nail bed pale

**Playgrounds & Pools**

### Immediate Treatment at Home:

1. Lie child on flat surface, or begin first aid in the water.
2. Check ABCs (Airway, Breathing, Circulation). This means you have to clear the airway, restore breathing, optimally by mouth-to-mouth resuscitation, and restore circulation, optimally by external cardiac compression/CPR.
3. Open airway and start mouth-to-mouth resuscitation.
4. Check pulse and begin full CPR if necessary to restore circulation.
5. When breathing and pulse have been restored, treat for shock.
6. Have child lie on his side to allow water to drain out of the mouth.
7. Restore child's body heat by removing wet clothing and covering with warm blankets.
8. *Do not give up* if breathing and pulse are not restored. Continue CPR until help arrives.

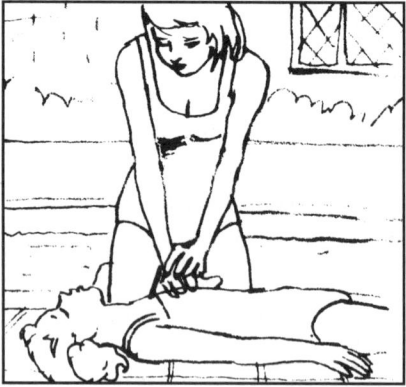

From *The Children's Emergency Handbook*, ©1993 Edward Hospital, Naperville, Illinois.

What else can you do? First, take time to learn everything you can about water safety. Then learn how to educate your kids properly. A healthy respect for water can lead to many hours of fun for you and your family.

**Playgrounds & Pools**

# Very *Important* Tips

**PLAYGROUND SAFETY**
The American Academy of Pediatrics recommends:
1. Supervise young children using playground equipment to prevent shoving, pushing, or fighting.
2. The surface under playground equipment should be energy absorbent, such as rubber, sand, wood chips, shredded cedar, or bark. Preferably, there is pea gravel available that is better than sawdust or wood chips. The latter tend to compress and lose their absorbent characteristics.
3. Swing seats should be made of something soft, not wood or metal.
4. Instruct your child not to twist swings, push empty seats, or walk in front of moving swings.
5. Put home playground equipment together correctly. It should sit on a level surface and be anchored firmly to the ground.
6. Cap all screws and bolts. Check for loose nuts and bolts periodically.
7. Do not buy equipment with S-hooks, sharp edges, or five- to ten-inch rings. A child's head may get caught in rings that size.
8. Install playground equipment at least six feet from fences or walls.
9. Check equipment such as slides for hot metal surfaces that might cause burns.

**POOL SAFETY**
1. Never leave your child alone in or near a pool, even for a minute.
2. Pool fencing is an important preventative measure. Be sure that the fence surrounds the pool on all sides and that the gate is self-latching, with the lock out of your child's reach. Be sure, too, that the gate is always locked.
3. Install a gate alarm or other sensitive alarm in the pool.
4. Use a pool cover when pool is not in use. (A motorized pool cover operated by a switch that meets the standards of the American Society for Testing

**Playgrounds & Pools**

# Very Important Tips

and Materials adds to the protection of your child, says the American Academy of Pediatrics.) Always remove cover completely before using the pool.

5. Learn CPR and know how to get emergency help.

6. Teach safety precautions at an early age. Tell your small child he always needs adult supervision. Advise an older child to swim with a friend, never alone.

7. Mark pool depths clearly.

8. Establish pool rules, post them, and stick to them.

9. Always drain kiddie wading pools. Turn the pool over or store when not in use.

10. A child too young to swim on his own should wear an approved life vest when playing around any water or at the beach.

11. When several adults are watching children, there is no guarantee that they won't all stop watching at the same time. To avoid this, assign one person at a time to do nothing but watch.

# Chapter 9

# "Stranger Danger": The Child Stands Alone

CRIME PREVENTION BEGINS AT HOME. While no parent wants to scare a child when it comes to discussing what many schools and police departments call *stranger danger*, children and parents must communicate on this issue.

Scare tactics are one thing; street savvy is another. It no longer matters whether you live in a big city, a tiny hamlet, or a mid-sized town. Tragically, there are people everywhere who do not respect the rights of others, not to mention the rights of children. And try as parents might to refute their existence, denial is a foolish way to tackle the problem. Sad as it is to risk destroying the innocence of children, these times necessitate doing precisely that.

**Stranger Danger**

Julia Cartwright, public affairs spokesperson for the National Center for Missing and Exploited Children (NCMEC) based in Arlington, Virginia, cites statistics contained in a NCMEC study by Daniel D. Broughton, M.D., and Eric E. Allen, J.D.

- The American Humane Association estimates 100,000 to 500,000 cases of child sexual abuse per year.
- ChildHelp USA estimates that one in three girls and one in six boys will be sexually abused or victimized before age eighteen.
- The National Committee for Prevention of Child Abuse reported that there were 2.4 million child abuse reports in 1989, of which 16 percent—more than 380,000 cases—involved sexual abuse.
- Fifty-four percent of sexually abused children are victims before age seven, 84 percent before age twelve. Most victimization occurs between the ages of ten and twelve.
- While most abuse cases occur in the home, there is also a major problem outside the home. The *FBI Law Enforcement Bulletin* reports that "like rape, child molestation is one of the most underreported crimes, only 1 to 10 percent are ever disclosed."
- The rape rate for girls under seventeen is four times the adult rate.
- The U.S. Department of Justice's *National Incidence Studies of Missing, Abducted, Runaway, and Thrownaway Children* (NISMART) found that as many as 114,600 children reported attempted abductions by nonfamily members in 1988. There were an additional 3,200 to 4,600 successful abductions reported to police, though the researchers noted that the estimate is almost certainly understated due to the low likelihood of reporting.
- The Justice Department found that two-thirds of the cases of nonfamily abductions involve the taking of a child for a relatively short period of time for sexual purposes. For a variety of reasons, these cases are rarely reported:
  The child is the only witness
  The child is frightened, embarrassed, or humiliated

**Stranger Danger**

The child has been threatened or intimidated
The child feels no one will believe him or her.

From *A Lesson for Life* by Daniel D. Broughton, M.D., and Ernest E. Allen, J.D. Arlington, VA: National Center for Missing and Exploited Children, 1992, pp 1–2.

Every normal parent will loathe reading these frightening statistics. Why must they be aware of these unhappy facts? In a changing world, where dangers seem to grow more pronounced daily, where headlines may frighten parents, not to mention their children, reason and its partner—a certain amount of healthy apprehension—walk a narrow tightrope. Today, children must not only be warned, but their fears must be discussed rationally.

The Polly Klaas Foundation, based about fifty miles north of San Francisco in the town of Petaluma, California, was originally established to locate twelve-year-old Polly Klaas, who was kidnapped in 1993. According to Dr. Gary J. Kinley, director of the foundation, "When Polly's body was discovered, a decision was made that children in this country, in general, are at risk, and we decided to continue the work of the foundation but to really focus on child safety. The mission of the organization is to make America safe, in the broader sense, for children."

The foundation works in three areas:
1. Responsively. Working with parents, friends, and law enforcement agencies, the foundation aims to bring missing children home. It has assisted in searches for more than 230 missing and abducted children. Foundation volunteers designed, printed, and assisted in the distribution of flyers for thirty-five of these search efforts, and all but four have been returned safely.
2. Legislatively. For example, the foundation lobbied for the passage of California's "Polly Klaas Memorial Habitual Offenders Bill," which will strengthen sentencing requirements for serious and violent felons.
3. Educationally. The foundation has just funded a grant for Sonoma County schools to provide training and a

**Stranger Danger**

curriculum called *Kids and Company*. It is produced by the Adam Walsh Children's Fund, with materials and concepts that can be taken into the classroom, grades kindergarten through six. (See page 250 for more information on this program.)

Dr. Kinley is grateful for the considerable media attention that the Polly Klaas Foundation has received because he feels the foundation's message must be continually reinforced: "I have a ten-year-old son. For years, his mother and I have talked about how to be safe, though I don't think we'd said anything about it for the past year and a half. Well, recently he was in a situation where he could have been at risk. And what it made us realize was that you have to keep talking about it. It isn't something you say to your kids once or twice."

Since the murder of Polly Klaas, fifteen states (bringing the total to forty) have adopted sex-offender registries to help law enforcement and community members know where a paroled sex offender is living. As well, the foundation uses computers aggressively to transmit images of missing children across the country, becoming a model for similar search efforts. The foundation received even more attention when actress Winona Ryder, who hails from Petaluma, added her support, both financially and emotionally, wishing to dedicate the film *Little Women* to Polly Klaas.

## What Is a Stranger?

Most adults over forty grew up hearing, "Don't talk to strangers, don't take candy from strangers, don't go anywhere with strangers." But many believe those admonitions don't work any more because children don't understand the meaning of the word *stranger*.

In 1992, the National Center for Missing and Exploited Children commissioned a study called *A Lesson for Life*. The study quotes British psychologist Dr. David Warden: "No matter how intelligent the child, he or she does not see the world through skeptical adult eyes. . . . children live very much in the present. They can't foresee someone's actions or judge their intentions, certainly not at primary school age. They have a very weak understanding of motives, they simply take someone at face value. The concept of stranger danger is difficult, because it clashes with the social constraints on children to be polite to adults. Research suggests that children don't really know what a stranger is. They feel that once someone tells his name, he ceases to be a stranger." (Broughton and Allen, 1992, p. 2)

When parents and their children begin to talk about the problem, they might start with the fact that some bad guys don't look like bad guys. The evil queen in *Snow White,* for instance, *looks* evil. No problem with her. But what about people who don't look threatening? How do you teach your child to watch out for them?

# Low-Risk vs. High-Risk Adults

As Dr. Gary Kinley says, children can't simply be expected to be able to judge who might endanger them "because sometimes strangers are the people that we have to go to, and sometimes strangers are the people who may abuse us or put us at risk. What we need to talk about with children is, instead of strangers, the whole concept of 'low-risk adults.' Generally, Mom and Dad are low-risk people we can trust, in most cases. I have to qualify that because many children are abused by their parents.

"Maybe Grandma or Grandpa fall into that category. Maybe their school teacher or school principal. It will vary for every single child. In all probability, a police officer is a low-risk adult. Or, as someone pointed out to me, a pregnant woman with another child is probably a low-risk adult. We need to teach children that if indeed they find themselves in a situation where they need help that they need to go to a low-risk adult.

"If someone approaches a child and offers him something, it's okay to say no. And he should leave and tell a trusted adult. We have to help children identify who those trusted adults are and have them realize that just because an individual is an adult, they don't have to do what that adult says."

**Stranger Danger**

**Low-Risk Adult**     **High-Risk Adult**

Parents need to be comfortable with setting limits, and they must encourage children to do so as well. Dr. Kinley gives as an example the difficult-to-handle circumstance of a grandparent attempting to kiss a child, and having that child say no. Grandpa has to realize that the child is setting limits. It's a hard one for all who love children, but the ultimate goal is to help children develop skills to keep themselves safe. Does this mean that a rarely seen out-of-town grandpa is a stranger? Are Uncle Joe or Cousin Sue trusted adults? They are, if you trust them and your child has seen your trust in those people and also feels comfortable with them.

But no matter how familiar the child is with the person you think is a low risk, it's a good idea to test your child's reaction. Does your child seem to feel uncomfortable or fearful of any adult he knows? If so, find out why. Talk with your child. Then, if you hear, "He touched me—here," or, "He said this to me. . . ," you know what to do.

A younger child may not wish to talk to you about such things, but if you sense something wrong when you observe your child's behavior around the person in question, intercede if you suspect a problem. *Don't* ask, "Did Uncle Tim touch you or hurt you?" *Do* ask, "Do you feel uncomfortable around Uncle Tim?"

## Stranger Danger

Of course, sometimes a completely innocent situation can create an entirely different problem. Let's go back to the case of the out-of-town grandfather who comes to visit. Dad, who is not only a good father but a good son, says, "Give Grandpa a goodnight kiss." The child says no, and Dad says he must. Dad is right in this case, because Grandpa really is a good man and loves the child, and Dad wants the child to show the love he should feel. So the child accedes to Dad's and Grandpa's request. If the child soon after comes to be with a "stranger" who *isn't* a good guy, and the latter demands that the child do this or that, what are we to think if the child does so? After all, that is what Dad taught him to do, even against his wishes.

Discuss with your preteen the case of an older child who goes to a friend's house. The friend's father tells her that her friend isn't there yet and asks her to wait. What should she do if, while she is waiting, the father touches her hair and her back? The child recognizes that something is wrong with this touching. The best advice is: "Say that you don't feel well and go home. Trust your instincts. If you feel that something is wrong, act on what you feel and tell someone."

It is not necessary to go into detail with little children about such problems; they need only know that some people in the world do not treat children right, and that it is not only strangers who might "bother" them. As is clear, *stranger danger* can be a misnomer, because children may be in danger from someone they already know. However, many protection agencies, including police departments throughout the country that are sophisticated enough to concur with the NCMEC, still use the terms *stranger* and *stranger danger*, even though they are aware of their inaccuracy. A better description has yet to be found. So, bearing all of the above in mind, for clarity's sake, *stranger danger* will be used throughout this chapter to describe the threat from people known *and* unknown. However, it's a good idea to apply the word *stranger* interchangeably with other terms such as *high-risk adult* or *bad guy*. Of course, the bad guy could be a woman, as well as a man.

**Stranger Danger**

# Programs That Make Children "Stranger Aware"

## McGruff, the Crime Dog

Many states with criminal justice information authorities use McGruff, the Crime Dog, to help older children and teens avoid becoming "fund-raisers for crooks." McGruff encourages boys to carry a wallet safely in a specific pants pocket or coat breast pocket and girls to carry a purse close to the body. Kids who walk confidently, who are alert and mindful of their packages, learn to shop in safety. McGruff teaches younger kids to tell a cashier if they're lost or separated from their parents at a store or in a mall, instead of going to the parking lot to look for the parents or their car.

Other excellent tips for children from McGruff include:

1. When returning home, the child should look for signs of a possible break-in, such as a broken window or broken screen, a door left ajar, or a ladder placed against an upstairs window. If she suspects a break-in, the worst thing to do is enter the house, and the best thing to do is go to a neighbor's home and dial 911.
2. If she's being followed, she shouldn't go home. She should go to a safe place like a store, the school, or "the nearest McGruff house" (a safe place in the neighborhood).
3. At home, she should know how to work door and window locks, and lock the door after entering. She should check in with parents (she should know how to reach them at work) or a trusted neighbor. She should never open the door for anyone she doesn't know, and she should never tell anyone who comes to the door or calls on the phone that she's home alone. If someone is at the door, without opening it, she should tell them, "My parents can't come to the door right now. Please come back later."
4. She should always learn how to use both home and public phones to make local, long distance, and emergency calls. She should always know her complete address—city, state,

# Stranger Danger

phone number, and area code—by heart. She should learn emergency numbers (police department, fire department, doctor, or 0 for operator).
5. If anything happens to her while she's alone that makes her feel uncomfortable, she should tell an adult she trusts. Every time.

## Play It Safe

Another fine contribution to the field is *Play It Safe*, an extraordinarily helpful booklet originally produced through the efforts of Sheriff Ralph Froelich of Union County, New Jersey, and now distributed as a public service through the B'Nai B'rith Commission of Community Volunteer Services, based in Washington, D.C. Through role-playing exercises and guided discussions, this twenty-five-page child safety guide helps teachers, parents, and all adult caregivers instruct kids on being cautious by encouraging youngsters to develop their own sense of safety awareness without terrifying them. Topics include "Who Is a Stranger?" "What you Should Know About Child Molesters," and "Trust Your Feelings." One theme focuses on teaching kids it's okay to say no to an adult (what to do "If You Feel Like Something Is Wrong"). Particularly interesting are the exercises that parents can do with their kids. Here's one of them, titled "Alone in the Car":

Role #1: A stranger (Mom plays this part.)
Role #2: You (The child plays this part.)
Scene: Your Mom leaves you alone in the car for a few minutes while she runs into the store. A woman knocks on the window and says your mom wants you to come into the store. The woman tries really hard to get you to get out of the car and come with her. What do you say and do?

The book encourages everyone to act out the scene and then sit down and discuss what happened, using the questions and points as a guide. The answers aren't given right away; parents should guide the discussion so that kids come up with their own answers in their own words, after thinking the situation through.

**Stranger Danger**

The questions to be considered here are: (1) "What else could the woman say to trick you into getting out of the car?" and (2) "Why should parents never leave little kids alone in the car?" The points to be made are: (1) "If you're in the car alone, even if only for a few seconds, lock the doors and roll up the windows; (2) If you need to get attention, honk the horn and keep honking it; (3) Mom (Dad) would never send a stranger to get you; (4) Women as well as men sometimes try to trick children."

Another interesting exercise is "When You're Mad at Mom or Dad."

Role #1: An adult you know—a teacher, a coach, or someone from your church

Role #2: You (the child).

Scene: You've just had a fight with your mom and dad and you're mad at them. You're talking to an adult about it. He offers to take you to the movies and then lets you come to his house to stay for a while. He tells you your mom and dad don't love you any more and don't want you to live with them any more. What do you say and do?

Question: "Where else could the adult offer to take you?"

Points:

(1) We *all* get mad at other people sometimes. That doesn't mean we don't love them. Make a list out loud of the times you remember being mad at somebody; (2) Mom (Dad) would never want you to live anywhere else; (3) The adult is trying to trick you, so tell Mom (Dad) what the adult said to you.

The booklet concludes with ideas on "What Do I Do If Someone Is Missing?" and "What Is My Prevention Plan?"

## The Polly Klaas Foundation

One tool parents have in the fight to keep their children safe is communication. The more children know, the safer they'll be. To that end, the Polly Klaas Foundation has published *8 Rules for Safety,* which you should share with your kids:

1. Before going anywhere, your child should always check with you or the person in charge to tell where he is going, how he will get there, who will be going with him, and when he'll be back.
2. He should check with you for permission before getting in a car or leaving with anyone, even someone you know. He should check with you before changing plans or accepting money or gifts.
3. It is safer for him to be with other people when going places or playing outside. He should always use the "buddy system."
4. He should say NO! if someone tries to touch him in ways that make him feel frightened, uncomfortable, or confused. Then he should go and tell a grown-up he trusts what happened.
5. He should know that it is not his fault if someone touches him in a way that is not okay. He doesn't have to keep secrets about those touches.
6. He should trust his feelings and talk to grown-ups about problems that are too big for him to handle on his own. A lot of people care about him and will listen and believe him. He is not alone.
7. It is never too late to ask for help. He should keep asking until he gets the help he needs.
8. He is a special person and deserves to feel safe. His rules are:
   - Check first.
   - Use the buddy system.
   - Say no, then go and tell.
   - Listen to your feelings, and talk with grown-ups you trust about your problems and concerns.

**Stranger Danger**

The former Adam Walsh Center, now a branch of the National Center for Missing and Exploited Children, publishes the *Kids and Company* program specifically for grades five and six, which gives parents practical suggestions for helping kids avoid dangerous situations. *Kids* contains three basic premises:

- Children should always check with their parents before going anywhere.
- "No! Run! Tell!" If a suspicious adult, someone you know or don't know, attempts to engage a child, he should say no, leave the area, and tell a trusted adult.
- Children should use the buddy system, so that they will not go anywhere alone.

In addition, the program teaches these rules:
1. Use Your Brain. Do your kids know how to make safe decisions and avoid dangerous situations? Do they know what to do when in a dangerous situation? Do they know how to choose the best helpers?
2. Train Your Body. Do they know how to use eye contact, effective facial expressions, and an assertive tone of voice, and how to avoid a potentially dangerous situation?
3. Trust Your Feelings. Do they know how to recognize confusing or uncomfortable feelings, and what to do when they have those feelings?
4. Remember Your Friends. Do they realize they are not alone? Can they identify people they can trust? Do they know how to access help when confused or frightened or in trouble?

Used with permission from the Polly Klaas Foundation.

# Keeping Your Kids Safe Away from Home

With all the help parents are getting in school from McGruff, *Play It Safe,* and, perhaps, local community programs, is there anything more you can do to keep your kids safe? The answer is yes, of course. Here are some ways to do just that.

## Stranger Danger

### Bolstering Self-Esteem

Self-esteem plays an important role in keeping children safe. A child who feels good about himself is less likely to be open to the advances of a stranger or a high-risk adult. For parents, from the day a child enters their lives, strong "yes messages" should be sent: "Yes, I love you," "Yes, you're an important person," "Yes, you're valuable."

That's not to say parents shouldn't say no to children; they have to set limits. But very strong yes messages build a child's self-esteem and position that child so that a stranger who says, "Aren't you a pretty child," or, "Gee, I'd like to give you this," is not going to have an unfair advantage over that child. The child doesn't need to seek that kind of gratification from strangers because he already has a strong sense of his own worth.

### Knowing the Basics

If you and your child become separated in a public place, he will need to be able to tell someone—preferably a police officer—some basic information. Be sure your child knows his first and last name, a parent's name, your complete address (not just the apartment building, but the number of the apartment), and your telephone number. This will give him confidence when speaking, and it will help reunite the two of you more quickly.

### Giving the Password

Just as you issue your "don't talk to strangers" directives, circumstances force you to confuse the issue. Let's say, for example, you have a meeting and you can't pick up your son from school, as promised, so you must send a co-worker to do it. Your child knows you work with a woman named Joan, but he's never seen her before. Should he get in the car? He (thank goodness) thinks not.

You could send an item of yours with Joan that your son can identify easily and that might reassure him. Better yet, prepare in advance for such an emergency. Decide, with your child, on a password any stranger sent to pick him up (or approach him in any way) must use.

**Stranger Danger**

Choose two words that don't go together, as *big mouse* or *little lion* do. Colors and animals are always easy to remember: *green cat, pink bear,* and the like. One way young children learn is by repetition. Once everyone in the family has learned the words, test your child every so often over a period of months by using the password (often for fun).

Bill: Mom, can I go over to David's house?
Mom: Sure, if you tell me the password.
Bill: What password? Oh! Green cat.
Mom: That's it. Now you can go.

Tell your son what will happen if you ever have to send your co-worker to pick him up: Joan pulls up in the car, she will say, "Mom says to tell you 'Green cat,' and all is well."

## Establishing a Landmark

Whether your child is a city child, accustomed to blocks crowded with stores and businesses, or a country child, who passes only farm gates and trees on the way home, choosing a *landmark* is important. Drive with your child between school and home, and choose a tree or sign that marks the halfway point. Then tell your child that if he's approached before the landmark on his way home from school, run back toward school like a deer. If he has gone beyond the landmark, run in the direction of home.

Reverse the sequence on the way to school, or your child can head for a lighted or populated area. In the city, a child is wise to duck into a store or a neighbor's house. Wave or call out, as if to a friend. Tell your child never to run into a home that's empty; be sure lights are on, and if there are no people there, keep on running.

## Combating Older and Bigger Aggressors

Go over some moves your child might make if he is approached by bigger kids who frighten him. If he can run fast, that's always best. Even a big bruiser will be momentarily stunned if the child throws his books and bags at him and runs away fast.

**Stranger Danger**

Acting weak can make your child seem like an easy mark; at the opposite end of the spectrum, hostility will cause anger and fail, too. Being clever and talking might help: reasonably explaining he hasn't any money on him ("Sorry, my dad just got laid off," or, "Sorry, my folks are in the hospital, but you can have this candy bar") may persuade the assailant to move on. These suggestions are, of course, not guaranteed.

## Providing Children with Identification Cards

Some parents, particularly those who live in urban areas, investigate the idea of identification cards for their children to carry, just as adults carry driver's licenses. The laminated cards offer photo and fingerprint identification, and also contain annually updated information: blood type, address and phone numbers, nicknames, height, weight, age, eye and hair color, and distinguishing physical characteristics. Kid-ID in Chicago and Futronix, Inc., of Forest Park, Georgia, which use the Kid-Shield ID system, charge about seven to nine dollars for the cards. Some police departments provide this same service to schoolchildren. Ask your local department about this service, and if it's not offered, check the phone book in your area for a company that can provide an identification card for your child.

Photograph

Name, address, phone number, and date of birth

Fingerprints

Physical characteristics and blood type

Stranger Danger

## **Encouraging Two-Way Communication**

Children with self-confidence and high self-esteem who have a solid grounding in safety competence are less vulnerable targets as victims, and parents can help create confidence through communication. But a parent's job doesn't stop with telling children these practical points. Communication is a two-way street, and children need to trust parents so that they feel comfortable discussing troubling problems.

This trust follows when you take the time to talk to your child about scary things, such as stranger danger, drug use, and the possibility of sexual assault. No responsible parent wants to face (and would rather avoid hearing about) the fact that infants as young as two months and women as old as ninety-six have been raped. Data indicates that 683,000 women were forcibly raped in the United States in 1991. (This number includes only the rapes that were reported; imagine how many more were not.)

How do you tell your child about rape? The concept is not appropriate for young children (under junior high and high school ages); tell them only about stranger danger or the high-risk adult or whatever you've chosen to call the "dangerous someone." Deal with older children by discussing the existence of such a crime, and reiterating the need to protect themselves.

Your child should understand the different types of touching. Teach him to recognize "private parts of the body" and to be able to distinguish between appropriate and inappropriate physical contact. If someone touches him in a way that he judges to be inappropriate (that makes him uncomfortable), he should tell you or another trusted adult immediately.

Talk frankly about drugs before your child has reached the age when drugs are discussed at school or when someone they know will offer them some. If you've brought up the subject in advance, you (and your child) will reap the benefits.

In the end, the key word remains *communication*. If you can keep a lifeline of communication open throughout the difficult years that often plague parents and teenagers, you've accomplished a lot. Don't avoid discussing such issues as crime just because you're uncomfortable talking about unpleasant things. There's nothing wrong with saying, "I'm uncomfortable talking about this, because I wish there was no crime. I wish kids never had to be victims of crime, and I wish you didn't have to know that things like this can happen. But there are crimes, and there have been crime victims, and things like this can happen. That's the way things are. Period."

# Home Alone

Children whose parents work often belong to that massive group known as *latchkey children.* Employing household help is not possible for many working mothers and fathers, and there may be any number of reasons why friends, family, or neighbors can't house your child. As a result he may be home alone, at least periodically. But no matter why they stand alone, children need not stand as innocents who don't know how to handle themselves. Indeed, that's what we're out to prevent. Children home alone either infrequently or on a regular basis pose special safety problems, as do young baby-sitters. Here are some points to remember about keeping these kids safe.

### Knowing Your Child's Schedule

Be aware of where your child is at all times. It goes without saying that you know who his friends are. If you know your child walks a short distance to his after-school piano lesson, and that the lesson takes an hour, you should know when he'll be home.

### Giving Your Child a Key

Your schedule and your child's may not coincide, so you may find it necessary to give him a key. Hang the key on a chain low around his neck so that it is not visible, or pin the key inside a pocket. Remind him that this is a great responsibility, and with that responsibility come some rules:

- Never display the key in or out of school.
- Never lend the key to a friend or stranger.

If the key is lost, direct him to use a second extra key that you have placed in a very safe place—under a doormat or flowerpot on the front step or at a neighbor's home. When you get home, he should tell you about the lost key immediately so you can replace it at once.

## Answering the Door and Phone

Kids must learn how to answer the door and phone safely when parents are out.

If a delivery comes to the door, your child should keep the door locked and tell the stranger to come back; never open the door to sign for a package. If a visitor says, "It's an emergency, and I need to use the phone," tell your child to say, "I'll call 911 for you; I'm not allowed to let you in to make the call."

If a child is home without an adult and the phone rings, the child should answer and say simply: "My mom can't come to the phone right now." If you have an answering machine, tell him to wait until the machine picks up and listen to discover who is leaving a message. It may be you, and in that case, you want the child to pick up the phone and talk to you. What if a child does answer the phone and is on the receiving end of a prank or obscene call? Tell your child to hang up at once; never engage in conversation. (Remind him not to leave the phone off the hook in case you want to reach him.) In any case, if he does pick up the phone, your child should *never* tell *anyone* that he's home alone.

## Using the Phone in Emergencies

Nobody loves the telephone more than preteens and teenagers, whether they're home alone or not. However, the younger child who is home alone should learn that the telephone can be a helper in case of need; thus, he must learn to use the phone correctly.

Prepare your child for an emergency by posting a list of important names and numbers in a conspicuous place. Let your child know that the list includes both Mom's and Dad's work numbers and/or beepers, as well as trusted neighbors' and grandparents' numbers. It's also a good idea to post the number for the family doctor, police, fire department, poison control, and ambulance. Discuss calling 911 for a medical, police, or fire emergency. If 911 isn't available in your area, teach your child to dial 0 for Operator, and to tell the operator what the emergency is and what his address and phone number are. Tell him not to hang up until the person on the other end has said it's okay. Remind your child that he should never call 911 or 0 unless he thinks there's a real emergency. Explain that the people who answer are busy and don't have time for pranks or games.

## Tips from Police and Educators

From Jane Bolek of the Phoenix, Arizona, Police Department:

- Repetition is important. Begin when your child is in kindergarten to teach stranger danger and by second or third grade, children will have learned the term.
- If your child is grabbed, tell him to kick, scream, and yell things like "I do not know you!" "You are not my mommy!" "You are not my daddy!" or "Get away from me!"
- Tell your child not to talk to anyone that you don't know, but clarify with them that not every stranger is bad.

From the Chicago Police Department (Preventive Programs Section):

- Tell your child never to go into anyone's house without your knowledge and permission.
- Tell your child never to play in isolated places.
- If a stranger is following your child, tell him not to hide but to run to where there are other people.
- If someone talks to your child about sex or love, tell him to tell you at once.
- If an older child says, "I know these things already," simply say, "I'm reminding you so you can share these thoughts with your younger brothers and sisters."

### Stranger Danger

From Chicago detective J. J. Bittenbinder:
- Pre-teens should never dangle a purse carelessly.
- Tell teenagers not to walk alone in the mall: muggers are discouraged if you're accompanied by someone. People and lights discourage attackers.
- Children old enough to make a phone call should have enough money to make a call from a pay phone.
- If your neighborhood has "safe homes," teach children to recognize them by the sign in the front window.
- No matter what, teach children never to accept gifts from strangers.

From Sgt. Lawrence Deck of the Columbus, Ohio, Police Department:
- Teach children that if anyone—a stranger or an acquaintance—attempts physical contact the child should report it to you.
- Strangers are not necessarily bad people. But the general rule is to trust the people you know and don't trust the people you don't know.

From Gertrude Williams, principal of the Barclay School in Baltimore, Maryland:
- Tell your child always to keep walking if she is being followed by someone in a car. Older children can try to remember any numbers or letters on the license plate.
- Parents should reinforce what their children are learning about stranger danger in school.
- Older siblings should be reminded to watch over their younger siblings on their way home from school.

From Linda Sharkey, Glenwood School in Short Hills, New Jersey:
- Role-play with your children so they know how to act with a

## Stranger Danger

stranger. Use specific examples of things that can really happen. Most children love animals, so remind them not to fall for the gimmick of "Help me find my little dog who is lost in the woods."

From Anne Green, RN BSMS:
- Teach children in first grade or younger that their bodies are private. By the time your child is in fourth grade and into sports, it is important to discuss privacy in greater detail.

## Stranger Danger

# Very Important Tips

### For Younger Children

The National Center for Missing and Exploited Children, based in Arlington, Virginia, offers these suggestions to help you prevent abduction or exploitation of your child:

1. Above all else is the need to communicate properly with your kids. Kids who aren't listened to, or don't have their needs met at home, become more vulnerable to abduction or exploitation.
2. Be sure your child knows her first and last name, a parent's name, your complete address (not just the apartment building, but the number of the apartment), and telephone number.
3. Discuss what you mean by "a stranger." When you and your child are out on the street, at the grocery store, or at the theater, and a woman you know approaches, your child may wonder who this woman is. She becomes okay—no longer a stranger—after she has seen you laughing or talking together.
4. If someone or something makes your child uncomfortable, she should tell someone he trusts.
5. If a stranger approaches and tries to talk to your child or doesn't use the password, she should run away as fast as she can.

### For Older Girls

1. If your child's handbag or book bag is snatched, she should not fight. Instruct her to throw it at the culprit—give it up, rather than incur injury—and run. This will be easier to do emotionally if she doesn't carry much money and leaves her valuables at home.
2. To prevent rape and assault, your child should scream and make a scene. She can scratch, poke, and bite hard if a hand or arm comes near her mouth and kick with her shoe, hard. She should swing any object she's carrying into an attacker's face, and jab with her elbows (backwards, if she's grabbed from behind). Tell her to do anything to break away and run.
3. Finally, consider giving your daughter a personal alarm to carry. Many parents believe this to be the first and best line of defense.

# Chapter 10
## Seasonal Safety

THE ART OF PRACTICING SAFETY IN OUR DAILY LIVES is not an occasional pastime, but one to live with every day of every month. Up to now this book has discussed guidelines in general: what to do about fire safety throughout the year, how to childproof your home against preventable injuries every minute of every day, the constant need to buckle up for safety, and so on.

Now, however, let's get seasonal, for some safety practices are appropriate only at certain times. This chapter will discuss some of your most commonly asked seasonal and holiday-related safety questions and offer some helpful answers.

**Seasonal Safety**

# Winter Wonderland

## How to Dress for Outdoor Activities

Nothing could be worse for children or adults than missing the outdoor winter fun because you're shivering with cold. In winter, as mothers are fond of repeating, "You have to dress for it." First, layer, layer, layer! Three layers are better than one to insulate the body and prevent heat loss. Kids out sledding, parents pushing strollers on frigid days—anyone can benefit from layering. Alan K. Roberts, who teaches cross-country skiing in Aspen, Colorado, offers "Three Ws" for layering. Begin with wicking perspiration moisture away from your skin. To stay dry and warm during any cold-weather activity, start with a snug-fitting base layer of silk and certain spun polyesters. Materials such as cotton or cotton blends (which soak up moisture and retain it) are not good wicking-layer clothes. Layer number two should warm or insulate. "Pile (thickness) retains warm air from your body heat. Materials to layer such as wool or thick woven synthetic fibers which trap dead air spaces are good insulators. Cotton and acrylic are less efficient choices for insulating layer clothing," says Roberts. The outside layer offers wind protection to keep the weather away from you. Water-resistant and loosely fitting for ease of movement, this outer layer should be made of specially treated, weatherproof fabric such as polyester microfibers or nylon. Waterproof materials such as plastic or rubber will trap moisture in all of your clothes as your body releases heat and sweat, and that isn't good. Perspiration, according to Roberts, calls for adjusting your body temperature at once. "Dry is warmer. Adjust with a hat, zippers, or your warming layer clothes."

A second rule of winter is to wear a hat. Everyone has heard how hats "hold in the warmth." They cause your body to warm the blood and send it from top to toe. If, for any reason, your household furnace or heating goes off, or your home feels too cold for comfort, the first item of extra clothing you should put on a baby or an infant is a warm hat. Bedtime nightcaps, like Grandpa used to wear to cover his bald pate, are another good idea. (And you don't have to be balding to wear one!)

## Seasonal Safety

Third, children who have a tendency to spend winters coughing—and this goes for the rest of the family, too—profit from wearing a scarf or a warming mask across their mouths and noses outdoors. A toasty scarf warms the air the child breathes and cuts down on stress to the heart and lungs.

Don't let your child walk around in wet clothes. Adults are usually so uncomfortable that they'll come in, exchange their wet togs for dry ones, and go out again, without fuss or muss. It's another story with kids who love to play in the snow and get their jackets and pants good and damp. One snowball fight, and they're soaked. Skaters' socks are likely to get damp, as well. Difficult as it is to bring them in, do so.

Children with sensitive skin (especially those with very fair complexions) are undoubtedly going to be exposed to chap. This is particularly true of babies who drool and kids with runny noses from colds or allergies. Doctors advise putting a thin layer of petroleum jelly or gentle moisturizing cream on their faces before they go outdoors to prevent chapping.

Finally, Alan Roberts offers the following general rules for staying warm, comfortable, and safe outdoors in winter:

1. Use good quality sunscreen on your child (carried with you for reapplication).
2. Make sure your child wears a hat to hold in body heat.
3. Your child should drink water or juice during activities.
4. Your child should wear good quality gloves and boots (and keep them dry between uses).

**Seasonal Safety**

5. Buy quality sunglasses for everyone in the family, as sun reflected on snow is damaging to the eyes.
6. Don't rub, slap, or pinch cold fingers, toes, or ears. Warm water is the best for heating them.
7. Don't put cotton next to your child's skin if he's going outdoors.

## Smart Sledders

Kids who are smart about sledding have usually learned the hard way. Better to cue your kids in on the dangers as well as the pleasures of sledding. *Parents'* magazine has reported that about 33,000 children between the ages of five and nine are injured in sledding accidents annually in this United States. Here are tips smart sledders should know, based on information from Dr. William E. Boyle, Jr., M.D., former chairman of the American Academy of Pediatrics' Injury and Poison Prevention Committee:

1. Teach your child to plot his course. Avoid hazards. Check for big rocks, tree stumps, ice (which increases speed), bare spots (which can bring the sled to a sudden halt), and other hazards. Examine the path to be taken and the surrounding territory, not just the direction the sled is aimed. Where will the ride end? Are there any fences or wall that could impede a ride?
2. Be sure the slope has a gradual decline, and a long, flat bottom so that the sled can stop on its own.
3. Sit tight, sit right. Your child should sit facing forward, feet first. Sliding downhill on his stomach, headfirst, is dangerous. If he crashes, head or abdominal injuries can result.
4. Hold on to the ropes on the sled. If he doesn't wish to, tie the ropes to the top of the sled so they don't slide underneath and cause a sudden stop.
5. Get off fast if a collision can't be avoided. Roll sideways off the sled. Your child should practice this, so that if a crash is inevitable, he'll know how to fall off properly.
6. Your child, who is unable to judge speed or force, should move out of the way of other sledders as soon as he reaches the bottom of the hill. Most kids learn this instinctively. They know they like a clear track ahead, without having

**Seasonal Safety**

to yell, "Get out of the way!," so they give that courtesy to others, as well.
7. Your child should avoid using his feet as brakes. Just as you've often told him that, learn that the same goes for you too. "Parents who ride with their kids often put a foot out to stop the sled and end up spraining or breaking their ankle or knee," notes Dr. Boyle. This won't happen if you practice the same safety tips you gave your child. If you take a little one on a sled, place him snugly in front of you between your legs.
8. Never sled alone. It's more fun to sled with friends or family and it's a lot safer in case of an accident.

## Snowboarding

Snowboarding is like skiing, skateboarding, and surfing all wrapped up in one winter sport. Snowboarders "ride" a snowboard in one of three styles: alpine, freeride, or freestyle. No matter which style you choose, you need the fundamental skills and proper equipment for this sport. This equipment includes a board, boots (not ski boots), thermal undergarments, warm layered clothing, gloves, headgear, goggles or sunglasses, and sunscreen or lip balm.

According to Julee Roth, snowboard instructor at Snowmass Mountain in Aspen, Colorado, "The number of injuries you'll find in snowboarding are less than you'll find in skiing. It's less severe because the child (or adult) is always in an athletic position (knees bent), so they're less likely to get tangled up as skiers do with their skis and poles." Roth says that most people adapt well to the sport, which has been around for about fifteen years, but became popular only around five years ago. Your child doesn't need a skiing background to try snowboarding, but make sure he:

- Always wears wrist guards. Wrists are the number-one place on the body to be injured in snowboarding, and the most commonly fractured. Wrist guards can prevent such injuries.
- Always wears knee pads and a helmet.
- Takes a lesson. Learning the basics and correct techniques will make snowboarding safer and more fun for your child.

**Seasonal Safety**

## Skating

The President's Council on Physical Fitness and Sports has rated ice skating as one of the top sports for maintaining physical fitness, and this is one sport Mom and Dad can enjoy equally with children. Of course, acquiring skating skills adds to the enjoyment, just as passing Ice Skating Institute of America (ISIA) tests at any age can add to a skater's sense of accomplishment. But if there was ever an area in which safety comes first, it's on the surface of a pond or lake where children come to skate.

How old should a child be before learning to ice skate? Most instructors say that any child who has learned to walk well can learn to skate, but very young children should be limited to classes of their age-group peers. Children should be able to take direction and, because preschool children do not have long attention spans, limit their time spent on the ice.

Here are a few safety pointers to consider when you and your children take to the ice:

- Check your child's skates for proper fit. Select skates that offer durability and value for the money, but don't skimp; the child's comfort is paramount, and no child will enjoy skating if his feet hurt. Experiment with sock thicknesses; thin socks are better, because thick socks impede the snug fit of the boots. If he wears thick socks, your

## Seasonal Safety

child will have to lace boots very tightly, which could be very uncomfortable.
- Snug-fitting boots give support. Experts usually tell you to buy a girl's skates a half to a full size smaller than her regular shoe size. Boys' sizes seem to run truer to shoe sizes, but they still may wear boots a half-size smaller than shoes. Skates fit when toes come close to the end of the boot.
- Some instructors tell you to pull skate laces very tight up to the instep, then loosen them a little so the skater can bend forward slightly. Be sure to tuck in the ends of the laces to prevent tripping over them.
- Maintaining balance and mobility on the ice can be difficult. Tell your child to take his time when learning to glide and to stop, and to rest when he needs to.
- Tell your child he doesn't have to be a champion skater to do what the champs do before skating: a few bending and stretching exercises to keep from straining muscles and joints after you go onto the ice. Do these bends and stretches before removing the plastic guards from the blades of the skates.
- Have your child dress for warmth, not glamour. On a brisk day, gloves or mittens, hats, leg warmers, and short scarves can make for more outdoor comfort. Sweaters may be better than coats; an open jacket can act like a sail, making it difficult to skate against the wind.
- Artificial ice is generally safer, but the beauty of a frozen pond in winter has a wonderful nostalgic charm families enjoy. When skating outdoors, check to be sure the ice is safe and obey all signs. Your child should skate with a buddy, and even with a buddy, adults should be present to supervise children.
- Don't skate at night, unless it's a public rink rimmed with lights. In the country or at a neighborhood pond, your child should stick to daylight hours.
- Advise your child not to skate where he's unsure of the depth of the water under the ice. If thin ice results in an accident, he can go under.

**Seasonal Safety**

- If a skater does fall in, the rescuer should never stand up on the ice, but lie flat and inch only close enough to reach the victim with an object: a pole, a branch, even an article of clothing. When the victim has firmly grasped the object, the rescuer should pull him to safety by inching backward carefully across the ice. If others are present, form a human chain by lying on the ice with everyone grasping the ankles of the next person.
- Of course, skaters at rinks may also fall; they may not get as wet, but falls can certainly be as painful. Tell your child to relax and go with the fall; don't fight it. He should get up quickly so other skaters don't collide with him.

**Seasonal Safety**

- For safe skating, teach your child courtesy on the ice. Roughhousing and horseplay should be forbidden. Don't skate too close to others; try to avoid cutting in front of people, but expect people to cut in front of you, so be prepared to stop.
- On a busy rink, tell your child not to get in the way of more experienced skaters practicing advanced moves. They are likely to be skating in the center of the rink.

## Skiing

Do children and skis mix? Many say no: "My child isn't old enough to handle the necessary coordination skills." You know your child, of course, and that should always be your number-one guide. But there are many who believe that the younger you start a child on skis, and teach him correctly, the better skier you'll develop. And if skiing is a passion in your household, the experience can be among the most exhilarating in the world.

Ski resorts are augmenting their programs for children, and, as a result, family ski vacations are increasingly popular. In Colorado, for example, Arrowhead Mountain in Aspen, and Lionshead and Golden Peak Children's Centers in Vail offer specialized ski instruction for children ages three to twelve; there are also full- and half-day programs for all skill levels at Vail and Beaver Creek. Big Sky and Big Mountain in Montana sponsor a Big Sky day camp for kids six to fourteen and the Big Mountain Kiddie Korner. Most other ski areas provide ski lessons for kids, as well.

Chi-Chi Gustafson, manager of the Snow Cubs in Snowmass, Colorado; Faye Grearson, a Snow Cubs team leader; and Charlotte Woodward, ski instructor, offer some advice about skiing and kids two to twelve years old.

### Two- and Three-Year-Olds

Woodward says, "Two-year-olds can take only private lessons at Snowmass; once they've turned three, they may take classes, which consist of two children and one instructor. Children learning at two years of age must first feel comfortable putting on their boots, skis, and clothes, and enjoy going outside in all that gear."

## Seasonal Safety

When starting out, it's important to work with children so they feel comfortable and confident around the instructor; then, once outside, they'll trust their teacher. "Two-year-olds," Woodward continues, "should have ski tips tied together so legs don't split on their own, and the child can control going into the snowplow position and then straight. The most important safety tip is to watch the child out on the hill and stay focused."

Kids as young as two begin wearing their skis and boots to get comfortable. Then they navigate a carpeted ski hill to get the feeling of going down a slope with the equipment. Then they move outside and practice going down a small hill; the child practices the snowplow position and straight legs.

Time limits are very important, says Gustafson, "especially for the very young child—two or three years old—but also for all kids. Don't over-ski a child. If you overdo it, they may never want to ski again, because if you push it, the child gets tired, weak, and scared. Children are not capable of going for long periods of time."

Grearson adds, "For parents of three-year-olds who are taking a class: (1) Be sure your child knows the instructor's name. (2) Your child should be able to follow in line. (3) The child should know about the ski patrol. (4) The child should look both ways before crossing a hill (just like on the street). (5) The child should not stop under a chairlift. (6) If the child becomes separated from the teacher or the group, he should wait at the bottom of the lift." Grearson recommends helmets for children, "because you don't know who may ski into you. Be sure, however, that the child can hear with the helmet on."

Children must learn to turn. This is important not only for children but also for their teachers. "Kids are distracted easily," says Grearson, "and they go toward that distraction. This applies to three-year-olds up to twelve-year-olds, even to adults. But as kids get older, their control is better, so they can avoid accidents when and if they're distracted."

The instructors advise, "Tell kids positives—what to do, not what not to do, because then they'll do the right thing, not the wrong thing." Finally, on long lift lines, kids get tired and cold.

## Seasonal Safety

Then they fall more easily or can't stop when coming downhill. At the top of the hill, your child should stretch and hop on his skis to wake up and warm up before skiing down.

Parents who push kids exhaust them. Very young children need rest time to recover, or they may become afraid if they fall and reject skiing. Why do parents push? Perhaps because they want the kids to ski with them. "But," says Grearson, "more skiing is not always better. On a skiing vacation, three- and four-year-olds should go skiing no more than twice a day. And the length of time a child is out each time really depends upon the child's skiing capabilities."

If the child is three years old and potty trained, Aspen Ski School recommends a class, not a private lesson. In a class situation, kids watch other kids, follow them, and help each other put on their boots, hats, and skis.

### Four- to Six-Year-Olds

When it comes to ski safety for four- to six-year-olds, the most important things to remember are to teach your child to look uphill before skiing out onto the mountain and to look for others. In general, make your child aware of what's out there.

Four-, five-, and six-year-olds need an indoor facility to retreat to when they are tired and cold, or if they simply do not like skiing. If skiers don't have this type of facility where you're going, find someplace else to vacation.

No child should feel he has to do what others of his age are doing. Some children are stronger than their peers. Others may have grown up around snow and skiing and are more likely to be used to the procedures.

In a private lesson, your child receives all of the instructor's attention and no pressure from other kids. In a group, one child may be crying or lose a mitten, and this is distracting to other children. A child can feel overwhelmed in a group of other children and by their abilities, as well. Choosing private or group lessons for a child should be based on his ability and what's best for him.

**Seasonal Safety**

### Seven- to Twelve-Year-Olds

Children are always learning, Chi-Chi Gustafson says, and at twelve years of age, they begin skiing and socializing. "It's important that they stay in classes and socialize, not go off on their own. It's also important for kids to learn boundaries on the mountain. This is taught in classes."

At Snowmass, the instructors work slowly and don't believe in pushing children up to the next level. "Structure is very important. We want kids to follow the steps, the rules, and levels of skiing, and we teach them, 'don't break the rules,'" finishes Woodward.

### Some Additional Tips

- Don't give poles to your three-year-old. The poles only get in the way, and the pointed ends are hazardous.
- Use modern bindings that release well and fast, in case of a fall. Always use up-to-date equipment.
- Always check equipment every time your child goes skiing. The Aspen Ski School has a ski technician on staff to check equipment before kids put on skis and boots.
- Your child should familiarize himself with equipment before skiing, especially if he's never used that equipment before.
- Discuss clear rules that emphasize safety first.
- Choose terrain for your child carefully.
- Provide choices: "You may do A or B," rather than, "Do what you want to." Make choices real and fair.
- Be consistent in guidelines and language.
- Repetition is important.
- Be specific: "We're going to slide as far as we can," not, "Let's slide."
- Expect confusion and hesitancy.
- Young children are egocentric—their point of view is the only point of view. Remind your child to be considerate ("It's someone else's turn to slide down the hill first"), but don't be surprised if he struggles with the concept.

## Seasonal Safety

# Winter Injuries and Dangers

### Frostbite

Frostbite is caused by exposure of inadequately protected flesh to sub-freezing temperatures. It's important to recognize its symptoms. First comes a tingling or burning sensation or, worse, no feeling at all in the frostbitten area. It won't hurt until the thawing begins. Watch for red skin that turns dead white—pale and waxy—and feels firm to the touch. The nose, cheeks, ears, fingers, and toes are most commonly affected.

Discuss with your child how to treat affected areas so that he can learn what to do if the need arises. He must not rewarm near a flame or a concentrated heat source such as a stove or a fireplace. Do not rub the frozen part. Handle the tissue gently. To prevent infection and the possibility of amputation, get to the doctor as soon as possible.

### Hypothermia

Hypothermia is nothing to treat lightly. Defined as a subnormal temperature of the body that occurs when the body is exposed to cold (aggravated by wet, wind, and exhaustion), it is the number-one killer of outdoor recreationists. And it can happen to adults as well as to children. The best defense, according to ski instructor Alan Roberts, is to stay dry.

"When clothes get wet, they lose about 90 percent of their insulating value. Wool loses the least. Beware of the wind. Wind drives cold air under and through clothing. Wind multiplies the problem of staying dry. Again, wool is the best. Most hypothermia cases develop in air temperatures between 30 and 50 degrees. Put on rain gear before you get wet. Put on wool before you start shivering." The surprise in Roberts's message is that hypothermia can develop in such relatively warm conditions.

How do you know if you or your child is in trouble? Look out for:
- Drowsiness
- Uncontrollable fits of shivering

**Seasonal Safety**

- Vague, slow, slurred speech
- Memory lapses, incoherence
- Immobile, fumbling hands
- Frequent stumbling, lurching gait
- Apparent exhaustion, inability to get up after a rest

## Seasonal Safety

The symptoms can be more evident in adults, who are also likely to describe them later. Interestingly, however, adults often try to deny they're in difficulty, and are even less willing to accept help ("I'm all right; keep going") than children, who are more likely to complain about their discomfort.

The most important thing you can do for anyone whom you suspect is suffering from hypothermia is to get that person out of the rain, wind, or snow as soon as you can and remove those wet clothes. Even mild symptoms demand quick treatment. If you can, position the sufferer between two other people to create "skin-to-skin contact," says Roberts. Keep the person awake if he is semiconscious and give him warm cocoa, coffee, or tea.

### Other Potential Hazards

1. Wind chill is not as severe a problem, but it can cause much misery. Whether clothing is wet from perspiration or rain, sleet, or snow, cold and wind only intensify the discomfort. Cross-country ski instructors advise their students to try to stay as dry as they can, encouraging them to stop as often as necessary to rearrange clothing layers to stay comfortable.
2. Altitude sickness may strike on the ski slopes. If a child is listless, nauseated, drowsy, or dizzy, it could be the altitude. Other symptoms include apathy and weakness. Time might take care of the problem, but the child should stop and rest, breathe deeply several times, and drink a little fruit juice. Some nourishment from simple sugar, as in candy or fruit juice, is good for altitude sickness, as is moving down to a lower elevation. It can happen to anyone, though it's less likely to strike someone in good physical condition. Don't arrive one minute and hit the slopes the next; give your body a chance to adapt to the new altitude.
3. Can a child become dehydrated at winter play? Yes, though it is more difficult to identify dehydration in winter for the simple reason that people don't feel as thirsty as they do in warm weather. But children who are sledding, skiing, and skating—which in most cases can be called strenuous activities—do need some form of liquid such as water, Pedialyte®

### Seasonal Safety

or Gatorade® (which return needed electrolytes to the body quickly), all of which are good for preventing dehydration. Since adults at rest should drink two quarts of water daily, ask your pediatrician how much your active child should be drinking. It will vary from child to child, depending on size and degree of activity.

4. Can seasonal affective disorder occur in children? Yes, and children with this condition seem to carry the weight of the world on their shoulders, a real safety hazard because their behavior can be careless and they may be more accident prone, says Dr. Michael Young of Rush-Presbyterian-St. Luke's Hospital in Chicago. Studies show that when less sunlight passes through the eyes to the brain, hormonal mechanisms that regulate mood, appetite, and sleep may be disrupted. Exposure to bright artificial light seems to relieve symptoms, says Dr. Young. The condition shows up in October or November and lasts throughout the winter months. Sufferers feel tired and lethargic. Usually, their appetite increases; they may gain weight and crave carbohydrates and sweets; they tend to sleep more; and their everyday functioning becomes impaired. They sometimes have trouble concentrating or carrying out their usual daily routine, and they may lose interest in favorite activities.

The syndrome is at its worst in January and February. Then, by March or April it starts to go away, and in the late spring, through summer and early fall, people return to normal. Sometimes, the problem can be misdiagnosed as chronic fatigue syndrome, even though it's only occurring at certain times of the year, says Dr. Young. "Sometimes, the seasonal component of it is missed and it's diagnosed as depression, or some other kind of psychiatric disorder." If you or your child or adolescent tend to suffer from extreme winter doldrums, look into "winter depression"; you just might have discovered the solution for a formerly "impossible" problem.

**Seasonal Safety**

## *Winter Driving Tips*

Here's a list of winter-ready rites for drivers:

- Check your tires (they lose one pound of pressure for every 10°F drop in outside temperature). Inflate tires to the pressure that's recommended.
- Check your brakes.
- Check your battery and transmission (transmission fluid should be fresh, not appear discolored; it is best to follow the owner's manual in checking the fluid levels).
- Check exhaust system for leaks, belts that are tight and not frayed, hoses that don't leak and have no cracks or bulges, and an air filter that's clean.
- Check windshield wipers and antifreeze wiper fluid, and fill radiator with antifreeze and water.
- Replace leaky pipes or muffler, and lubricate your locks, hinges, and weatherstripping so you won't be frozen out of your car.
- If your car stops dead and you have to start your car with jumper cables, wear eye protection and watch out: hydrogen fumes that ignite easily concentrate around the battery, and a spark from a jumper cable could blow the battery into your face.
- If you live in an ultra-wintry climate, and you're often elected to do children's car pools, keep a lock de-icer in your purse, coat pocket, home, or office.

### Seasonal Safety

## Winter Holidays

Here are a few tips for surviving the winter holidays:
- Check all holiday lights (indoor and outdoor) for any loose connections, frayed wires, or broken sockets.
- Make sure to use only indoor lights indoors and outdoor lights outdoors.
- As you go to bed or leave the house during the day, turn off all tree lights and holiday decorations.
- Use tinsel made only of nonleaded and nonflammable materials.
- Place a menorah or any other candles out of the reach of all children. You may want to guide a child's hand during the actual lighting of the candles, but remove the menorah to safe ground immediately afterwards.
- Never leave burning candles unattended and extinguish candles on the menorah before going to bed.
- If buying an artificial tree, read the label to be sure it is fire-resistant.
- Don't attach more than three sets of lights to one extension cord.
- Use only light sets that are approved by Underwriters Laboratories.
- Keep any and all holiday plants, such as mistletoe, holly berries, amaryllis, and azalea, out of children's reach. They can all cause severe stomach problems or skin irritations.
- Are poinsettias poisonous? One botanical garden official said she had never heard of a child becoming allergic to poinsettias. A plant information source noted that there is disagreement over whether it is toxic. One scientist said that you have to eat four pounds of it before there's any danger. The Rush-Presbyterian-St. Luke's (Chicago) Poison Control Center Toxic Plant List notes that poinsettia causes contact dermatitis only. Finally, a small notation in the material for 1994's National Poison Prevention Week offered this summation: "Question: Is the poinsettia still considered to be extremely toxic? Answer: The poinsettia was blamed for a death in 1919; however, recent studies indicate that the

## Seasonal Safety

plant is not as highly toxic as was thought at that time. It is unlikely that ingestion of a poinsettia would be fatal, although it may cause some gastric irritation and burning in the mouth."

- If you purchase a living Christmas tree, make sure it is as fresh as possible and water it daily; if it's dry, it becomes more flammable. As the tree grows older and more brittle after the holidays, dispose of it. Some parents put a gate around the tree because tree needles can seriously injure a child's eye. And about those lights on the tree: the Consumer Product Safety Commission (CPSC) reported about 3,000 emergency room visits that involved shocks and burns from Christmas tree lights in 1993. Another 4,000 visits were caused by cuts from handling broken tree decorations. Be sure that your tree lights don't exceed Underwriters Laboratories standards. And don't string lights on an artificial metal tree because of the potential for electrical shock.
- Keep the tree away from any heat source that can cause a fire, such as fireplaces, radiators, vents, and candles.
- Common holiday cookie ingredients (such as vanilla and almond extract) contain levels of alcohol that may be harmful to an infant, so they should be kept out of the baby's reach.

## Seasonal Safety

- When entertaining at home, be sure your guests don't leave alcoholic drinks or ashtrays within the baby's reach.
- Advise visitors and grandparents who are in the home over the holidays to keep vitamin supplements out of the baby's reach. Iron supplements are the leading cause of childhood poisoning.
- Keep the fireplace area clean and well covered. Don't leave any firewood or utensils within your child's reach. And, most important, don't forget to remove the key to all gas fireplaces. (Of course, it goes without saying what to do with those matches you keep near the fireplace.)
- Never burn tree branches or wrapping paper, as they emit hazardous fumes.
- Keep tree ornaments off the bottom part of the tree so that a crawling baby or a toddler can't get at them. It may be a good idea to hang them with yarn rather than hooks.
- Babies can choke on toys with small parts; therefore, make sure that older siblings don't leave their new toys (or their old ones, for that matter) within your baby's reach.
- Be careful of games and clothes that come in plastic bags with ribbons. Plastic can suffocate a baby, and ribbons may strangle.
- Toys can involve batteries, and batteries can cause chemical burns. Since 1988, the Consumer Product Safety Commission has received more than a hundred reports of household batteries overheating, rupturing, and leaking. About one-third of the incidents caused injuries, a number of which were chemical burns to children from the corrosive battery liquid. Carelessness—something as simple as putting batteries in backwards—can cause them to overheat and rupture. Parents should install batteries in household appliances and their children's toys. (See Chapter 4 for more information on battery safety.)

Remember, if you're feeling that too-much-to-do-no-time-to-do-it-in stress, think how your baby or child can sense it. With the coming of the holidays, excitement mounts, and children need to be watched more than usual—in spite of your lack of time.

**Seasonal Safety**

# Summer Sense
## Sunburn and Sunscreen

Think of balmy breezes, the doffing of coats and mufflers, and the delights of a June moon. Healthy enjoyment of the outdoors means that families head for backyards, playgrounds, and local swimming holes. As a result, children spend a lot of summertime outdoors and get three times more exposure to the sun's harmful rays than adults. Specialists say that 50 percent of the sun damage a person experiences over a lifetime is believed to occur before the age of eighteen. The Skin Cancer Foundation notes that the sun is responsible for 90 percent of all skin cancers. The first thing you can do is shield your child from these rays. Keep a baby out of the direct sun, particularly at the noon hour. Actually, between ten in the morning and three in the afternoon—the heart of a child's play day—the sun is at its most damaging. A light-skinned tot can burn in ten minutes during these midday hours.

Note the "sneaky factor." If the sun goes behind a cloud, with that nasty radiation blocked, the temperature down, and the bright light gone, is everything okay? Sorry. The sneaky factor means that those ultraviolet rays aren't gone. The clouds have scattered them, but they're there. And they can burn just as badly as they do on cloudless days.

The best thing you can do for your baby is to bring him indoors during those hours of heightened solar intensity. What about sunscreens and sunblocks? Ask your pediatrician if your baby under six months of age should be treated with sunscreen. Some say that is too young because the chemicals are not good for a baby's skin.

For babies over six months of age, lotions and creams that contain the chemical PABA are not likely to harm sensitive skin. If your child is particularly allergic, do a spot test. Take a couple of your favorite sunscreens (or one sunblock and one sunscreen) and place a half-dollar-sized dot of each on your child's arm. Cover with a bandage for forty-eight hours. There should be no rash, but if there is, do not use that product.

The difference between sunblock and sunscreen is that sunblock does what it says: it blocks out the sun. No harmful ultraviolet rays go through completely, and 97 percent of one's skin is

## Seasonal Safety

protected. Sunscreen, on the other hand, does not completely block the sun. Some ultraviolet rays can go through.

The sun protection factor (SPF) number on the sunscreen container indicates its strength. For example, an SPF 30 sunscreen delivers thirty times the protection that using no sunscreen would give you. That means it takes thirty times longer to burn under SPF 30. Let the SPF guide you in purchasing the correct sunscreen. The SPF can be as low as 2 or as high as 45. Select one with a minimum of 15. Sunscreens come in many child-friendly and hypoallergenic varieties. A good dab of zinc oxide cream on the baby's fair-skinned, freckled nose will also provide a total block.

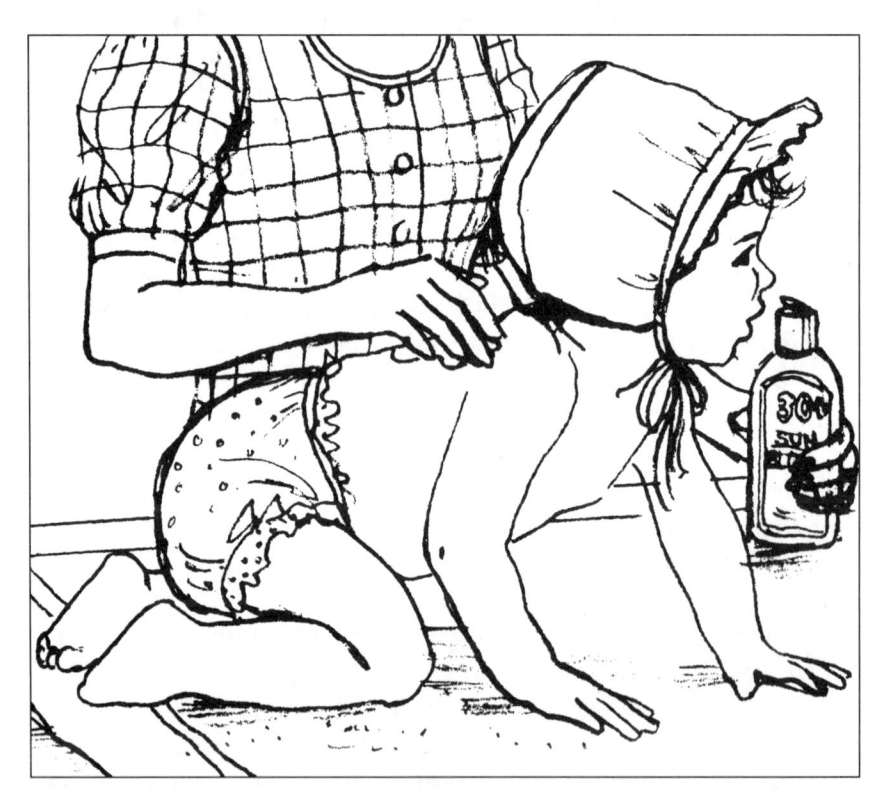

Apply sunscreen to your child's face, neck, and ears—common sites for skin cancer. Is a T-shirt enough protection for the baby's torso? No. A cotton T-shirt has an SPF of only 8, and even with a shirt, that highly sensitive area between the shoulders can burn in two hours. If the T-shirt is wet, after a dip in the baby's wading pool, the SPF goes down to 5. Apply a good protective sunscreen before dressing the baby. And encourage your older child to do the same before he goes off with his friends. Make sure he carries some in his bag to reapply when he climbs out of the water.

Feet burn almost as fast as the area between the shoulders. Socks and sneakers should be protection enough. But on a bright sunny day, you may dress the baby in sandals. These provide excellent protection from hot sand and stray seashells and shell fragments on the beach, but they're no protection at all from the burning sun. Be sure to apply sunscreen here.

Legs need sunscreen, too. The kid fad of oversized baggy shorts isn't a bad idea on a hot day. Loose clothes are (literally) cooler, and the bigger they are, the more skin they cover.

Reapply your child's sunscreen every ninety minutes, and even if your town borders on cornfields instead of the Pacific shore, make sure that your child's sunscreen is waterproof. However, after a dip in the water, reapply even waterproof sunscreen.

Find a hat for the baby and don one yourself. Dads, put those baseball caps to some use. However, since baseball caps and visors are usually too small to shade more than the top half of the face, it's not a bad idea to wear a hat. A golf hat is as good for your child as it is for Dad.

Should your child wear sunglasses? During the baby's first year, you should try to shield his eyes at all times from the bright sun. Use a brimmed stroller or sun hat. In an air-conditioned car, when baby is traveling in his car seat and the sun is streaming into his eyes, provide protection.

## Summer Injuries and Dangers

### Sunburn

You may have had an aunt who doused sunburn with vinegar and water. This could help, but it can't take away the sting any more than you can hurry the healing. When you've been unwise enough to visit the beach without sunscreen and your child has burned, the best thing to do is to place him on cool linen and apply cool compresses every few hours to help carry the heat away from the skin. Cool doesn't mean cold, however. Ice cubes feel good, but they may be harmful. And under no circumstances should the child become chilled. In the average air-conditioned summer room, be sure those cool compresses aren't applied continually.

Plenty of liquids help. They not only taste good going down, but the fluids replace those that were lost. At bedtime, baby aspirin, aspirin, or acetaminophen may lessen the pain and allow your child to sleep better. A hydrocortisone-type cream, applied gently, soothes the skin and can take away some of the redness. Don't use a heavy ointment that can block the heat's escape from the skin. And sunburned kids, who've got enough to contend with, don't like the messiness at all. If your child is totally nonallergic, try a cooling anesthetic spray.

### Heat Exhaustion, Heatstroke, and Overheating

Heat exhaustion may occur when a person loses fluids as a result of sweating or because a body's cooling system has sent so much of its blood supply to the skin. As a result, the decrease in blood flow to the brain can bring on confusion or even cause unconsciousness. Heat exhaustion is serious; it may suddenly appear after vigorous exercise, or it can come on slowly over a period of days or weeks because of the dehydration that may build up.

Signs of heat exhaustion include pale, moist skin that is cool to the touch and profuse sweating. Victims may also suffer from headaches, dizziness, nausea, vomiting, and heightened body temperature. Their pupils may be dilated.

The best way to avoid heat exhaustion is to give a child enough liquids, plain and simple. If he is very young, frequent drinks of breast milk, baby formula, or water will do it. If he is six months or older, use juice diluted with water. Be careful not to use formula or juice that has been in the sun; it may have spoiled. Keep both cool if you want to use them.

Heatstroke is a more severe and more advanced version of heat exhaustion. An estimated 200 deaths occur every year from heat stroke, but because some cases have been attributed to heart attacks or other conditions, the actual figures are probably higher.

## Seasonal Safety

How will you recognize heatstroke? A victim's body temperature can rise as high as 110°F. His skin is likely to be hot and dry and he may be dizzy and confused and suffer from diarrhea or vomiting. A baby will be woozy, unsteady when crawling, irritable, and lethargic. If you see these signs, get immediate medical attention. If you can't get to a doctor or have to wait, go immediately to a cool place, loosen his clothing, and fan him. You can also place him in a tub of cool water. Apply cool compresses on the "heat points"—head, underarms, groin—to cool the body. Giving liquids to the lethargic baby is likely to result in choking or fluids in the lungs. Only after the child is more alert should you give fluids.

If you have parked the baby under a tree at a playground in a stroller while doing sandbox duty with an older child, check to be sure the angle of the sun hasn't changed, and move the stroller if necessary. Don't ever leave baby in a parked car in hot weather, even with an open window, and *never* leave baby in a car alone. Cars can become dangerously hot, and so can baby.

Overheating is less serious. It may manifest itself only in prickly heat, a rash common to babies in their first summers. When your baby is overdressed and he's perspired until the small red pimples appear, your best bet is to bathe him in baking soda, sprinkle a bit of the baking soda on the rash, wrap him comfortably in cotton, and keep him comfortable in a cool, dry place.

### Bee Stings

Whether it's a hornet, a honeybee, or a wasp, flying insects that sting head for anything that smells like a flower. And a baby is no exception. Forego scented lotions when you're dressing the baby for a stroller ride in the park or the woods. Don't use floral-scented powders or soaps, either. Avoid bright clothes, too, which attract bees; they think the baby looks like a flower in his bright red or yellow sunsuit. Stay away from places likely to attract bees: flower beds, clover, and grassy areas. Bees are the reason many city officials say they don't plant flowers right up against playground areas and why grass is likely to be eliminated.

It's extremely rare for a baby under a year old to have an allergic reaction to a bee sting, but if your baby develops more than the usual reaction of a localized swelling, such as trouble breathing or vomiting, go to a doctor immediately; your baby may be fighting for his life.

The localized swelling is not difficult to treat if you act at once. Never scrape the stinger off with your fingernail. It may be better to use a credit card at a forty-five- or ninety-degree angle, which avoids pulling the stinger out or pinching it out; pinching releases the venom. Wrap some ice in a cloth and apply to the swelling. You can also apply a paste made of baking soda and water. Calamine lotion is usually ineffective for pain. If a sting affects the tongue, mouth, or throat, go immediately to a professional, as swelling in these areas can cut off the passage of air.

**Ticks and Lyme Disease**

Summer brings out deer ticks, which can carry Lyme disease. Early detection of Lyme disease is key to a cure; the longer a child has the disease, the more damage to the heart or nervous system can result. Symptoms include redness around the tick bite, nausea, fever, headache, lethargy, and muscle pain. Learn to recognize the signs of a tick bite: a red rash that expands into a doughnut shape with a clear center. Ask your family doctor for a photo or picture of a tick bite.

To keep from picking up ticks, avoid grassy wooded areas, including marsh grass and underbrush near the beach during tick season. If you can't avoid grass or woods, dress the baby in long-sleeved shirts and long pants. Tick repellent is available, but don't use it on babies younger than one year. Apply the spray to your baby's clothes (not in areas he might put in his mouth). If you've been in the woods, check your baby nightly for ticks, especially on skin folds. Dress him in light-colored clothing, so it's easy to see the tick. Ticks are dark and can be only as big as a dot the size of a period on this page.

If you find a tick and remove it promptly, there's less danger of Lyme disease. If you're confused about whether that tiny brownish black dot on baby's skin is a tick or a mole, scrape the area lightly. A tick will lift off the skin. That's your cue to remove the tick with tweezers. Be very careful to pull straight out, or you may break the head off inside the skin, which causes many more problems. Put it in a jar of alcohol if you can for medical examination. Removing a dead or a live tick with tweezers is the best method. Ask your pediatrician if your baby should have a Lyme test.

## Mosquitoes

Though mosquito bites are not dangerous or life threatening, they can cause children (and adults) great discomfort. Mosquitoes especially like to congregate where there's water. If your child has a kiddie pool, try to spray the area when he's not around, before he takes a dip. Stagnant pools are breeding areas. If you're picnicking by a stream, watch out. Any area around garbage cans is a breeding ground for mosquitoes (in fact, for any insects). Spray your garbage area, too, when your child is not around; sprays are poison. For treatment, use hydrocortisone cream or calamine lotion.

## Poison Ivy, Poison Oak, and Poison Sumac

Knowing what poison ivy looks like doesn't always keep your child safe, because sometimes it's hidden among weeds he may be walking through; it can even be disguised by a tangle of low bushes and shrubs. Its three leaves are usually tinged with red and trampled leaves have shiny black spots where the poison ivy resin has been exposed to air. It's this resin on the leaves that causes the rash.

Two out of every three people whose skin comes in contact with the resin on the damaged leaf can expect the rash to appear anywhere from twenty-four hours to as much as a week later. Its red spots look like minuscule blisters that appear to be leaking. This blister ooze (or liquid) doesn't carry or spread the poison ivy; it's just like the liquid that usually appears with any blisters. The rash can appear on any part of the exposed body or wherever the victim has scratched. (The resin may be on or under the fingernails.)

Poison oak is the name given to poison ivy in the bushy form; it looks like poison ivy, with its three leaves. Poison sumac doesn't resemble this. It has more than three leaves that are long and narrow and grow from a common stem. Sumac also has clusters of white berries.

### Seasonal Safety

This is what poison ivy and poison oak look like.

This is what poison sumac looks like.

The first line of defense against all three is to dress properly. If you or your child are going out walking through areas of heavy brush, wear long pants, socks, and long sleeves. If you think your child has been exposed, wash his hands and the exposed skin at once. If you can do so within five or ten minutes of exposure, you may be able to wash away most of the resin before it binds to the skin.

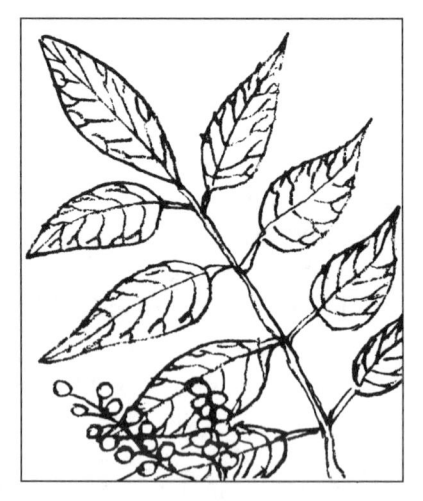

Though you can't immunize a child against a reaction to poison ivy, there are several things you can do. Many physicians believe that a good calamine lotion can control most poison ivy itching. Select a plain calamine without other ingredients that could cause a skin reaction.

## Seasonal Safety

According to Dr. Jeffrey L. Brown, Clinical Associate Professor of Psychiatry at New York Hospital-Cornell University Medical College, pain relievers, like acetaminophen, and analgesics taken by mouth can sometimes bring surprisingly effective relief. Caladryl® lotion may be recommended, and some physicians specify Ivy-Dry® cream for six- to twelve-year-olds to dry the itchy areas caused by poison ivy, and Benedryl® elixir (liquid) to help the itchiness. If the itching worsens, your physician may prescribe steroid tablets or liquid.

### Barbecue Grills

Many families like to celebrate the first really warm day of spring on the patio. Your next stop is the garage or basement where you stored the grill; now, after getting it out and cleaning it for a trial run, you're ready to create.

This brings up the problem of kids and grills. Better engage some safety rules right now, so that summer fun is not ruined.

First of all, assign one adult to do the barbecue honors and one adult to watch young children. The former does the cooking, and the latter keeps all young children away from the grill. That means keeping them away from the charcoal briquettes, ignition sources, the grilling tools, lighter fluids, and the cover of the barbecue unit. Keep adequate water available to douse any itinerant sparks.

## Safe Holidays

### Fourth of July Fireworks

Unless you're in the business, stay away from fireworks. Period. Kids who pride themselves on their daredevilry have been known to end up fingerless. Unbelievably, many people don't heed that advice. About 56 million pounds of fireworks sell annually, and most are bought by private citizens. What this adds up to are severe burns, blindness, amputation, even death. Every year, about 6,000 children seek emergency room treatment because of injuries caused by fireworks. Two-thirds of these result from legal fireworks, and 20 percent from sparklers. About a thousand emergency room visits are made by preschoolers injured by fireworks every year.

Fireworks most often cause facial burns. Hands can also suffer damage, and eye injuries have been known to cause blindness. As if all of these weren't bad enough, sparks that land on a child's thin July clothing can catch fire. Even sparklers burn fast at high temperatures and can ignite clothing quickly. None of these injuries is worth the risk of setting off fireworks in your own backyard for the fun of it.

Many states prohibit or limit the sale and use of ordinary fireworks, including wheels, Roman candles, sparklers, M-80s, party poppers, and missile-type rockets. Tell your kids that handling fireworks is better left to professionals who really know how to light them. If your child is curious about the colors, tell him that minerals and metals make up most firecrackers. When these metals and minerals are heated to high temperatures, they produce the bright colors you see in the sky. For example, calcium turns a deep red, sodium a vibrant yellow, and hot phosphorous, green. Explain that setting fire to these materials is dangerous. Children only see the fireworks as pretty and don't understand the dangers; they also don't know how to react quickly and effectively in an emergency situation.

If you must light fireworks, light them outdoors, away from the house, away from flammable items, and with a bucket of water handy. If a firecracker is malfunctioning, throw it out. If you must store fireworks, keep them in a cool, dry place, and out of a child's reach (a locked cabinet or toolbox). But it's far better not to store them, nor light them at all. Leave it to people who do it for a living.

## Happy Halloween

The happiest Halloween is a safe one. If only those miniature witches, ghouls, and ghosts were the worst monsters children had to face. The plain fact is that they're not, and parents would do well to have a little talk with their trick-or-treaters before they're off and running.

## Seasonal Safety

All costumes must be flame retardant (that includes masks and wigs, too), and your child should never carry a pumpkin with lit candles inside. Costumes should fit loosely enough to accommodate warm clothes underneath; many a Halloween night has been spoiled by chilled feet and fingers. Young trick-or-treaters should wear flat, comfortable shoes; heels can cause a fall. If it's raining, boots won't ruin a witch's outfit and may make it possible for the witch to feel comfortable on her neighborhood rounds.

## Seasonal Safety

If your child wears a flowing cape, be sure it isn't long enough to trip him. (Capes may also pose a strangulation risk.) If the fairy princess refuses to wear a hat, warm earmuffs (temporarily covered with satin to which sequins have been glued) could be enchanting.

Use reflective tape on every costume, so motorists can see your child. A flashlight can help him to see and be seen.

All kids like to wear masks, but many shouldn't. If your child insists, cut ample eye, nose, and mouth holes. That fairy princess (or witch) would look much more fetching, however, wearing makeup instead of a mask. The makeup should be as washable as possible (though Mom's lipstick is sure to be oil-based) and make very sure all face makeup and paints are nontoxic.

Your child should never eat candy that has been opened. Inspect all treats, and if any treat is opened or suspicious, throw it away. All fruit should be cut open and examined for any foreign objects. Call the police if you're suspicious of food tampering. Call your local Poison Control Center if your child has swallowed something harmful. If your child is given toys rather than treats, be sure they aren't small enough to choke the child if placed in the mouth.

Watch out for allergies. Children who don't know they are allergic to certain foods may ingest something seemingly harmless with disastrous results. As many as 4 percent of children under three years old suffer from food allergies. Those sufferers older than three make up only 1 to 2 percent of the population. Still, make sure your child checks with you regarding allergies.

If your child ingests a Halloween candy and exhibits an allergic response, treat those symptoms with a dose of liquid antihistamine. Try to reach your pediatrician immediately. If the symptoms are so severe that the child can't breathe, call 911.

Have your trick-or-treater eat something yummy at home before he takes off; that way, he won't be so hungry and will save the goodies he's collected till he gets home and you can inspect them. Many parents like to give their kids early dinners so that the kids can go in the early evening; others send them out right after an

## Seasonal Safety

afternoon snack, so that they are home before dinner. That way, parents can check the candy before it becomes dessert.

Accompany your young child trick-or-treating. Older responsible (teenage) siblings may also be pressed into service to escort tots who are making the rounds only of their own block or cul-de-sac. No young children should be wandering a several-block radius without Mom or Dad.

Remind your older children never to enter cars or accept treats from people in cars. They should remain in the neighborhood. Caution them to obey traffic lights, to use sidewalks (not the street), to wait at the curb and look both ways before crossing the street, and to cross only at the crosswalk. In a bulky costume, it's best to walk, not run. Give your older child a time to return home.

Some neighborhoods are not safe enough to allow a child of any age to go trick-or-treating. If that is the sad case in your area, seek out supervised Halloween parties and events planned at schools, churches, or park district facilities.

**Seasonal Safety**

# Very Important Tips

## WINTER SPORTS

1. When sledding, be sure the area is free from obstacles such as fences, rocks, and trees. All young children should sled with an adult. Older children should ride with another child.
2. Snowboarding requires practice, proper equipment and clothes, and lessons.
3. When skating, children should wear skates that fit. They should never skate at night. If outdoors, watch for any warning signs about the ice. All skaters should be courteous to others on the ice.
4. It is not true that little children (three years old) have no fear. They do get scared.
5. Make skiing practice inside fun, so that when they go outside, they're not afraid.
6. Have kids walk around inside and practice wearing heavy boots and skis. Then, when they go outside, they won't be intimidated by them.
7. Two- and three-year-olds need one-on-one instruction. It is important for a child and an instructor to bond and build trust.
8. Instructors should ski in front of a three-year-old, so that the child doesn't ski by them.
9. If you go skiing in high altitudes, expect that your child will feel it. Between that and the time zone changes, he'll be tired and thirsty. Provide plenty of rest and liquids to drink.

## WINTER WARNINGS

1. The key to dressing for winter is layer, layer, layer. A few necessities for wintry days are hats, gloves, boots, sunblock, lip balm, sunglasses, and juice or water for hydration.
2. Hypothermia occurs when the body is exposed to cold aggravated by wet, wind, and exhaustion. Symptoms of hypothermia include drowsiness, uncontrollable shivering, slow speech, incoherence, and apparent exhaustion. When children get wet while playing in the snow, call them in and dress them in dry clothes or keep them in to rest and warm up. (This goes for adults too.)

## Seasonal Safety

# Very Important Tips

3. A key frostbite warning sign is red skin turning white and waxy. Watch for this on the nose, cheeks, ears, fingers, and toes.

### SUMMER SUNNING
1. For maximum benefit, apply sunblock to your infant's skin every time he is in the sun—at beaches, parks, or every day in your own backyard.
2. For swimming protection, choose a waterproof sunblock and be sure to reapply every ninety minutes.
3. Sunblock is more effective than sunscreen, but if you use sunscreen, choose a moisturizing sunscreen with an SPF of at least 15.
4. For children with allergies or ultrasensitive skin, choose a hypoallergenic sunscreen.
5. Protective clothing blocks reflected light. The sun's rays bounce off sand, concrete, and water (even on cloudy days), so it's a good idea to cover your baby in a shirt and a hat. Even so, use a sunscreen under your baby's clothes.
6. Some medications can cause increased sensitivity to the sun's UV rays. If your baby is on a medication, ask your doctor if you should decrease his sun exposure.

### SUMMER WARNINGS
1. Heat exhaustion occurs when the body loses fluid as a result of sweating. To avoid heat exhaustion, drink plenty of liquids.
2. Heat stroke is more severe than heat exhaustion. Some common signs are hot and dry skin, dizziness, diarrhea, irritability, and vomiting.
3. To prevent bee stings, avoid wearing perfumed lotions and stay away from flower beds. If you or your child is stung, never scrape the stinger with your fingernail.
4. Tick bites can cause Lyme disease. Some warning signs are a migrating rash, fever, and joint swelling and soreness. To avoid ticks, apply tick repellent (but not on babies under one year old) and stay away from grassy, wooded areas.

## Seasonal Safety
# Very Important Tips

5. To prevent mosquito bites, spray your child's clothes, not his skin, with insect repellent.
6. Teach your child what poison ivy and poison oak look like so he can avoid touching those when he sees them.

### HOLIDAYS
1. Never, never play with fireworks on any occasion.
2. On Halloween, dress your child in a costume with reflective tape on it. Teach him to stay in well-lit areas, and inspect all candy before he eats it.
3. During winter holidays, keep festive plants away from children. Many are poisonous if eaten. Be sure to extinguish all candles when leaving home or going to bed. Check all indoor and outdoor lights for frayed wires and loose connections, and do not plug in more than three sets of lights on one extension cord.
4. Keep Christmas trees well watered so they don't dry out, and place ornaments high up and out of reach of children.

# Chapter 11
# For Pet's Sake

RAISING AND CARING FOR ANY PET can be one of the most valuable, memorable, and rewarding activities parents and children can share. Helping to select and take care of a pet can give a young child important early insights into what it means to be a responsible, compassionate person. A good pet can be not only a good companion, but also an anchoring force in a child's life, offering structure in the form of its physical needs and opportunities to learn from its habits and behavior. Growing up with unconditional love from a happy and well-cared-for pet can provide some wonderful memories for your child, even after she reaches adulthood.

You'll want to be sure your new pet doesn't pose a risk to your child's safety. To ensure that bringing a pet into your home is a positive experience for everyone, make your choice of pet a safe and realistic one. Marla Minuskin, president of the Chicago Veterinary Medical Association, notes that "one should never assume anything when it comes to pets. For example, the assumption that little dogs are better than big dogs for children, or that you should be careful of certain breeds of cat, is not always right. I've known a lot of little dogs that are much more aggressive than big dogs."

Watch for behavior that shows how the animal responds to the child, and note whether it tends to protect the child or to be jealous of the child. "Many times," says Minuskin, "when the pet and the child are raised together, you're going to have the best luck. They're going to be like sister and brother, as much as that can sometimes be a hassle! Mixed breeds [of dogs] are your best breeds, your basic mutts."

Along the same lines, you may have heard stories of cats suffocating children, but the only explanation Minuskin can think of is "that the baby had milk on its breath and the cat came to investigate. In years of practice, I can say that yes, there are aggressive cats and cats that will scratch, bite, be jealous, or be angry, but most cats will just retreat and will not be an unsafe animal to have around the house or be with children.

You just have to be cautious. Nobody even thinks of a parakeet being dangerous. But a parrot could break a finger! If I'm not careful how I handle a parrot or a macaw, they can crunch my finger in their beak and break it. So when you use the word 'bird,' think: do I mean a canary or do I mean a macaw?

"Educate yourself and the family about every animal, and keep your eyes open and be cautious, based on knowledge about that particular animal. Take warning signs seriously. There have been enough documented attacks on children by specific dogs. You read about them, but incidents are rare. If you have a dog that snarls at a child or bites a child once, if you think the child is in real danger, then that's not a risk you should take. You also need to be very, very careful about warning whomever that pet goes to, about what the dog or cat has done. Accept warning signs and take heed before something else happens."

## Selecting a Pet

Your first move in making an intelligent, informed decision about what type of animal to select starts with learning what type of animals can be dangerous if left unsupervised with children. Make sure the family learns the safest ways to care for a new pet. Select the safest cages, hutches, or aquariums and find out where and how to display them so that a child can enjoy them without the possibility of them toppling over or otherwise harming her. And, of course, it's important to store your pet's food, medications, choke-hazardous toys, and other pet care products out of your child's reach.

Start your pet search with animal shelters, pet stores, animal breeders, or private owners located through newspaper advertisements. Word of mouth is another good way to locate a pet. If a friend or acquaintance has a dog or cat whose looks and temperament you like, ask if they got it from a specific breeder. Learn more about what kinds of animals to look at and where to find them at pet shows, usually sponsored every few months by various pet organizations in most cities.

It's important to find a pet that will suit your family's lifestyle. If your family travels often or spends a lot of time out of the house, you may want to opt for a lower-maintenance animal, such as a cat, or a cage-confined animal, such as a hamster or rabbit. A dog demands more time. If your family doesn't want to put the time into housebreaking and training a puppy, you may want to look into adopting an older dog that's already trained and housebroken. If a member of your family has allergies, consider pets with less allergic potential, such as fish, reptiles, or birds, rather than a furry pet that could contribute to health problems.

Be aware also of the risks inherent in mixing pets in a household. Compatibility can be an issue when introducing Fido into a home where a cat (or another dog) already lives. Unfortunately, it's hard to predict how the two animals will get along, and whether or not the jealousy of one pet poses a threat toward another or even toward other members of your family. In selecting a new pet as an addition to your family, a little common sense goes a long way.

## Dogs

Dogs become part of the family very quickly, so you'll want to choose your "best friend" wisely. Though thousands of adult dogs in pet stores, animal shelters, and private homes are available for adoption, many parents prefer buying a puppy for their young child, so the child and the dog can "grow up together." Bringing a dog home is a big commitment; if you adopt the dog specifically for your child, make sure the child is mature enough to understand the responsibility of pet ownership and is capable of helping with, if not entirely assuming, the care of the dog.

### Selecting a Dog

Before you even set out to look for a dog, consider the breed you'd most like your child to be around. Descended from wolves, different breeds have been developed by humans throughout history to fulfill specific needs. Some dogs are bred for hunting, while others are developed to be strong (even vicious, to fight other dogs and animals for people's perverse entertainment). Other dogs are bred to be "living tools": guards, rodent-catchers, animal herders, rescuers, and, yes, lovable house pets. Make sure the dog you consider is the right size, has the correct features, and, most importantly, displays the right temperament. To help you find a good match for your "family type," spend some time in research. If you are looking for a breed with a typically gentle disposition that's good with kids, the Chihuahua may be too small, but consider labs, golden retrievers, shelties, shih tzus, and basset hounds, all dogs that acclimate well to a child. Keep in mind, though, that any dog can and will bite.

Many veterinary associations recommend buying a mid-sized (around forty pounds) female dog for preschool-aged children. Select a healthy, sturdy older dog with a gentle disposition. Make sure the dog doesn't exhibit excessive guarding behavior or become angry or agitated when something is taken away. Why select an older dog? For one thing, puppies of all breeds have small but very sharp milk teeth (teeth used for nursing) and don't know how to control their biting.

If you feel you can manage a puppy's boundless energy and unpredictable biting, look for a friendly, well-proportioned, and healthy puppy. Try to find out as much as possible about the puppy's parents. Did either of them have any temper problems, or a health problem the puppy may inherit, such as hip, eye, ear, or skin problems or allergies to certain foods, chemicals, medications, or plants? Stand back and watch the puppy interact with other people and dogs. Is it easygoing and friendly, or overly shy, jealous, hostile, or hyperactive? Try to overcome your initial reaction to the puppy's cuteness and small size and imagine the puppy as it might look and act when it grows up. Will it be too big or tough to handle? Is it a dog you wouldn't mind having as a companion for yourself? It may still be alive when your child has left home for college or career.

Inspect the puppy to make sure its eyes are clear, properly aligned, and free of mucous or matted discharge. Make sure the dog isn't sneezing or coughing and has reached the proper size and weight for its age. The puppy should be very energetic and have healthy-looking fur and skin. Inspect the home or facility where the puppy was raised to make sure it was a clean, warm, reasonably happy place where it got the proper nourishment and attention from its mother, and was not abused. Try to find out the exact age of the puppy and whether or not it has had its first coronavirus, parvo, and distemper vaccinations.

If all of these issues check out all right, try to arrange a test meeting to see if the puppy will get along well with your child and your other pets before you make a final decision. See how the puppy reacts alone with you or with your child, out of the presence of its siblings or other pets. When you think you've found the puppy that you simply must take home, immediately set up an appointment with a veterinarian to give the puppy a physical exam. The vet will thoroughly examine the puppy's teeth, eyes, ears, nose, throat, heart, lungs, joints, and skin. Try to make an arrangement with the puppy's previous owners that will allow you to return the puppy if it is diagnosed with any serious or life-threatening medical conditions.

The vet will also give the dog whatever vaccinations it needs along with worming medication. The doctor can also recommend various obedience schools or individual trainers who will come to your home. Obedience school benefits the owner as much as the dog; training both is the responsible thing to do. Train any child who will be caring for and walking the dog. Trainers will also teach you how to feed, housebreak, and socialize your dog properly. At your veterinarian's office, look for pamphlets about how to feed and care for your dog. Don't hesitate to leave with an armful.

## Bringing the Dog Home

Once home, keep the dog's movements confined to specific parts of the house where it can be watched and won't damage furniture or other items. You can easily set up confined "dog areas" in a kitchen, family room, or another room by fitting one or more adjustable dog gates in doorways. Made of wood, plastic, or metal, dog gates come in a variety of sizes and heights. Most are reasonably priced and well designed to prevent causing accidental injury to you, your child, or the dog.

A wire pet cage makes a good investment. Far from being a cruel device meant to punish your dog, a pet cage can serve as a useful way to contain your dog when young guests unfamiliar with your pet are milling about the house. Many dogs, particularly when they're young, treat their cages as indoor doghouses, "time-out zones" where they can voluntarily retreat when they want some time to themselves or a familiar place to sleep. In many areas, dogs do quite well outside in doghouses. Also, a well-designed fence will contain the dog so it doesn't run away while keeping strange dogs from wandering into your yard.

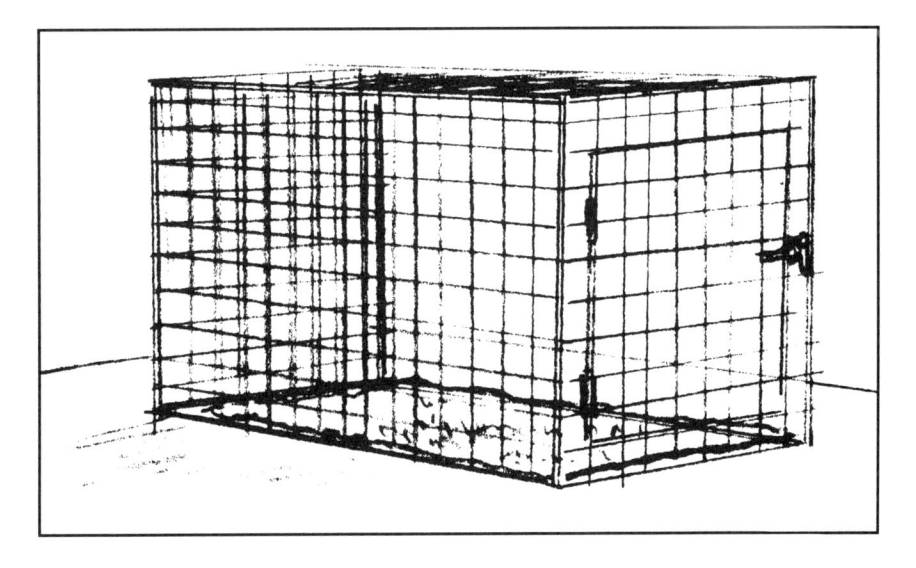

Establish a regular place in your home where the dog or puppy can eat and drink. Though you may have your dog on a set feeding schedule, make sure it always has access to fresh water. (Dogs rely heavily on the water they drink; they lose a lot of water by panting, which helps regulate their body temperatures and keep their skin and fur healthy.)

The best water dish for your dog would be a flat, heavy dish from a pet supply store made of ceramic, plastic, or metal. According to Dr. Glenn Meyer, former president of the Chicago

Veterinary Association, you should "never use containers such as buckets, wastebaskets, or other tall plastic or metal containers as a water bowl for your dog, especially if you have toddlers or young children. Any container that your child could get his head, face, or upper body caught in should be strictly off limits. Children have been known to drown in as little as one inch of water." No need to panic if your toddler eats a piece of the dog's dry dog food (although be alert for choking), but you should still prevent the practice by feeding the dog at specific times and storing dog food in a secure plastic container, on a shelf or in a pantry to which the child has no access.

Dr. Meyer also suggests that as a new dog eats, an adult should pat it on the rear to accustom it to the feeling of being bumped by a child. In this way, the dog learns not to snap at the child. Part of the dog's socialization and training will be to teach it to be gentle with children. Watch out for dogs that turn aggressive when approached while eating, or that aggressively guard a bone or toy; they require patient training and very close supervision. Remember, hunger fuels a dog's behavior at feeding time and often prompts unpredictable behavior. Never let your child come between a dog and its food at feeding time.

Keep pet maintenance items such as heartworm medicine, vitamins, shampoos, ointments, and grooming tools strictly out of reach of children like all medications and sharp implements that adults may use. Keep your Poison Control Center's phone number near your telephone, as well as numbers of your family physician, veterinarian, and emergency services, and briefly familiarize yourself with the symptoms to look for and the treatments to administer should your child accidentally ingest or otherwise come into contact with your pet's medicines.

## Training

To be sure that your dog doesn't become a safety risk to anyone in the family, invest some time in obedience training either through an obedience training school, an owner-pet training program, or a diligent training regimen in your home. A well-mannered and even-tempered dog is a safer dog, less likely to bolt off into dangerous traffic or brush.

Training also strengthens the bond between a dog and its owner. A well-trained pet regards you as the "top dog" and the one to be obeyed, especially important with large or potentially aggressive or dominant breeds. If such a dog doesn't respect you as the leader, you both could be in big trouble farther down the line, especially in situations involving children. Training can make your dog fun to be around and more likely to earn approval from passersby, visitors, and family members than a rowdy or ill-mannered animal.

### Dogs and Babies

Think of bringing home a new baby to meet the family dog in the same way you'd bring her home to meet an older child. Before the baby comes home, let the dog smell some of her layette things. Practice holding a baby doll, so the dog sees that it's not always going to be the center of attention.

Dogs can be jealous; that's why it's important to know what breeds get along with children. When the baby arrives, one parent can hold and play with her while the other parent plays with the dog. Keep a regular routine with the dog; Fido still needs special times for play.

For the most part, dogs, though curious about babies, adjust without incident. Here are several more things you can do to prepare your dog before the baby comes:
- Be sure your dog knows how to sit, stay, lie down, and come when called.
- Practice "baby activities": command the dog to sit and stay while you pick up a doll, hold it, rock it, and so on. Then reward and praise the dog for remaining in the correct position. Show the doll to the dog. If you're feeling particularly wary about your pet, it might be wise to acquaint the dog with recorded baby sounds (crying, babbling, etc.).

Take things slowly when baby comes home from the hospital:
- Allow time for the dog to get used to the smells, sounds, and presence of the baby.
- Allow the (leashed) dog to see the baby from about ten to fifteen feet away. Then bring them closer. If the dog remains

calm and under control, you might allow it to sniff the baby. You know your dog, so it's a judgment call.
- Monitor your dog's behavior closely. The best of dogs can act up under stress or when a baby is crying uncontrollably. Talk to the dog as you begin to do something with the baby. This allows the dog to associate pleasant experiences with the baby and gives the dog extra attention.

## Walking Dogs Safely

Making the time to walk the dog with their children can be a great opportunity for parents to put some "quality time" into a busy schedule. It gives parents and children a chance to enjoy being outdoors and share the unabashed joy dogs take from running, playing with their masters, and exploring new surroundings. Letting your child "take the reins" by holding the leash and guiding the dog is not only fun, it also empowers her with some responsibility for the well-being of a member of the family. When another dog passes, an adult should take hold of the dog's leash to avoid contact between the two dogs. If a child is holding the leash when another dog gets close, and one or both dogs react, the child can end up getting hurt too.

The size and temperament of your dog in relation to the size and temperament of your child should guide you in deciding whether to let the child take the leash. Does your child have the necessary knowledge and skill to keep the dog under control? (You wouldn't turn your five-year-old loose for a scamper around the park clinging to the leash of your untrained, eighty-pound rottweiler. On the other hand, from the perspective of the dog's safety, you wouldn't let your rambunctious ten-year-old drag your miniature poodle behind her like a rag doll.)

The key to a successful child-dog walking relationship is mutual respect. A child needs to know the responsibility of having a dog depend on her. The dog must be made to realize that this small person holding its leash requires as much respect and obedience as you do. For this reason, you must supervise the first several walks your dog takes with an older child (as well as every walk

**For Pet's Sake**

your dog and a younger child take, especially if the dog's route takes you places off limits to your child alone.)

Teach your child the commands you give the dog when walking and emphasize the importance of using a firm tone of voice when necessary. Assure your child that she won't hurt the dog's feelings by sternly ordering the dog to heel or sit (especially if the dog becomes overly excited by traffic, other dogs, a squirrel, or a rabbit).

The two major hazards to dogs are traffic and other dogs. If your child isn't physically or emotionally strong enough to contend with either of these situations, she should not walk the dog alone outside your property. Make sure the child knows that your dog depends on her to keep it safe, and that she must take care of the dog and keep it out of danger in very much the same way you take care of the child and keep her out of danger.

As another child approaches, tell her not to rush up to the dog and ask her to talk to you and your child before petting the dog. Kids should learn not to run from a dog, because it may follow.

To help a younger child learn how to manage a leashed dog, let her hold onto one side of the end loop of the dog's leash while you hold the other. This will allow the child to feel the tug of the leash without the danger of the child losing her balance or her grip on the dog. As the child gains experience, it's okay to let her walk the dog in a safe, open place such as a park, field, or yard—a place where you can see the dog, and more importantly, where the dog can see that you are keeping an eye on things.

The safest leash by far is the popular nylon strap variety, looped at one end for a handhold and connected at the other end to a clip that hooks to the dog's collar. Nylon is light, strong, affordable, and easy to clean. Its soft, slightly slippery texture makes a friction burn less likely should it slip through the child's hands. Because they can cause burns, scrapes, and scratches, materials such as rope, twine, chain (other than some specialized dog chains), wire, or electrical cable should never be used as a makeshift leash for your dog, especially if your child will be holding it.

**For Pet's Sake**

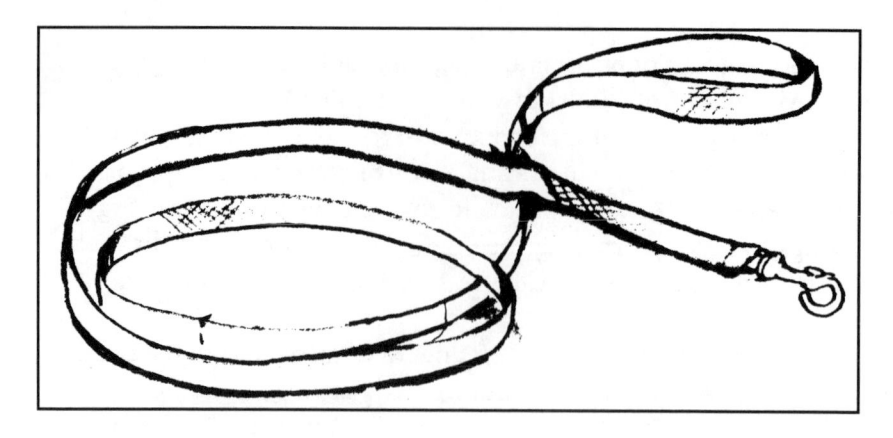

Beware of the "fishing reel" leash. Designed to give the dog more freedom and the master more rest, such leashes consist of a spring-loaded spool of cord enclosed in a plastic handle-shaped casing. The owner holds the enclosed spool device and lets the cord feed out as the dog runs or walks away. The owner can stop the dog at any time by pulling a trigger or pressing a button built into the handle to activate a catch. Risks to a child, however, include rope burn from accidentally grabbing the line while it is feeding out, or possible hand, arm, muscle, or joint injuries if the child pushes the catch and is jerked or knocked down while the dog is running away from him.

A dog leash can be as dangerous off the dog as on. A child should never be allowed to swing a dog leash around or otherwise use it as a toy. Injuries could result from being struck by the metal clip at the end, being tripped by a swinging leash, or being scratched, bruised, or possibly cut by a leash being used during rough play. Don't leave dog leashes hanging from coat hooks, doorknobs, or kitchen cupboard door handles in between walks; an unsupervised child might strangle or suffocate by becoming entangled in an idle leash.

## Diseases

Dog owners must deal responsibly with sanitation and the prevention of pet-borne diseases. Keeping your dog outside reduces the spread of diseases and infections to family members. Housebreaking a puppy means indoor accidents are inevitable.

Internal parasites such as tapeworms, roundworms, and giardia can be spread to animals and humans through contact with an infected dog's feces. Bacteria such as salmonella and campylobacter can also be carried in the stool of dogs and can cause intestinal infection. Symptoms of such bacterial infection include loose stool or diarrhea. To prevent the spread of these parasites and bacteria, keep the dog's feces from accumulating either outside or in your home. If your dog suffers from parasites or a bacterial infection, give it the proper medication to clear them up and prevent the possibility of a more serious illness.

To dispose of your pet's waste, you may want to consider one of the many dog waste clean-up systems available on the market today. Most systems consist of a ventilated canister or tank that you bury under the ground, leaving only the opening or lid exposed—much the same principle as a home septic system. (Some even have a handy foot-operated opening lever.) A premixed enzyme solution added to the tank "digests" your dog's waste, converting it into harmless organic material that then gets absorbed into the ground.

Ringworm and scabies mites are two skin infections that can be passed from dogs to humans. Ringworm (a fungus not caused by worms) transmits easily to people, especially to children. Symptoms include dry, scaly, itchy skin in red patches that sometimes develop in a circular pattern (hence, the name ringworm). Once you recognize symptoms, call your doctor. Left untreated, the infection may cause long-term harm. Depending on how bad your pet's or child's infection is, it can be treated with antifungal creams, ointments, baths, and possibly oral medication. Ringworm infection usually takes between four and six weeks to clear up.

Scabies might be the itchiest parasite a dog or person could suffer. A dog might pick up scabies mites from your boarding kennel, your veterinary clinic, or from playing in the park or a yard with other dogs. To rid the dog of scabies, you must kill the mites with special medications and use antibiotics to control the skin infections.

## For Pet's Sake

Diseases carried and transmitted by fleas and ticks have long been a serious concern for dog owners, especially with the growing public awareness of the dangers of Lyme disease. Both humans and dogs can contract Lyme disease from ticks (usually after walking, hiking, or romping in wooded areas), but not from each other. Flu-like symptoms of this bacterial infection may include fatigue, headache, hot and swollen joints, and sometimes a skin rash. Left untreated, Lyme disease can cause serious long-term health problems in the heart and joints of children and adults. Remember that early detection is a must, although for many individuals there is no treatment. Luckily, Lyme disease vaccine is available for dogs. Have your dog tested if you have even the slightest suspicion that it might have been exposed. Take extra precautions when you remove ticks from your dog, or allow a veterinarian to remove the ticks and apply a residual tick repellent to prevent the risk of further exposure.

All dogs must be vaccinated for rabies by law. Ideally, a dog should first be vaccinated at three months and receive a booster at one year. (After that, shots come due every three years.) An outbreak of rabies could be deadly for humans, as well as animals. You must carry a rabies certificate while traveling with your dog within the United States. It would be wise to check for similar regulations if you are planning a trip abroad.

Incurable in dogs, rabies is a viral infection that can be transmitted through the saliva of an infected animal. Unless vaccinated, your dog could pick it up by being bitten by a bat, a skunk, or a raccoon. Examining its brain is the only way to determine whether an animal has contracted rabies. Since it is probably impossible to test the animal that attacked your dog, there is no way to know whether it has been infected until symptoms begin. A rabid dog must be euthanized.

Symptoms of rabies in dogs include excessive thirst and therefore excessive urination, occasionally bloodshot eyes, and lethargic and/or aggressive behavior. They may hide or growl, and in the later stages, they may become antisocial with people and other dogs. They do froth at the mouth.

When your child is bitten by a dog she knows, you or the owner of the dog should call the local animal control center to pick up the dog immediately, and then call the vet to verify the currency of the dog's rabies vaccination. Cleanse your child's wound with lukewarm or hot water for ten minutes using an antiseptic soap. If bleeding cannot be stopped, go immediately to the emergency room at the nearest hospital.

If wild, the biting dog will probably be identified as a rabies risk and sacrificed immediately so that its brain can be examined for signs of rabies infection. Fortunately, according to the American Academy of Pediatrics in 1993, rabies from a dog bite was so rare that no more than five cases per year had been reported in the United States since 1960.

## Strays

Sometimes you and your child don't even need to go out and look for a pet dog. Sometimes the dog picks you. Teach your child that she must not automatically trust strange, unfamiliar, and unattended dogs, even if a dog engages her. If you see an unfamiliar dog roaming your neighborhood, keep your child away from it until you've determined whether it wears a collar, a registration tag, or a vaccination tag. If it does have tags and seems to like you and your child, give the dog some water and call the dog's owner. If the dog has no tags but appears healthy and good-natured, you must decide whether to take it to an animal shelter, house it for a while and advertise its whereabouts, or keep it permanently. If you decide to keep it, take it to a veterinarian right away for a physical examination to determine its good health.

If a stray dog bites your child, call the animal control center immediately, giving them as exact a description of the dog and its whereabouts as you can. If the dog is considered at risk for rabies when captured, it will be destroyed and tested for the rabies virus and other diseases. If the dog tests positive for rabies, your child will need to undergo rabies treatment to prevent her from contracting the dangerous disease. If the bite breaks your child's skin, clean and dress the wound and take the child to an emergency room or physician's office so a doctor can determine the need for stitches and a tetanus shot.

## Cats

Though cats are just as furry, four-legged, and popular as canines, they tend to be more reserved and self-sufficient than dogs. Many people and families who travel often or lead very active lives opt for cats rather than dogs, since they can fend for themselves for several days at a time if left with enough food, fresh water, and a proper litter box or similar facility.

While dogs, being extremely social creatures, see themselves as part of your family and strive to be included and well liked, cats remain independent, often acting completely indifferent to the relationships within the family. However, though independent and sometimes aloof, cats can also be warm and affectionate companions.

## Selecting a Cat

Many of the principles that guide finding a pet dog apply to finding a pet cat as well. Most communities have animal shelters and even specific cat shelters full of healthy cats in need of a good home. Pet stores can also be good places to locate a pet cat, or at least to windowshop to determine what sort of feline would best suit your lifestyle. When cat hunting at a pet store, check the store's reputation. Does it obtain its animals from clean, humane breeders or other sources, or from inhumane kitten and puppy "mills" that churn out unhealthy animals raised in unsanitary, and often abusive, conditions?

**For Pet's Sake**

The pet section of your local newspaper's classifieds probably includes several advertisements by people whose cats have had kittens or who can no longer keep or take care of their healthy, well-behaved cats.

Some cat owners purchase a purebred cat from a cat breeder. Purebred cats are potentially valuable as breeder cats; you might even take home a prize if you enter your cat in shows. And, if you own a purebred cat, you'll most likely have access to information on your pet's parents and breeding history, which can help you to identify possible health and behavioral problems.

## Cats and Babies

Should a cat owner (or a potential one) have serious concerns about children in the household, when it comes to a cat's sharp teeth and sharp claws? Most felines will lash out if they're in the mood, creating an unpredictable risk of injury, especially to small children who might not be aware of the warning signs a cat sends when it's agitated. If a cat exhibits defensive body language when children approach it, they should leave the cat alone and try petting or playing with it some other time when it is in a better mood. Some clues a cat may give to show it doesn't feel like socializing include hissing, growling, or meowing in a low tone, arching its back, spitting, flattening its ears against its head, or slitting its eyes. When annoyed, cats often wag or twitch their tails, as well.

As a rule, parents shouldn't leave a very young or small child unattended in the same room with a cat—especially if the cat doesn't know her. Playful and curious herself, a child won't be able to resist the opportunity to make a new friend out of the cat. When a new baby arrives, a cat will be naturally curious. Wait until your baby is a few weeks old, used to her surroundings, and stronger before introducing her to your cat. After that, you should never leave your baby and cat together in the same room unattended as your cat might approach the child to investigate, become startled, and accidentally bite or scratch the baby.

Introduce your cat to a young child or toddler by holding the cat on your lap or at a level where the child and cat can see each other. While stroking the cat gently to calm it, speak softly to the child, encouraging her to stroke the cat gently as you are doing.

Thanks to your familiar touch and sound, the cat will probably revel in the extra attention given by the child rather than hiss, bite, or scratch.

Being standoffish toward strangers and sometimes finicky even around people they know, most cats will react negatively to being surprised or handled roughly by anyone, but especially by someone they don't know. If that person happens to be a small child, the cat could lash out, biting or scratching, instead of simply retreating, as they might when facing an adult. When guests visit your home, whether adults or children, it might be best to put your cat or dog on a leash.

## Claws

Sheathed within the cat's toes, claws can be extended or retracted whenever the cat wants. Cats use their claws for a variety of reasons including climbing, hunting, maintaining a grip on slippery or uneven surfaces, and keeping themselves balanced, as well as for self-defense.

Many cat owners opt to have their cats declawed, whether they have children or not. Besides reducing your child's risk of sustaining a nasty cut or scratch from your cat's front claws, declawing will also stop a cat from damaging your furniture while attempting to sharpen its claws.

Declawing—onychectomy—is a simple surgical procedure from which your cat needs only a few days to recover. Declawing can be done while the cat is under general anesthesia for neutering or spaying. Most vets remove the front claws but leave the back claws intact so the cat can use them for traction and as a last-ditch defense against an aggressive cat or other attacker.

If your cat spends a lot of time outdoors, your veterinarian will probably recommend against declawing. Outside, cats act very much like they would in the wild and depend on their claws for defense and climbing trees to escape predators. A cat with no front claws would be at a serious disadvantage in the outdoor world. A good compromise would be to clip your cat's nails often to limit the serious cuts and scratches that untended razor-sharp claws can inflict. Clipping the claws every week or two will dull the nails enough to prevent severe skin, face, or eye injury if the cat scratches someone. (This option makes sense especially for purebred cats, since declawing will disqualify them from cat shows.)

If the family cat scratches your child and you're certain that the cat is relatively clean and has had all of its vaccinations, soothe your child and treat the wound as you would any other cut or scratch by washing and disinfecting it and applying a bandage if necessary. If the cut is deep, take your child to the emergency room or a doctor's office; stitches or a tetanus shot may be needed.

Sometimes a cat can accidentally injure a child's eye or eyes with an improperly aimed swipe of the paw. Such scratches can be extremely painful and can cause serious and sight-threatening injury to the eye. Go immediately to a physician; medication will soothe the pain as well as prevent infection and aid the healing process. A severe eye injury may also require minor surgery or a supervised period of recovery to prevent any loss or impairment of vision.

## Diseases

Cats can host numerous infections caused by protozoans, or one-celled organisms. The most dangerous of these protozoans to humans causes toxoplasmosis, which can lead to birth defects and even stillbirth. Cats are exposed to the organism either through contact with rodents or other small animals it hunts, or by eating raw meat (possibly the meat of its prey). Because an infected cat will pass millions of the organism's microscopic eggs in its feces, pregnant women should never clean up after a cat indoors or change the cat's litter. If yours is an outdoor cat, the soil in flowerbed or garden areas could create a risk as well.

Keep the cat's litter area clean to prevent the possible spread of disease, and for obvious reasons, keep young children—especially when they're at the age when they'll put anything in their mouths—away from the cat's litterbox. Toddlers may mistake it for a sandbox.

The protozoal infection coccidiosis can cause persistent diarrhea in both humans and cats, especially kittens. If your kitten suffers frequent diarrhea, take it to the veterinarian at once for diagnosis and to prevent the spread of disease. Cats are also susceptible to many different types of worms that shouldn't be left untreated, though transmission to humans is rare. Roundworms are common in kittens, and lungworms in hunting cats. And of course, if your cat takes medications for worms or any other infectious illnesses, keep them out of the reach of your children, as you would with any type of medicine.

Cats sometimes transmit a disease to humans that has earned the nickname "cat scratch fever" or "cat scratch syndrome." This infectious disease, caused by a bacteria that occurs naturally in a cat's mouth and spreads by scratching or biting, exhibits flu-like symptoms: swollen lymph nodes, fatigue, headache, fever, loss of appetite, vomiting. Cat scratch fever affects up to twenty-two thousand people a year and accounts for approximately two thousand hospitalizations. Cat owners with children should be aware of this disease, as should the elderly and the immunodeficient or those who have weakened immune systems, such as people undergoing cancer chemotherapy or taking long-term steroids. The disease is associated more with kittens than with adult cats, but veterinarians are unsure if this means that kittens are more prone to the infection, or that they simply bite and scratch more.

### Strays

If a stray cat bites or scratches your child, clean and dress the injury and take your child to an emergency room or doctor's office. The animal should be caught so that it can be tested for rabies.

Report the cat to your animal control agency; give them its description and the location in which your child found it. It may be necessary to entrap or possibly even kill a stray animal if it's vicious and poses a threat.

## Birds

Although less popular than dogs or cats, birds can live comfortably in closer quarters, making them common pets among apartment dwellers and families who don't want a pet with the bulk or the roaming range of a dog or a cat.

**For Pet's Sake**

## Domestic Birds

Most birds sold as pets are of the hook-billed variety: parrots, parakeets, macaws, cockatoos, cockateels, and conures. Called hook-bills because of the particular curvature of their strong beaks, these birds can be highly personable, easy to feed and care for, and the most likely to learn to talk. Popular non-hook-bills include pigeons, toucans, finches, canaries, and mynah birds.

For a household with children, select smaller birds that can be comfortably confined in a cage most of the time: parakeets, finches, or canaries, all small-billed, generally passive, and relatively quiet or pleasant-sounding birds.

Because of their physical delicacy, birds probably shouldn't be introduced into a household with young children who don't yet understand the risk they pose to the bird and vice versa, or basic ideas about sanitation and droppings (not to put feathers, seeds, and bird droppings in your mouth, for example). Children living with birds should already know basic household safety rules such as keeping out of medicine cabinets and other storage places for pet-related medicines and chemicals and not throwing toys or other objects that could break or topple a bird cage in the house.

### For Pet's Sake

A bird is probably not an ideal pet to have around an infant or very small toddler; she may enjoy watching and listening to domestic birds when she visits a bird owner's home, but she should be supervised at all times in the bird's presence. Make sure the child doesn't touch or stick her fingers between the bars of a bird's cage. Birds normally allowed to fly or roam about the house should probably be caged during the child's visit.

When acquiring a bird, make sure you have consulted with a veterinarian, bird breeder, or a friend who keeps birds to make sure the breed you are considering has the proper temperament, noise level, and space and diet requirements for your household. Purchase an easy-to-clean cage of the right size and strength made of a nontoxic material.

Highly social and surprisingly intelligent creatures, domestic birds crave attention from their owners to replace the steady stream of input their active brains would be processing if in the wild. New bird owners often shower their pet with attention at first, tapering off as the novelty of the new pet wanes. This can cause negative behaviors such as repeated squawking or screaming, thrashing around inside the cage, feather picking, food throwing, biting, and pecking. The bird's intense need to be integrated into the life of your family rather than being "quarantined" makes it absolutely essential that your child is mature enough to be trusted around the bird without constant supervision.

Place the cage so that the bird can participate in the household hustle and bustle. And, since pet birds like to be kept busy, you may want to provide safe toys such as bird-specific chew toys, pieces of rope or rawhide, and cardboard paper towel and toilet paper tubes.

After bringing a new bird into your home, let it adjust to the frightening rush of new sights, sounds, and smells from the safety of its own cage for about a week. Interact with it using a calm, soothing voice and slow, even motions until it appears relaxed and adjusted to its new environment.

After a comfortable adjustment period for both the bird and your child, begin to train your bird in a quiet room free from distractions. To ensure that the bird does not fly away and stays focused and attentive to your training efforts, it may be wise to have its flight feathers clipped by a veterinarian qualified to treat birds. If the child wants to train the bird to sit on her and take food from her, an adult must be present. Also, make sure that you don't allow the bird to sit on your shoulder or your head. Birds may scratch your face, transmitting diseases through the scratch. Also, humans can pick up some diseases from birds by breathing in skin material from them.

## Wild Birds

Rather than keeping pet birds, many parents and their children choose to attract wild birds to their yards or outdoor areas so that they may watch them in their natural habitat. It's fun to offer food and water for drinking and bathing. If you provide good nest-building locations and materials, you and your child can make friends with the wild birds that live in your area.

But don't forget about your child's safety. Will more birds in your yard create a risk for your infant or toddler, who might try to eat seeds or bird droppings off the ground? Here's a good rule of thumb: If the child still puts things in her mouth, don't leave her alone in the yard. The feather of a wild bird, while fascinating, could be host to parasites or bird-borne diseases; this goes for eggs and nests, too. Are the bird feeders or birdhouses you're using made of safe materials? Are they designed not to harm anyone if they accidentally break or are knocked down? Consider too that bird feeders or birdhouses may attract other animals to your yard.

Some pet supply stores offer advice on how to attract the types of birds you want and directions on how to select or build a feeder to do the job. Many experts and pet stores recommend setting up a birdbath or similar water source so that birds will be inclined to drink and bathe in your yard. Be sure the birdbath is child-safe as well. (Place it high enough to keep the baby away from the water, and remember that a heating element to warm the water for the birds may create a risk of shock for a toddler. Many birdbaths are made of a masonry material poured into two separate sections, a basin that sits unattached on a pedestal. By hanging on the edge, a child could very easily tip the birdbath. Be careful when selecting and locating your birdbath.

# Fish

The way fish swim and dart through their tiny underwater world will keep kids mesmerized for hours (it's also known to lower an adult's blood pressure), and fish are relatively easy for children to feed and maintain once their homes have been properly set up. Because of the inherent risks involved whenever children have access to a sizable container of water, aquarium expert Erich Hruda recommends waiting until a child is between the ages of six and eight to give her her own fish or introduce an aquarium into the home. Hruda notes that many aquarium setups consist of water and electrical equipment in close proximity. By the six- to eight-year age range, your child should be fully able to comprehend the risks of drowning and electrocution that a large fish tank can represent if misused.

If you plan for your child's fish setup to be no more complex than a fishbowl with a few rocks and goldfish in it, simply select an unbreakable plastic or vinyl fishbowl. Make sure the opening of the bowl measures a good deal smaller than your child's head or face, but not so small that she could get her hand stuck if she attempts (despite your firm orders otherwise) to reach into the water. And, place the bowl out of the reach of a crawling baby.

If you wish to establish an aquarium specifically for your child, Hruda recommends buying a small tank (ten to fifteen gallons or smaller) and starting with a freshwater setup. Besides being easier to start up and maintain, freshwater aquariums require less chemical treatment than marine aquariums and use less complicated filtering devices. Also, freshwater fish are usually hardier and less expensive than their marine counterparts and easier to replace should "experimentation" on the child's part unintentionally wipe out part of your fish population.

Select a less breakable vinyl aquarium rather than one made of glass. If a child should accidentally strike the aquarium with a toy or other object, vinyl reduces the risk of a flood, and, more importantly, the risk of a child being cut on a shard of broken glass.

Prevent access to your aquarium and cut the risk that a curious child could fall in or topple the tank by fitting it with a hood or other cover that can be fastened to the rim and secured shut with a latch. Most pet stores offer aquarium hoods with lights built into them. These provide both attractive lighting for the fish and a cumbersome barrier between the child and the water in the tank.

One of the most important issues a parent should be concerned about when setting up a home aquarium is its sheer weight. A gallon of fresh water weighs approximately seven pounds, and salt water weighs almost nine pounds to the gallon, making a small tank weigh easily near a hundred pounds, and a large aquarium as much as five hundred pounds! To display your aquarium safely, place it on a sturdy steel or wood stand designed especially to support it. You can purchase one from a pet store, aquarium shop, or previous aquarium owner. Never put an aquarium on an end table, a bookshelf that could topple over on a child, or an entertainment center shelf not designed to support it.

Remember to follow the manufacturer's recommendations for placement of your aquarium. Keep it away from TV sets and other electronic equipment; there's a real risk of electrocution should the tank develop a leak or if water spills during cleaning. (Also, many "mist"-style filtration devices cause the aquarium water to evaporate at a rapid rate, and salt residue from marine aquariums could deteriorate metal circuitry and other parts of your electronic equipment.)

Keep aquarium chemicals, like all household chemicals, out of the reach of children, especially in the case of marine aquariums, which may require a greater number of more toxic chemicals. Many of the chemicals used to simulate salt water are poisonous in their stored forms. (Copper sulfate, for example, used to kill aquarium bacteria, can be fatal to adults as well as children.) Keep these and fish medications strictly off limits for children. Store them in a locked place.

Inexpensive filtration systems for freshwater tanks tend to be simple affairs, but those for marine aquariums can become complicated, utilizing potentially dangerous parts and chemicals that should be treated seriously and with thoughtful safety precautions. One type of water filtration and sterilization system, for example, exposes aquarium water to ultraviolet radiation to kill bacteria and other parasites present in the water.

If you decide to invest in such complicated electrical and chemical filter systems for your home aquarium, lock the components for these systems in some sort of cabinet either below, behind, or near the aquarium and secure the water tubes leading to and from the systems so that curious children won't disturb them.

Though you wouldn't think that a fish confined to an aquarium could represent a safety risk to your child, you should think twice before bringing certain species into your household. Don't buy piranhas! These freshwater fish do "attack" hands and fingers reaching into their tanks, and they're an unwise choice for a child's pet. Avoid poisonous lion fish and fox face fish (with sharp spines full of venom on their dorsal fins capable of killing a small child). Sharp teeth and ferocious tempers make moray eels especially dangerous. (Your child could easily lose a finger to one!) Several varieties of beautiful, flowerlike invertebrate sea anemones, while attractive to look at, have no place in the aquarium of a family with children since they, too, can produce a poisonous sting.

For Pet's Sake

## Hermit Crabs

Though not underwater animals, hermit crabs are widely popular aquarium or terrarium-type animals available for a reasonable price at most pet stores. Normally docile land crabs ranging in size from a half-inch in length to the size of an adult man's fist, they carry their homes on their backs. When threatened or approached by a quickly moving human or other animal, a hermit crab will draw itself up into its shell for protection. Hermit crabs are hardy creatures, easy to care for and feed. They survive best and are most active in a warm, humid terrarium. Though many hermit crab owners fill their crab terrariums partially with fresh water to create a "lagoon" effect, it is important to provide plenty of above-water space and several things to climb on, since hermit crabs will drown if kept underwater constantly.

Since hermit crabs are scavengers, they will eat practically anything, even pieces of leftover pizza your child throws in. The hermit crab's powerful claw (one is bigger than the other) constitutes the biggest safety issue. Mistaking an inquisitive child for an attacker, the crab can lash out and pinch. Always pick up a hermit crab by its shell, keeping fingers clear of its claws.

While sitting in the palm of your hand, a hermit crab can easily grasp a flap of skin in its claws and give it a painful pinch. Although rare, cases of cat scratch fever have resulted from wounds inflicted by hermit crab pinches, so wear protective gloves to eliminate the risk in handling hermit crabs.

## Reptiles

Kids love dinosaurs, and things that look like dinosaurs fascinate them. Many species of reptiles, however, have extremely specialized environmental and dietary needs, so they're often difficult to care for and therefore usually don't make good pets for young children. They can be better enjoyed at the reptile house of your local zoo or natural history museum.

If you are a reptile enthusiast or a first-time reptile owner, consider the following safety issues to be sure your exotic pet doesn't injure your child. Many elements of the reptile's vivarium setup, display, and upkeep mirror those involved in setting up or maintaining an aquarium full of fish.

If your vivarium will be displayed in a part of the house where children frequently play, make sure that it is made out of shatterproof plastic and is supported in such a way to prevent it from being toppled over. Use a lid to discourage children from reaching or falling into the vivarium. Electrical heating elements, water filtering devices, and other electrical life-support equipment must be set up or sealed off to prevent young children from accidentally burning or electrocuting themselves.

Store the many chemicals, medications, and vitamin supplements needed to sustain captive reptiles and amphibians in a locked cabinet out of the reach of children. Administer them when children are out of the room so that they will not come into contact with these potentially hazardous substances.

Reptiles are not cuddly or personable creatures; most won't allow you to pick them up or touch them without a struggle, and those reptiles that will do so only grudgingly. The builds of reptiles such as turtles and tortoises (with their easy-to-grip shells) make them relatively safe and easy to handle, while large, exceptionally strong, extremely quick, aggressive, or poisonous reptiles can be dangerous or even deadly to handle. Perhaps you are thinking about bringing one of these home:

THE AMERICAN CHAMELEON, ALSO KNOWN AS THE ANOLE OR GREEN ANOLE. These small lizards are found throughout the southern United States and are often called American chameleons because they can change colors. Anoles can be easily kept in a small aquarium. Their expressive eyes and keen reptilian intelligence make them enjoyable to watch, but their care is still complicated enough that they should be bought only for children well into their grammar school years. (Even then, supervise them as they care for their anoles.)

Anoles eat crickets and mealworms, live creatures that could escape and wreak a small havoc in your kitchen or living room. Mealworms are the larval stage of a type of beetle. You can keep several dozen mealworms for an extended period in a jar full of cornmeal or oatmeal with air holes punched in the lid. Some reptile keepers (called herpetologists) recommend keeping your jar of mealworms in the refrigerator, since the cooler temperature will slow the mealworms' metabolism and the rate of their maturity into less-edible beetles. Keeping crickets in the refrigerator, however, will kill them, and if you keep crickets and mealworms in the same container, the mealworms will eat the crickets.

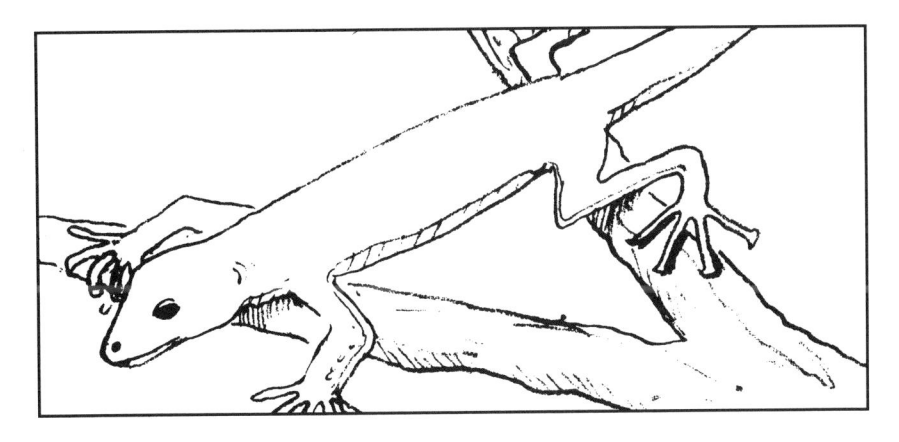

Because anoles are difficult to handle, they make good pets to watch rather than touch. Male anoles can be very territorial and aggressive toward one another and therefore should not be kept within sight of each other in the same vivarium. If you choose to take your green anole out of its cage, be sure a child never grabs it by its tail. Like many lizards, anoles can detach their tails and escape, tailless. (Their tails do grow back, but they never look as nice as the originals.) Though keeping anoles can be an enjoyable pastime for you and your child, to succeed it should be a cooperative effort. Because of the small payoff in terms of child-pet bonding, the reptile suffers from neglect when its upkeep stops being fun.

**GREEN IGUANAS.** While popular for their reptilian good looks and easy-to-manage vegetarian diets, green iguanas can grow to be up to six feet long. Iguanas are equipped with sharp teeth, sharp claws, sharp and scaly spines running down their backs, and exceptionally strong whiplike tails. If a green iguana does not want to be handled, it will use all these tools to try and wrench free of a person's grip. Though many pet iguanas are domestically bred and many adult iguana owners let their pets roam freely outside of their cages, they should never be allowed to do so in the presence of small children or toddlers. If allowing a child to examine an iguana up close, be sure to hold the reptile firmly.

GECKOS. The gecko is another species of reptile widely popular because of its expressive-looking eyes and dramatic coloration. Quick and capable of delivering nasty bites, geckos should be left in their cages in the presence of young children. They've been known to grip a finger or other appendage and not let go until submerged in water almost to the point of suffocation.

SNAKES. Snakes in small to large sizes, both poisonous and nonpoisonous, live all over the United States, though as a general rule, more venomous varieties inhabit the South and Southwest. Many nonpoisonous snakes are harmless and make interesting house pets. However, most of them consume live or recently killed mice, and it can be tricky to get them to eat in captivity. Take the normal safety precautions regarding the make and setup of your snake's cage and heating and lighting equipment. For the safety of both the snake and children who view it, limit the snake's time outside the cage in the presence of children to a few minutes while you hold it to give a child a closer view. Let her briefly touch its skin to feel that it is clean and dry rather than slimy. The best advice you can give your child about snakes and other reptiles is "All lizards and reptiles have mouths. Don't let the reptile get at you with it."

Outside, concentrations of poisonous snakes vary depending on the region of the country you live in. Familiarize yourself with the density of the poisonous snake population in your area and establish "snake rules" that will increase your child's awareness. Many nonpoisonous snakes mimic venomous snakes by taking on similar colorations and behaviors, so the safest bet is to establish a "hands-off" rule for all snakes in the wild unless your child is especially good at deciding which snakes are dangerous and which are not. Parents are advised to follow the same rule.

If you and your child encounter a snake while hiking or walking outdoors, the snake will most likely beat a hasty retreat before you even have to worry about it. However, a few identifiable traits most venomous snakes share include a triangular or diamond-shaped head, eyes with slits instead of round pupils, and heat-sensing pits between the snake's snout and eyes. If a poisonous or nonpoisonous snake bites you or your child, call your local Poison Control Center to determine if immediate treatment is needed, and see a physician as soon as possible.

## Rabbits

Members of the order *Lagomorpha* (which includes hares, too) are quiet, clean, and relatively easy to keep (but not uncaged in a child's bedroom, where little pellets have a way of ending up all over the floor). In its hutch, a rabbit will probably dirty only a little corner. Children love to pet a rabbit's soft fur, and bunnies seem to love being petted.

For safety's sake, check the cage for protruding wire that might cause injury to child or rabbit. Rabbit food purchased at your pet store goes in a deep heavy dish, as does water, though some owners serve bunnies water in a bottle that attaches to the side of the cage where it can't become soiled by droppings or bedding material. Don't overfeed, and forget what you've heard about carrots; bunnies like them only on a limited basis.

Buy a rabbit that is between eight to ten weeks old. Its eyes should be bright and its coat sleek. Staining or discoloration around the vent indicate diarrhea—a sure reason not to buy this one.

Explain to children that this bunny isn't stuffed, like the one in their toy box, and they should never pick a rabbit up by his ears. If he's still a baby, he should be picked up with two hands, one under his chest and the other to support his hindquarters. Older bunnies can be picked up with one hand on the rump and the other holding the loose skin over his shoulders.

## Hamsters

A hamster isn't very demanding, but it does take some care, as do gerbils, hamster relatives. Both need a home large enough to move about in and exercise, a quiet place to hide and sleep; clean dry living conditions; a well-balanced diet; and love and attention from the kids.

Hamsters are nocturnal creatures who sleep when the kids are in school, arising shortly after they come home from school (or in the late afternoon). Children can play with them before dinner and after homework time.

Pick up a hamster in cupped hands, holding gently but securely. Don't let the child pick up the new hamster right away; he should just stroke the fur a little every day and then feed some treats to calm it. When both are less nervous, allow the child to pick up the hamster. (Hamsters are so sensitive, they can smell the child and recognize her voice.) When a hamster makes repeated jerking motions, or suddenly washes its face, it is frightened. Yawning and stretching with sleepy eyes indicates contentment.

Like rabbits, hamsters need clean quarters and appreciate separate areas for sleeping, eating, and eliminating waste. Food and water containers; soft, fresh wood shavings and bedding; and a workout wheel to run on are all they require. Be sure, for safety's sake, that when your child feeds her hamster, no grains, seeds, nuts, vegetables, or insects go into her mouth; it's not an awfully good diet for kids. Neither are any cleaning supplies, wood chips, or "bed fluff."

**For Pet's Sake**

# Very Important Tips

1. Be cautious when selecting a family pet. Investigate the animal and its temperament, along with what type of food and care it will need. Consider your family's schedule and choose a pet that best fits that schedule.
2. Before bringing home a new pet, discuss with children the many responsibilities involved in owning a pet. Who will feed it? Who will exercise it, if necessary? Who will clean up after it? Also discuss the importance of not being aggressive with any pet.
3. Pets can spread disease, so remind children to wash their hands after handling any pet.
4. Never bring home a stray animal.
5. Keep animal food out of the reach of children, and, if possible, keep children away from a pet who is eating.

# Appendix

# Resources

## Agencies and Publishers

The following agencies and publishers offer additional resources for information and publications related to the topics in this book:

American Academy of Pediatrics (AAP)
141 Northwest Point Boulevard
P. O. Box 927
Elk Grove Village, IL 60009-0927
847-228-5005
800-433-9016

American Association of Poison Control Centers, Inc.
3800 Reservoir Road, N.W.
Washington, DC 20007
202-784-4666

American Automobile Association
Traffic Safety Department
8111 Gatehouse Road
Falls Church, VA 22047

American Lung Association
1440 W. Washington Boulevard
Chicago, IL 60607
312-243-2000

American Medical Association
P. O. Box 10946
Chicago, IL 60610
312-464-5000

American Red Cross National Headquarters
17th and D Streets, N.W.
Washington, DC 20006

B'nai Brith (Play It Safe program)
1640 Rhode Island Avenue, N.W.
Washington, DC 20036-3278

Boats U.S.
Foundation Department
880 S. Pickett Street
Alexandria, VA 22304
800-336-2628

Brain Injury Association
1776 Massachusetts Avenue, N.W.
Washington, DC 20036
800-444-NHIF

Canadian Toy Testing Council
22 Hamilton Avenue North
Ottawa, Ontario, Canada K1Y 1B6
202-466-6272

Child Magazine
110 Fifth Avenue
New York, NY 10011
212-463-1000

Closure Manufacturers Association
1627 K Street, N.W., Suite 800
Washington, DC 20006
202-223-9050

Coast Guard Customer Information Hotline
U.S. Coast Guard Headquarters
2100 Second Street, S.W.
Washington, DC 20593-0001
800-368-5647

Comprehensive Health Education Foundation (CHEF)
22323 Pacific Highway South
Seattle, WA 98188
800-323-2433

Council on Family Health
225 Park Avenue South, Suite 1700
New York, NY 10003
212-598-3617

Food and Drug Administration (FDA)
5600 Fishers Lane
Room 16-85
Rockville, MD 20857
301-443-3170

# Appendix

**Juvenile Products Manufacturers Association, Inc. (JPMA)**
236 Route 38 West, Suite 100
Moorestown, NJ 08057
609-231-8500

**KidsCare**
50 Victoria Street
Seventeenth Floor
Hull, Quebec, Canada K1A0C9
819-997-4776

**Kids Life Resources**
3816 Church Road
Mt. Laurel, NJ 08054
609-778-5433

**National Association for the Education of Young Children (NAEYC)**
1834 Connecticut Avenue, N.W.
Washington, DC 20009-5786
202-232-8777

**National Center for Missing and Exploited Children (NCMEC)**
2101 Wilson Boulevard, Suite 550
Arlington, VA 22201
703-235-3900

**National Crime Prevention Council**
1700 K Street, N.W., Second Floor
Washington, DC 20006-3817
202-466-6272

**National Fire Protection Association (NFPA)**
Batterymarch Park
Quincy, MA 02269-9101
617-770-3000
617-328-9290

**National Highway Traffic Safety Administration (NHTSA)**
400 Seventh Street, S.W.
Washington, DC 20590
Auto Safety Hotlines:
202-366-0123 and
800-424-9393

**National Injury and Violence Prevention Resource Center**
Education Development Center, Inc.
55 Chapel Street
Newton, MA 02158-1060
617-969-7100

**National Pesticide Telecommunications Network (NPTN)**
ag.chem extension
Oregon State University
333 Weniger
Corvallis, OR 97331-6502
800-858-7378

**National Safe Kids Campaign**
111 Michigan Avenue, N.W.
Washington, DC 20010-2970
202-939-4993

**National Safety Council**
1121 Spring Lake Drive
Itasca, IL 60143
Central Region: 800-621-7619
Northeastern Region:
800-432-5251
Southeastern Region:
800-441-5103
Western Region: 800-848-5588

**Nonprescription Drug Manufacturers Association (NDMA)**
1150 Connecticut Avenue, N.W.
Suite 1200
Washington, DC 20036
202-429-9260

**Operation Lifesaver, Inc.**
1420 King Street, Suite 401
Alexandria, VA 22314
800-537-6224

**Parents Magazine**
685 Third Avenue
New York, NY 10017
212-878-8700

## Appendix

Poison Prevention Week Council
P. O. Box 1543
Washington, DC 20013

The Polly Klaas Foundation
P. O. Box 800
Petaluma, CA 94953
800-587-HELP (4357)

President's Council on
Physical Fitness and Sports
450 Fifth Street, N.W.
Washington, DC 20001
202-272-3430

Robotronics
1610 W. 1600 South
Springville, UT 84663-3057
801-489-4466

Safe Moves
P. O. Box 9860
Calabasas, CA 91372
800-WEAR-IT

The Safer Image
P. O. Box 1444
Columbus, OH 43214
614-447-0000

SIDS Alliance
1314 Bedford Avenue, Suite 210
Baltimore, MD 21208
800-221-SIDS

The Soap and Detergent
Association
475 Park Avenue South
New York, NY 10016
212-725-1262

Toy Manufacturers of America
P.O. Box 866
Madison Square Station
New York, NY l0159-9866
800-851-9955

United States Consumer Product
Safety Commission (CPSC)
4330 East West Highway
Bethesda, MD 20814
301-504-0550
800-638-CPSC
Hearing Impaired: 800-638-8270

United States CPSC Division of
Poison Prevention and Scientific
Coordination
Washington, DC
301-504-0550

United States Department of
Conservation
524 South Second Street
Springfield, IL 62701
217-782-6431

United States Power Squadron
Headquarters
1504 Blue Ridge Road
Raleigh, NC 27622
919-821-0281

# Appendix

# References

American Academy of Pediatrics. *Caring for Your Baby and Young Child.* New York: Bantam, 1993.

Baptiste, M. S., and Feck, G. *Preventing Tap Water Burns.* Washington, DC: American Public Health Association, 1990.

Broughton, Daniel D., and Allen, Ernest E. *A Lesson for Life.* Arlington, VA: National Center for Missing and Exploited Children, 1992.

*The Children's Emergency Handbook.* Naperville, IL: Edward Hospital, 1993.

Glowacz, Dave. *Safe Bicycling.* Chicago: City of Chicago, 1994.

Green, Lyndsay. *Babies Aboard.* Camden, ME: International Marine, 1990.

*Growing Up Drug Free.* Washington, DC: U.S. Department of Education, 1990.

*Handbook for Public Playground Safety.* Bethesda, MD: U.S. Consumer Product Safety Commission, 1991.

*Know What You're Taking.* Washington, DC: Nonprescription Drugs Manufacturers Association, 1994.

McLoughlin, E., and McGuire, A. *The Causes, Cost and Prevention of Childhood Burn Injuries.* Chicago: American Medical Association, 1990.

Oppenheim, Joanne, and Oppenheim, Stephanie. *The Best Toys, Books, and Videos for Kids.* New York: HarperCollins, 1996.

*Pesticides and Child Safety.* Washington, DC: Environmental Protection Agency, 1993.

*Protecting Young Children from Poisoning.* Itasca, IL: National Safety Council, 1993.

Shrawder, Gail. *Skating Safe for Kids* (video). Chicago: Miracle Media Productions.

Statman, Paula. *On the Safe Side.* New York: HarperCollins, 1995.

*Tips for Child Safety.* Washington, DC: Closure Manufacturers Association, 1988.

*The Toy Report.* North Ottawa, Ontario, Canada: The Canadian Toy Testing Council, yearly.

# Index

## A

Adults, identifying low-risk vs. high-risk, 243–245
A-frame turn, 210
Aggressors, combating older and bigger, 252–253
Airbags, 163, 169
Airplane glue, 128
Alarms
 door, 157
 pools, 231
 smoke, 3
Allergic reaction
 to bee sting, 285–286
 to Halloween candy, 292
Altitude sickness, 275
American Academy of Pediatrics (AAP)
 on cardiopulmonary resuscitation, 44
 on fall surface, 218
 injury prevention program of, 87
 on lead poisoning, 96
 on sudden infant death syndrome, 34
American Association of Poison Control Centers, 80
American Humane Association, 240
American Lung Association on carbon monoxide positioning, 101
American National Standards Institute (ANSI) on helmet safety, 203
American Sensors and carbon monoxide positioning, 101
American Society for Testing and Materials (ASTM)
 on helmet safety, 203
 and setting of furniture standards, 151
Animal control agency, 311, 316
Anoles, 324–325
Appliances
 as family room hazard, 146–147
 as kitchen hazard, 140–141
Aquarium, 320–322
 chemicals in poisoning, 322
Arson, 2. *See also* Fire(s); Fire safety
Art supplies, 127–128
Asbestos, 104
Automatic seat belts, 169
Automobile safety, 162
 airbags in, 163, 169
 child safety seats in, 164–170

 features of, 173
 pedestrians in, 175–178
 seat belts in, 162–163, 170–172
 staying awake on the road, 175
 tips in, 172–175
 winter driving tips in, 277

## B

Babies. *See* Infants
Babysitters, and fire safety, 15
Baby walkers, injuries involving, 30
Balloons, dangers of deflated, 70
Banisters, stair, 144–145
Barbecue grills, 289
Basement, 156–157
Basements, safety checklist for, 16
Bathrooms, 148
 electrical appliances in, 150
 floors in, 150
 medicine cabinets in, 150
 poison checklist for, 88
 tubs, showers, and toilets in, 148–150
Batteries, as source of lead poisoning, 132
Batteries, chemical burns from, 21, 280–281
Battery acid, 132
Bed rails, 153
Bedrooms, 151–156
 children's, 151–154
 safety checklist for, 19
Bee stings, 285–286
Bicycle safety, 195
 injury statistics in, 195
 for older riders, 199–200
 rules for, 204–205
 selecting and inspecting a bike, 205–207
 using helmets in, 200–204
 for younger riders, 195–199
Biological pollutants, 104
Birdbaths, 319–320
Birds, 316
 domestic, 317–319
 wild, 319–320
Bites, dog, 310, 311
Bitrex®, 98
Bleach, dangers from, 79
Bleeding, treating, 36
Blinds
 venetian, 154
 vertical, 139
Blisters, burn, 27

Boat Registration and Safety Act, 184
Boat safety, 181–185
Bookcase tip-overs, 155
Booster seats, 165
Bruises, treating, 36
Buddy system, 249, 250
Bunk beds, 153
Burns, 20–22
 from barbecue grills, 289
 immediate care of, 26–27
 preventing, 22–26
Bus safety, 180–181

## C

Canadian Toy Testing Council, 126
Cancer, skin, 281
Carbon monoxide, 100–103
 as cause of death in fires, 3
Carbon monoxide detectors, 101–102
Cardiac arrest, 49–66
Cardiopulmonary resuscitation (CPR)
 instructions for performing, 49–66
 child, 58–66
 infant, 50–57
 and pool safety, 229, 235–236
Cats, 312
 and babies, 313–314
 declawing, 314–315
 diseases in, 315–316
 selecting, 312–313
 strays, 316
Cat scratch fever, 316
Chameleon, 324–325
Chapping, prevention of, 263
Chemical burns, 21
 treating, 27
Chemicals, household, 77–80
Child abductions, statistics on, 240–241
ChildHelp USA, 240
Childproofed home, 135–159
 basements, 156–157
 bathrooms, 148
 electrical appliances, 150
 floors, 150
 medicine cabinets, 150–151
 tubs, showers, and toilets, 148–150
 bedrooms, 151–156
 children's, 151–154
 dining room, 142
 doorstops, 138
 exercise rooms, 156–157

335

# Index

family room, 145
  appliances, 146–147
  electrical cords and outlets, 147
  fireplaces, 148
  furniture, 145–146
  gun cabinets, 146
  sliding glass doors, 148
fire ladders, 138
garage, 157
kitchen, 138
  electrical concerns, 141–142
  furniture and appliances, 140–141
  general hazards, 138–139
  poisons, 140
outdoors, 157
room monitors, 138
safety latches in, 137
stairways, 143
  banisters and posts, 144–145
  gates, 143–144
  stair steps, 145
Children Riding On Sidewalks Safety (CROSS) program, 198
Children's rooms, 151–154
Child-resistant packaging for pesticides, 80
Child safety, tips from police and educators, 257–259
Child safety seats, 164–170
Chin lift, 43
Choking, 41–44
  preventing, 69–70
  toys as danger in, 115, 116, 280
Christmas, safety tips for, 278–280
Closure Manufacturers Association, and child resistant packaging, 81–83
Coccidiosis, 315–316
Comic books as source of lead, 99
Communication
  encouraging two-way, 254–255
  importance of, in keeping children safe, 249
Compatibility in selecting pets, 299–300
Competitiveness, 130
Comprehensive Health Education Foundation (CHEF), 107–109

Consumer Product Safety Act, and regulation of toy industry, 116
Consumer Product Safety Commission (CPSC)
  and child resistant packaging, 81–82
  and in-line skating, 208
  and lead poisoning, 95–96
  and playground safety, 217
  poison checklist of, 88–89
  and pool safety, 227
  and regulation of toy industry, 116
  on sudden infant death syndrome, 35
  and tricycle safety, 196
Contact burns, preventing, 25
Convertible seats, 164
Costumes for Halloween, 291–292
Covers, pool, 231
Crabs, hermit, 323
Cribs, safety standards for, 152–153
Crime
  prevention of, 239
  statistics on, 240–241
Crotch straps for stroller, 194
Cut, treating, 36

## D

Deaths, drug-ingestion, 82
Deaths from bathtub scalds, 22
Deep wounds, treatment of, 37
Dehydration, 275–276
Denial of danger, 239
Dining room, 142
Dirt as source of lead, 98
Dishwasher, placing utensils in, 139
Diving boards and slides, 232–233
Dog bites, 310, 311
Dogs, 300
  and babies, 305–306
  bringing home, 302–304
  diseases in, 308–311
  selecting, 300–302
  strays, 311
  training, 304–305
  walking, 306–308
Domestic birds, 317–319
Door, answering, 246, 256
Doorstops, 138
Dresser tip-overs, 155
Driving tips, winter, 277
Drowning, 235–236

Drugs, 105–106
  prevention programs, 107–111
  telling children about, 254
Drug Abuse Resistance Education (DARE), 107

## E

Education
  drug, 107–111
  poison, 86–87
  toy, 123–125
*8 Rules for Safety,* 249
Electrical appliances, and bathroom safety, 150
Electrical burns, treating, 27
Electrical concerns as kitchen hazard, 141–142
Electrical cords and outlets as family room hazard, 147
Electrical injuries, preventing, 25–26
Electric toys, 131–132
Electronic toys, 129
Emergencies
  on the road, 174
  using telephone in, 246–247, 256–257
Environmental Protection Agency, and radon, 104
Exercise rooms, 156–157
Exit Drills in the Home (EDITH), 15
Extension cord, as safety hazard, 142

## F

Falls
  preventing, in the home, 30–32
  from windows, 155
Fall surface in playgrounds, 218–219
Family
  escape plan for, 14–15
  fire safety in, 1, 2
  first-aid kit for, 67–68
  safety checklist for, 18
Family room, 145
  appliances in, 146–147
  electrical cords and outlets in, 147
  fireplaces in, 148
  furniture in, 145–146
  gun cabinets in, 146
  sliding glass doors in, 148
Federal Aviation Administration (FAA), and plane safety, 186–188

# Index

Federal Hazardous Substances Act, and regulation of toy industry, 116
Feelings, trusting, 249, 250
Fences, pool, 231
Fire extinguishers, 12–14
Firefighter visits, benefits of, 5–6
Fireplaces, 148
Fire(s)
  anatomy of, 4
  good uses of, 4
  statistics on, 2–3
  temperatures of real, 5
Fire safety
  away from home, 20–27
  in family, 1, 2
  family escape plan, 14–15
  fire extinguishers, 12–14
  fire ladders in, 138
  heat detectors, 12
  at home, 5–6
  important tips in, 28
  at school, 7–10
  smoke detectors in, 10–12
  and use of room monitors, 138
Fire Triangle, 4
Fireworks, 289–290
  as source of chemical burns, 21
First-aid kit, family, 67–68
Fish, 320–322
Fit of ice skates, 266–267
Five-point harness seats, 164–165
Fixed temperature detector, 12
Flame burns, preventing, 23–25
Flashlights as source of chemical burns, 21
Floors, and bathroom safety, 150
Flotation devices, 231–232
Formaldehyde, 104
Fourth of July fireworks, 289–290
Fractures, treating, 38–39
Frostbite, 273
Furniture
  as bedroom hazard, 151, 154–155
  as family room hazard, 145–146
  as kitchen hazard, 140–141
Futronix, Inc., 253

## G

Garage, safety checklist for, 16
Garage as safety hazard, 157
Garbage, 139
Gasoline, leaded, 98–99
Gates
  pool, 231
  safety, 143–144
Gatorade®, 276
Geckos, 326
Germs, kitchens as breeding grounds for, 138–139
Get Out! Stay out! formula, 9
Glass doors, sliding, 148
Ground fault circuit interrupter (GFC), 142
*Growing up Drug Free*, 107
Gun cabinets, 146

## H

Halloween, 290–293
Hamsters, 327–328
Hats
  in summer, 283
  in winter, 262
Head injuries
  treating playground related, 226–227
  and use of helmets, 200–204
Heat, 4
Heat detectors, 12
Heat exhaustion, 284
Heatstroke, 284–285
Heimlich maneuver, 44–47
Helmets in bicycle safety, 127, 200–204
Hermit crabs, 323
Holidays, 289
  Fourth of July fireworks, 289–290
  Halloween, 290–293
  winter, 278–280
Home
  fire safety at, 5
  preventing falls in, 30–32
Home fires
  causes of, 2
  property losses from, 4
  statistics on, 2–3
Home safety, checklist for, 16–19
Hookbills, 317
Household accidents, and need for safety proofing, 135–159
Household poisons, 72
  chemicals, 77–80
  pesticides, 80
  plants, 72–77
Hypothermia, 273–275

## I

Ice skating, 266–269
Ice Skating Institute of America (ISIA) tests, 266
Identification cards, 253
Iguanas, 325–326
Immunizations, tetanus, 36
Indoors, safety checklist for, 16
Infants
  cardiopulmonary resuscitation for, 50–57
  and cats, 313–314
  and dogs, 305–306
  fall prevention, 30–32
  furniture for, 152–154
  injuries involving walkers, 30
  safety seats for
    in automobile, 164
    on bicycle, 195–199
  stroller safety for, 194
  and sudden infant death syndrome, 32–35
  toys for, 121–122, 129–130
Information, need for basic identifying, 251
Information resources, 331–334
Injuries
  preventing, from falls, 69
  to teeth, 39–41
Injury Prevention Program (TIPP) of American Academy of Pediatrics (AAP), 87
Injury treatments, 35
  fractures and sprains, 38
  Heimlich maneuver, 44–47
  minor scrapes, cuts, and bruises, 35
  puncture wounds and bleeding, 36–38
In-line skating, 208–211
Iron supplements, poisoning from, 89
Iron supplements as source of poisoning, 280

## J

Jaw lift, 43
Juvenile Products Manufacturers' Association (JPMA), and stroller safety, 194

## K

Key, giving to child, 255–256
Kiddie pools, 232
Kid-ID, 253
Kids and Company, 242, 250
Kid-Shield ID system, 253
KidsLife Resources, 109
Kitchen, 138
  electrical concerns in, 141–142

# Index

furniture and appliances in, 140–141
general hazards in, 138–139
poison checklist for, 88
poisons in, 140
safety checklist for, 16–18
Klaas, Polly, 241, 242
Klaas, Polly Foundation, 249–250
    purpose of, 241–242

## L

Labeling of Hazardous Art Materials Act, 116
Labels
    importance of reading, 78
    toy, 116, 119–120, 131
Ladders, fire, 138
Landmark, establishing, 252
Latchkey children, 255
    answering door and phone, 246, 256
    giving child key, 255–256
    knowing child's schedule, 255
    using phone in emergencies, 246–247, 256–257
Law Enforcement Travel Network (LETN), and automobile safety, 162, 163
Layering in dressing for winter activities, 262
Leaded gasoline, 98–99
Lead poisoning, 95–100
*Lesson for Life*, 242–243
Lifelines, 184
Life preservers, 182–184
Line conditioner, 24
Liquids
    need for, in summer, 284
    need for, in winter, 275–276
Living room, safety checklist for, 18
Loud toys, 131
Lyme disease, 286–287, 310

## M

Macfarlan Smith Ltd., 98
Maintenance of toys, 132
McGruff, the Crime Dog, 109–110, 246–247
Medicine cabinets, and bathroom safety, 150
Medicines, 81
    child-resistant packaging, 81–86
    safety in taking, 81
Merry-go-rounds, 223
Microwave operation by children, 17

Midas Project Safe Baby Campaign, 173
Million Dollar Machine Program, 109, 110–111
Mosquitoes, 287
Mouth guard, need for, in sports participation, 39–41
"Mr. Yuk" stickers, 87

## N

National Association for the Education of Young Children (NAEYC)
    and bicycle safety, 198
    and playground safety, 220
    and traffic safety, 178
National Center for Missing and Exploited Children (NCMEC), 240, 250
    commissioning of *A Lesson of Life*, 242–243
National Center of the American Heart Association, and seat safety checklist, 167
National Committee for Prevention of Child Abuse, 240
National Easter Seal Society, and safety seats for special needs child, 169
National Electronic Injury Surveillance System, 20
National Fire Codes, development of, 7
National Fire Protection Association (NFPA), 2, 7–10, 15
    Learn Not to Burn curriculum of, 7–8
National Head Injury Foundation (NHIF), and use of bicycle helmets, 200
National Highway Traffic Safety Administration (NHTSA), and traffic safety, 162, 178
National Incidence Studies of Missing, Abducted, Runaways, and Thrownaway Children (NISMART), 240
National Poison Prevention Week, 86
National Safe Kids Campaign (NSKC)
    on child pedestrian accidents, 175
    and pool safety, 227–228
National Safety Council (NSC) and automobile safety, 162, 163

    and bicycle safety, 195
    and playground safety, 219, 220
    and pool safety, 233–234
    and train safety, 178–179
Natural gas, 103
Netting and stairway safety, 144–145
Newspapers as source of lead, 99
Nonprescription Drugs Manufacturers Association (NDMA), and child resistance packaging, 84–86
Nontoxic plants, 75–77

## O

Onychectomy, 314
Operation Lifesaver, 179
Outdoors
    dressing for, 262–272
    safe toys for, 129–132
    safety, 215–238
    safety checklist for, 19
    as safety hazard, 157
Outlet plugs or caps, 147
Overheating, 285
Oxygen, 4

## P

Pacifiers, 122
Password, using, in providing identification, 251–252
Pedestrian safety, 175–178
Pedialyte®, 275
Personal flotation devices (PFDs), 182–184
Pesticides, 80
Pets, 297–329. *See also specific pets*
    selecting, 299–328
Plane safety, 186–188
Plants, 72–77
    toxic, 278–279, 287–289
Plastic surgical procedures, need for deep wounds, 38
Playground safety, 216–217
    away from home, 223
    background, 217
    fall surface, 218–219
    playground placement, 217–218
    equipment, 219–223
    public playground safety checklist, 224
    supervision away from home, 225
    treating head injuries, 226–227
*Play It Safe*, 247–248

# Index

Playpen, 153
Plumbing pipes as source of lead, 98
Poison Control Center (PCC), 90, 99, 100, 103
Poisoning, 71–114
 from aquarium chemicals, 322
 checklist, 88–89
 diagnosing and treating household, 89–90
 drugs and medicines, 81, 105–106
  child-resistant packaging, 81–86
  prevention programs, 107–111
  safety in taking, 81
 household, 72
  chemicals, 77–80
  pesticides, 80
  plants, 72–77
 as kitchen hazard, 140
 from pet maintenance items, 304
 poison control centers, 91–95
 poison education, 86–87
 systemic poisoning, 95
  asbestos, 104
  biological pollutants, 104
  carbon monoxide, 100–103
  formaldehyde, 104
  lead poisoning, 95–100
  natural gas, 103
  propane, 103
  radon, 104
  wood smoke, 104–105
Poison ivy, poison oak, and poison sumac, 287–289
Poison Prevention Packaging Act, and child resistant packaging, 81–82
Pool safety, 227–228
 diving boards and slides, 232–233
 drowning, 235–236
 flotation devices, 231–232
 home pool, 228
  adult supervision, 228–229
  children's swimming lessons, 229
  poolside precautions and rules, 229–230
 kiddie pools, 232
 pool alarms, 231
 pool covers, 231

pool fences and gates, 231
 in public pools and other bodies of water, 233–234
 submersion, 235–236
Posts, stair, 144–145
Power surge, 24
Pressure gate, 143
Projectiles, 131
Propane, 103
*Protecting Young Children from Poisoning*, 72
Puncture wound, treating, 36

## R

Rabbits, 327
Rabies, 310–311
Radon, 104
Rape, telling children about, 254
Rate-of-rise heat detector, 12
Refrigerator, disposing of old, 141
Reptiles, 323–324
 chameleon, 324–325
 geckos, 326
 iguanas, 325–326
 snakes, 326–327
Retroreflective material
 and bicycle safety, 204–205
 and pedestrian safety, 177
Riding toy, 127
Ringworm, 309
Rocking horses, 126–127
Role playing in teaching safety, 247–248, 258–259
Rollerblading, 208–211
Room monitors, 138

## S

Safe Kids Campaign, 176–177
Safety gates, 143–144
Safety guidelines for toys, 118–123
Safety latches, 137
Safety plates for electric outlets, 147
Safety-proofing, benefits of, 136
Sandboxes, 222
Scabies mites, 309
Scald burns, 20–21
Scalds, preventing, 22–23
Scald-safe devices, 149
Scare tactics, 239
Schedule, knowing child's, 255
School, fire safety at, 7–10
School firefighter visits, 4
Scrape, treating, 36
Seasonal affective disorder, 276
Seat belts, 170–172
 automatic, 169
 for stroller, 194

Seesaws, 222
Sex-offender registries, 242
Sexual abuse, statistics on, 240–241
Shoes, proper fit of, 31–32
Showers, 148–150
Skating safety, 208–211
Skiing, 269–272
Skin cancer, 281
Sledding, safety in, 264–265
Sleeping positions, and SIDS, 34–35
Slides, 221–222
Sliding glass doors, 148
Smoke, as cause of death in fires, 3
Smoke detectors, 10–12
 importance of, 4
Smoking, and SIDS, 33–34
Snakes, 326–327
Snowboarding, 265
Special needs child, safety seats for, 169
Splint, making, 39
Sports participation, need for mouthpiece for, 39–41
Sprains, treating, 38–39
Stair steps, 145
Stairways, 143
 banisters and posts, 144–145
 falls down, 30
 gates, 143–144
 stair steps, 145
Stop-drop-roll, 8–9
Storage, toy, 122–123
Stove shields, 141
Stranger, identifying, 242–243
Stranger aware programs, 246
 McGruff, the Crime Dog, 246–247
 *Play It Safe*, 247–248
 Polly Klaas Foundation, 24–250
Stranger danger, 239
 encouraging two-way communication, 254–255
 establishing landmark, 252
 giving password, 251–252
 knowing basics, 251
 providing children with identification cards, 253
 self-esteem bolstering, in keeping children safe, 251
 use of term, 245
Stray cats, 316
Stray dogs, 311
Street savvy, 239
Stroller safety, 194
Submersion, 235–236

# Index

Sudden infant death syndrome (SIDS), 32–33
  prevention of, 34–35
Suffocation, 41–44
  preventing, 69–70
Summer, 281
  injuries and dangers, 283
    barbecue grills, 289
    bee stings, 285–286
    heat exhaustion, 284
    heatstroke, 284–285
    mosquitoes, 287
    overheating, 285
    poison ivy, poison oak, and poison sumac, 287–289
    sunburn, 283–284
    ticks and Lyme disease, 286–287
  sunburn and sunscreen in, 281–283
Sunburn, 283–284
  and sunscreen, 281–283
Sun protection factor (SPF) number, 282
Supervision
  home pool, 228–229
  playground, 225
Swimming lessons, 229
Swing sets, 220–221
Systemic poisoning, 95
  asbestos, 104
  biological pollutants, 104
  carbon monoxide, 100–103
  formaldehyde, 104
  lead poisoning, 95–100
  natural gas, 103
  propane, 103
  radon, 104
  wood smoke, 104–105

## T

Teeth
  immediate care of knocked out, 40–41
  injuries to, 39–41
Telephone
  answering, 246, 256
  using, in emergencies, 246–247, 256–257
Tetanus booster, need for, 36
Thunderstorm, safety during, 157
Ticks and Lyme disease, 286–287
Tire, changing, 174
Toddler
  car seats for, 164–165
  fall prevention for, 30–32
Toilets, 148–150
Tongue-jaw lift, 43, 44
Touching, teaching children about, 249, 254, 258, 259
Toxic and injurious plants, 73–75, 278–279
Toxoplasmosis, 315
Toy box lids, 123
Toyland, 115–133
Toy Manufacturers of America (TMA), and regulation of toy industry, 116
Toys
  age-appropriate
    children over three, 126–129
    children three and younger, 125–126
  choking on, 280
  choosing appropriate, 123–125
  importance of maintenance, 132
  for outdoor fun, 129–132
  regulating, 116–118
  safety guidelines, 118–119
    for infants, 121–122
    selecting, 119–120
    storage, 122–123
    unwrapping and assembling, 120–121
  unsafe, 131
    electric, 131–132
    loud, 131
    projectiles, 131
Training of dog, 304–305, 307
Training wheels, 197
Train safety, 178–179
Treadmills, 156
Trick-or-treating, safety in, 290–293
Tricycle, 196–197
Truncated cylinder test tube for testing small parts for choking dangers, 120–121
Tubs, 148–150
Turpentine as source of chemical burns, 21

## U

Underwriter's Laboratory mark, 157
United States Coast Guard, 183
United States Power Squadrons, 182

## V

Venetian blinds, 154
Vertical blinds, 139
Vivarium, 323–324

## W

Walking of dog, 306–308
Walk in Traffic Safely program (WITS), 178
Walsh, Adam, Center, 250
Walsh, Adam, Children's Fund, 242
Wild birds, 319–320
Wind chill, 275
Window bars, 155
Window guards, 155
Windows, falls from, 155
*Winners Don't Use Drugs*, 109–110
Winter
  dressing for, 262–272
  driving tips for, 277
  holidays in, 278–280
  ice skating in, 266–269
  injuries and dangers in, 273
    altitude sickness, 275
    dehydration, 275–276
    frostbite, 273
    hypothermia, 273–275
    seasonal affective disorder, 276
    wind chill, 275
  skiing in, 269–272
  sledding in, 264–265
  snowboarding in, 265
Wood smoke, 104–105
Workshops, safety checklist for, 16
Wrist guards, need for, in snowboarding, 265